MW01170140

Class and the College Classroom

Hello Lee :
  Here's the latest collection
of essays from Radical Teacher.
  Many thanks for helping
to keep us alive.
  All on the board were distressed
by hearing about your eye.
  With best wishes for your
future health.
            Louis

Class and the College Classroom

Essays on Teaching

Edited by

Robert C. Rosen

BLOOMSBURY

NEW YORK • LONDON • NEW DELHI • SYDNEY

Bloomsbury Academic

An imprint of Bloomsbury Publishing Plc

1385 Broadway	50 Bedford Square
New York	London
NY 10018	WC1B 3DP
USA	UK

www.bloomsbury.com

First published 2013

© Robert C. Rosen and Contributors, 2013

All rights reserved. No part of this publication may be reproduced or transmitted in any form or by any means, electronic or mechanical, including photocopying, recording, or any information storage or retrieval system, without prior permission in writing from the publishers.

No responsibility for loss caused to any individual or organization acting on or refraining from action as a result of the material in this publication can be accepted by Bloomsbury Academic or the author.

Library of Congress Cataloging-in-Publication Data
Class and the college classroom: essays on teaching / edited by Robert C. Rosen.
pages cm
Includes index.
ISBN 978-1-62356-477-3 (pbk.) – ISBN 978-1-62356-320-2 (hardcover)
1. Critical pedagogy–United States. 2. Education, Higher–United States.
I. Rosen, Robert C., 1947- editor of compilation.
LC196.5.U6C534 2013
378.1'25–dc23
2013007765

ISBN: HB: 978-1-6235-6320-2
PB: 978-1-6235-6477-3
ePDF: 978-1-6235-6063-8
ePub: 978-1-6235-6047-8

Typeset by Deanta Global Publishing Services, Chennai, India
Printed and bound in the United States of America

CONTENTS

PART SIX Teaching About Class Across the Campus

PERMISSIONS

"Is Class an Identity?" by Richard Ohmann originally appeared in *Radical Teacher* #69, pp. 10–12. Copyright by Radical Teacher. Reprinted with permission.

"A Dream Deferred: Undocumented Students at CUNY" by Carolina Bank Muñoz originally appeared in *Radical Teacher* #84, pp. 8–17. Copyright by Radical Teacher. Reprinted with permission.

"Last In and First Out: Poor Students in Academe in Times of Fiscal Crisis" by Vivyan Adair originally appeared in *Radical Teacher* #73, pp. 8–14. Copyright by Radical Teacher. Reprinted with permission.

"Welfare 'Reform' and One Community College" by Susan Jhirad originally appeared in *Radical Teacher* #76, pp. 2–6. Copyright by Radical Teacher. Reprinted with permission.

"Teaching Freire and CUNY Open Admissions" by Kristen Gallagher originally appeared in *Radical Teacher* #87, pp. 55–66. Copyright by Radical Teacher. Reprinted with permission.

"A Teaching Temp Talks Back" by Michelle LaPlace appeared in *Radical Teacher* #39, pp. 28–9. Copyright by Radical Teacher. Reprinted with permission.

"Instruction" by Kat Meads appeared in *Radical Teacher* #44, pp. 24–6. Copyright by Radical Teacher. Reprinted with permission.

"Contingent Teaching, Corporate Universities, and the Academic Labor Movement" by Joseph Entin originally appeared in *Radical Teacher* #73, pp. 26–32. Copyright by Radical Teacher. Reprinted with permission.

"Anti-Intellectualism, Homophobia, and the Working-Class Gay/Lesbian Academic" by Carlos L. Dews and Carolyn Leste Law originally appeared in *Radical Teacher* #53, pp. 8–12. Copyright by Radical Teacher. Reprinted with permission.

"Stories Out of School: Poor and Working-Class Students at a Small Liberal Arts College" by Laurie Nisonoff, Susan J. Tracy, and Stanley Warner originally appeared in *Radical Teacher* #41, pp. 15–19. Copyright by Radical Teacher. Reprinted with permission.

"Class Privilege, Oppression, and the World in the Classroom" by Erin Smith originally appeared in *Radical Teacher* #68, pp. 23–6. Copyright by Radical Teacher. Reprinted with permission.

"Enforcing the Rules" by Taylor Stoehr originally appeared in *Radical Teacher* #76, pp. 7–12. Copyright by Radical Teacher. Reprinted with permission.

"Upward Mobility and Higher Education: Mining the Contradictions in a Worker Education Program" by Emily Schnee originally appeared in *Radical Teacher* #86, pp. 39–49. Copyright by Radical Teacher. Reprinted with permission.

"Working-Class Cultural Studies in the University" by Lawrence Hanley originally appeared in *Radical Teacher* #68, pp. 26–31. Copyright by Radical Teacher. Reprinted with permission.

"All That Hollywood Allows: Film and the Working Class" by Linda Dittmar originally appeared in *Radical Teacher* #46, pp. 38–45. Copyright by Radical Teacher. Reprinted with permission.

"Canon Issues and Class Contexts: Teaching American Literature from a Market Perspective" by Janet Galligani Casey originally appeared in *Radical Teacher* #86, pp. 18–27. Copyright by Radical Teacher. Reprinted with permission.

"Teaching *Howards End* to the Basts: Class Markers in the Classroom and in the Bourgeois Novel" by Ed Wiltse originally appeared in *Radical Teacher* #68, pp. 5–9. Copyright by Radical Teacher. Reprinted with permission.

"Empathy Education: Teaching About Women and Poverty in the Introductory Women's Studies Classroom" by Jennifer Scanlon originally appeared in *Radical Teacher* #48, pp. 7–10. Copyright by Radical Teacher. Reprinted with permission.

"Teaching an Interdisciplinary Course on the American Upper Class" by Richie Zweigenhaft originally appeared in *Radical Teacher* #85, pp. 5–11. Copyright by Radical Teacher. Reprinted with permission.

"Teaching About Class in the Library" by Emily Drabinski originally appeared in *Radical Teacher* #85, pp. 15–16. Copyright by Radical Teacher. Reprinted with permission.

ACKNOWLEDGMENTS

This book owes its existence to the members of the *Radical Teacher* editorial board who acquired these essays and worked with their authors. I would also like to thank William Paterson University for released time to work on this project and David Barker of Bloomsbury Academic for his encouragement and support.

Introduction

Suddenly people started talking about class. It had always been there, of course, but then it emerged into the light. The financial crisis of 2008, the rising unemployment and accelerating home foreclosures that came in its wake, the decision of Occupy protestors to target not government but Wall Street—all made class issues hard to avoid. Politicians of every kind, however implausibly, had to reassert their loyalty to those of their fellow Americans who were not—or at least not yet—on the upper rungs of the economic ladder.

Much of the talk of class, of course, obscured more than it illuminated; the inequalities that are inevitable in a capitalist society needed new ideological cover. But the facts themselves became increasingly familiar, harder to ignore: in 2011, for example, the typical top CEO (according to AFL-CIO statistics) earned 380 times as much as the average worker, up from 343 just a year earlier. Today, the top 1 percent of households have more wealth than the bottom 80 percent, and over 20 percent of children in the United States live in poverty.

Americans have long been encouraged to look to education, especially higher education, for the solution to social problems, especially as a way out of poverty for the talented and the hard working. In its appointed role as the path to upward mobility that makes inequality more acceptable, higher education has been faltering lately. As funds for public institutions were cut and tuition costs soared everywhere, as for-profit education raced into the breach, and as student debt grew wildly, the comfortable future once promised to those willing to study hard was beginning to fade from sight.

So now is a good time to take a more serious look at the ways class structures higher education and the ways teachers can bring it into focus in the classroom. In recent decades, scholarly work and pedagogical practice in higher education have paid increasing attention to issues of race, class, gender, and sexuality. But among these four terms of analysis—and clearly they are interrelated—class has often been an afterthought. From general education "race and gender" requirements to pedagogical panels at national conferences and academic books from university presses, class has been directly addressed far less than gender, sexuality, and race.

One challenge facing anyone who wants to teach seriously about issues of class is the widespread belief that just about everyone in the United States is "middle class," a way of thinking that masks the power and importance of class, and can make it seem as if there is little to be taught or learned. Another is the reality that most students who pursue higher education still do so with an eye to rising in social class; they may not be eager to think about the tenacity of class differences, the barriers to class mobility. And then, of course, there is the genuine complexity of defining just what "class" is; the traditional definition that mainstream social science offers— "socioeconomic status"—just doesn't do the job. Difficulties of these sorts may deter many faculty inclined to use the lenses of race, class, gender, and sexuality in their teaching from giving social class the emphasis they might wish to.

But some have been teaching and writing about class and higher education for a while. This volume collects 20 essays originally published in *Radical Teacher*, "a socialist, feminist, and antiracist journal on the theory and practice of teaching," that has, since 1975, been a leader in the field of critical pedagogy. *Class and the College Classroom* represents an attempt to address the interests, concerns, and pedagogical needs of teachers committed to social justice and to provide them with new tools for thinking and teaching about social class.

I What is class?

Richard Ohmann begins the first essay—"Is Class an Identity?"—by describing a Wesleyan University class on Jane Austen's *Emma*, in which he encounters great resistance to the novel's premise that the social status of the person one marries is of the utmost importance. Marriage, his students insist—at least for those inclined, or legally able, to marry—is not about class but about love, however much their "classist" parents might object were their children to marry down. Privileged, or on their way to privilege, living while at college in an almost utopian bubble, many of his students believe, at some level, that class will "go away if people just stop being snobs"; these students "manage to enact class without allowing its reality." Class, to Ohmann, needs to be understood not only in terms of larger structures of inequality, but also as a personal identity, "a complex and powerful identity, a script you act out daily," often without knowing it, "a bundle of habits and feelings and ways of relating lodged deep in your psyche and broadcast by your talk and conduct." To teach about class, he argues, is essential, a powerful thing, a perfect opportunity to challenge "the ideology we take in with every breath."

II Who gets to be in the classroom

"Selective" and less "selective" colleges and universities emphasize academic criteria in their selection process, but social class is always deeply implicated. The quality and reputation of the school that applicants come from, their access to cultural capital while growing up, their ability to pay for or even envision attending college—all these help determine who ends up where, if anywhere. Classrooms certainly can be diverse, but the center of gravity around which this diversity distributes itself will be very different at an elite private liberal arts school than at a community college. And the experiences of students once they get to the classroom—how they feel there, how much time they can devote to their studies, perhaps how they are seen or treated—will surely be shaped by their class backgrounds.

Getting into and staying in college, any college, is especially challenging for students who are undocumented. Of the tens of thousands who graduate high school every year—often having come to the United States as small children—only 5–10 percent are even able to start college. In "A Dream Deferred: Undocumented Students at CUNY," Carolina Bank Muñoz describes the struggles of those she teaches at Brooklyn College, students who are, she writes, "among the most self-motivated and focused students I have had." Bank Muñoz goes on to outline a variety of campus services and political actions that could significantly improve the situation of undocumented college students.

In "Last In and First Out: Poor Students in Academe in Times of Fiscal Crisis," Vivyan Adair analyzes not only the impact of government policy changes on poor students, but also the ways that the educational process can alienate and push them away. One student she interviewed told her that a class on the sociology of poverty taught her only one thing, that "my people, my family and I, and our culture are problems." Surveying poor students who had left college, Adair found that far too many had done so because they "had been made to feel 'shamed,' 'worthless,' and 'invisible' in their classrooms."

Even at colleges where faculty strive to honor all students and make them feel welcome, life can be difficult. In "Welfare 'Reform' and One Community College," Susan Jhirad describes North Shore Community College as "the place where students who never dreamed of going to college find an open door to college life." The challenge, though, for the "immigrants, laid-off workers, and displaced homemakers" she teaches, is *staying* in college, as both State and Federal "welfare deform" (as some of her students call it) have heightened the already intense time and budget pressures they struggle with. Jhirad and her colleagues do what they can, but it can never be enough.

Kristen Gallagher decided to make higher education access itself the subject of critical analysis and writing assignments in a composition class she taught at LaGuardia Community College. In "Teaching Freire and CUNY Open Admissions," she describes how, using documents from an on-campus archive, her students analyzed the debates and activism around the 1969 struggle by Black and Puerto Rican students for Open Admissions and found the issues raised back then very much alive in their own lives and education. The overt drama of that earlier period shed light on their usually more private dramas, and the connections they made to 1969 led to impassioned writing and real learning.

III Class and the working teacher

Class differences, of course, also matter in the working lives of faculty; the community of scholars and teachers we sometimes imagine we dwell in has its own hierarchies and inequities. An adjunct rushing madly from one campus to another, uncertain of his or her future, has little in common, as a worker, with a senior professor at an elite school, pursuing the life of the mind in leisurely security—especially at a time when the likelihood of climbing from the first position to the second is vanishingly small. Such a major difference in the lives of their teachers surely impacts students, even if those students aren't always aware of it.

In "A Teaching Temp Talks Back," Michelle LaPlace, a part-time instructor at a California community college, describes life for those underpaid instructors who "spend their off-hours scrambling for other part-time jobs that can support their teaching habit" and are "silently praying that enough of the old-timers will die so that we can get their job." She sometimes felt herself sliding toward despair, toward the "paralyzing malaise" that affected her fellow part-timers, but finally she was just "too fucking *angry* to give up" and instead began working as an organizer of part-time faculty.

In "Instruction," Kat Meads tells of her single semester teaching first-year composition as an adjunct. Far tougher for her than the poor pay, the packed classrooms, and the cramped and noisy shared office space, was the steady stream of suffering—"parental abuse, alcoholism, depression"— that swept over her as she read her students' often very personal writing. Their lives were difficult, and her ability to help, stretched as she was, remained severely limited. Of one struggling student, she writes: "I had been hired to correct Mark's comma splices, his dangling participles, his run-on sentences – that was my job, the duties for which I was being paid. But after reading *Luckily my dad died when I was small*, I could only set aside my pen."

"Contingent Teaching, Corporate Universities, and the Academic Labor Movement," by Joseph Entin, offers a broad overview and detailed analysis of the ways the class hierarchy in college teaching can damage faculty and students alike. For those teachers at the bottom of the pile, "low pay, high job turnover, institutional invisibility, little or no funding for research and professional development" can "discourage scholarly growth, pedagogical innovation, and individual attention to students." But Entin also believes that the trend toward greater use of "flex teaching" can be fought, and he provides a not entirely disheartening historical survey of graduate assistant and adjunct unionization drives.

Class, of course, often intersects with other identities in the educational and working lives of faculty. In "Anti-Intellectualism, Homophobia, and the Working-Class Gay/Lesbian Academic," Carlos L. Dews and Carolyn Leste Law write of growing up in conservative, southern working-class families where education was "believed to make men effeminate and women masculine." For these future academics, going off to college and becoming professionals seemed like a path toward sexual freedom as well as intellectual development. But things proved more complicated. Law discovered that, among colleagues, she had to "negotiate the class closet in higher education just as [she] was emerging from the queer closet," while Dews, as a new teacher at a largely working-class school, was surprised to find that revealing his working-class background helped him bond with his students, while revealing his sexual identity drove many of them away. For Dews and Law, class can combine with other identities to form a "tangle of fear" that faculty and students need to learn to untangle.

IV Students' class and classroom dynamics

No matter which students and teachers find themselves together at college, social class will be an essential component of their interactions. If teachers remain attentive to the contradictions this can produce, they may be able to minimize the potential harm and perhaps even use these contradictions to enrich their teaching. Class matters in college life, sometimes most when we realize it least.

Differences in social class can be especially glaring in very expensive colleges, where students on financial aid or working part time may feel alienated from (and perhaps subtly disparaged by) their better-off classmates. In "Stories Out of School: Poor and Working-Class Students at a Small Liberal Arts College," Laurie Nisonoff, Susan J. Tracy, and Stanley Warner explore class tensions at Hampshire College, a progressive institution dedicated to building a diverse student body, but where "class contradictions as an internal campus issue are seldom examined." They point out, for example, how students who had family members and close friends in the military— often as a result of what one called the "poverty draft"—felt alienated from what seemed to them like an easy antiwar stance on the part of faculty and fellow students. The authors suggest a number of ways to address this and similar problems that can arise when class issues are pushed aside.

Erin Smith, teaching mostly working-class students in a night class on Gender and Education at the University of Texas at Dallas, had no trouble getting her students to understand issues of class and power in education, at least at a theoretical level. But one day, while casually telling them about the ways the elite students she formerly taught at Duke often argued fiercely against her in class, she realized the extent to which her UT students had silently internalized the consequences of their own class positions. "Class Privilege, Oppression, and the World in the Classroom" describes her efforts to make class privilege, and its absence, visible—a significant challenge when we "are in no way encouraged by public discourse to think of ourselves as having class identities at all."

Class comes into the classroom at an unusual angle in "Enforcing the Rules." Taylor Stoehr writes of his work with probationers in the Massachusetts Changing Lives Through Literature program, where probation terms are shortened by 6 months for those who complete his 10-week course. Stoehr explores the impact of various traditional behavior rules—about absences, about tardiness, about homework undone—on the learning and personal development of students who are "certified 'failures,' whose report cards have both 'F' and 'Felony' inscribed on them." In doing so, he offers much to think about for teachers of other students whose class backgrounds might tempt these teachers to think their students would benefit from more rigorous external discipline.

In "Upward Mobility and Higher Education: Mining the Contradictions in a Worker Education Program," Emily Schnee analyzes the sometimes painful tension between "education for upward mobility and education for critical consciousness." Studying interviews with and writings by former students in a union-supported program connected to the City University of New York, she realizes that students' desire for individual upward mobility is more complex than she'd thought, that teachers can find ways to ally it with their own desire to encourage a broad social critique. Schnee urges teachers to have a serious dialogue with students about these possible tensions and to teach in a way that "honors the legitimacy" of students' class aspirations without abandoning the goal of "critical consciousness building."

V Teaching about class in the humanities

Many humanities faculty have eagerly integrated issues of race, gender, and sexuality into their research and teaching, and so courses in humanities departments are a natural place to give issues of class the attention they deserve. However, as Linda Dittmar writes in this section, "despite their emphasis on liberatory discourses as key to social change, both poststructuralist theory and identity politics ended up participating in the broader silencing of class-focused discourse in the United States." Teachers who have already been developing their critical analysis and pedagogy in other ways can only enrich their work by giving class the emphasis it deserves; we have nothing to lose but our chains.

"Working-Class Cultural Studies in the University," by Lawrence Hanley, represents an attempt to rescue this young field from the fate that has befallen multicultural studies, which he believes has left behind the radical impulses that initially created it. Despite its "attention to oppression and resistance," he writes, multicultural studies has suffered from "a repressed consciousness of its own participation in the reproduction of class relations." To avoid going down the same road, working-class cultural studies "needs to begin with working-class people's demands on institutions, curricula, syllabi, and pedagogy." Hanley describes his efforts to take his own advice.

Linda Dittmar finds film studies, "steeped" as it is "in Hollywood's glamour industry," especially oblivious to class issues. In "All That Hollywood Allows: Film and the Working Class," she describes a course that analyzes depictions of the working class in a wide range of classic films—films in which she sees a "shared practice of suppressing class consciousness, disempowering workers, discrediting collective bargaining, and invoking religion as a stand-in for social change." She argues for critical teaching about representations of the working class, something she hopes will help both students and faculty "reconceptualize working-class identities and politics."

Janet Galligani Casey found her students at an elite private liberal arts college eager to discuss literature by and about people whose lives were very different from theirs, but reluctant to entertain the "unsettling" idea that their own "behaviors, preferences, and even their decision to study literature might be related in part to class formations." In "Canon Issues and Class Contexts: Teaching American Literature from a Market Perspective," she outlines a final project she devised that asked students to design and to "sell" a "class-oriented American literature anthology"—a project that helped them see how literary "taste" can be shaped by class in ways that had been invisible to them.

In "Teaching *Howards End* to the Basts: Class Markers in the Classroom and in the Bourgeois Novel," Ed Wiltse describes his efforts to encourage his very diverse group of students to explore the contradictions in E. M. Forster's novel. "All of the standard American mythology about mobility and a classless society," he writes, "stood in the way of our discussion of class's structuring role in the lives of Forster's characters, and in our own." He found a way in, however, through the character of "poor Leonard Bast, a clerk living 'at the extreme verge of gentility,' but with a hunger for the easy cultural capital" that other characters "possess as a birthright"—and through a number of ingenious strategies that have application far beyond the specifics of his British literature course and Forster's novel.

VI Teaching about class across the campus

The small sampling of approaches outlined in this section can only hint at the potential for integrating issues of class into teaching outside humanities classrooms. But this potential is great, all across the campus—even, as Emily Drabinski demonstrates, in special lessons on using the library. Nothing, apparently, is safe from the critical eye of class analysis.

In "Empathy Education: Teaching About Women and Poverty in the Introductory Women's Studies Classroom," Jennifer Scanlon spells out her practical approach to helping her mostly middle-class students get beyond their quite unempathetic stereotypes of poor women. She began by creating hypothetical representative characters—a mother on welfare and food stamps, and an employed single mother of two, for example—and then asked students working in groups to come up with budgets and other strategies for dealing with the problems of daily living these women would face. Most students ended up more or less able to "identify with their character," and their follow-up presentations and their discussions of public policy options were often "light years away from the blaming-the-victim approach" many had begun with.

If any social class is the object of study in college courses, it is usually the working class. But in "Teaching an Interdisciplinary Course on the American Upper Class," Richie Zweigenhaft argues for the importance of focusing our attention on the top, in order to understand how this very small class reproduces itself, how it exercises power through key public and private institutions, and how its actions impact everyone else. In a lesson, for example, on Veblen's *Theory of the Leisure Class*, he asked his students (a diverse group) to take a "driving tour" around Greensboro, North Carolina, where his Quaker liberal arts college is located, and to analyze what they saw using the concepts Veblen provided. For many, this was a major step toward understanding "the way the class system is stacked in favor of those born into the upper class in America."

Finally, in "Teaching About Class in the Library," Emily Drabinski writes of the college library skills classes she conducts. She points out to students where the Library of Congress classification scheme places titles about class, what these titles are near and what they're far away from, and how this arrangement embodies a conceptualization of class as "something malleably related to the individual rather than causally related to economic theory or public financing." She also explores the ways that the invisibility of class in subcategories outside the social sciences might suppress its significance in these other areas—whether literature, or science, or the arts. Questioning this official categorization, she argues, "can help students understand class as something operating even if we do not see it," for unexamined structures "not only govern the library, but what and how we know, and in turn, what we can be."

PART ONE

What is Class?

1

Is Class an Identity?

Richard Ohmann

The word "class" can suggest many things at once— economic structure, power dynamics, family history, personal experience—and each essay in this collection embodies its own implicit definition of class. Here, Richard Ohmann directly confronts the question of what class is, discovering that teachers may see class very differently than their students do—and that this difference can make for an illuminating classroom exchange.

In my section of Introduction to Literature, we were discussing Jane Austen's *Emma*. I knew from experience that a lot of students would have silently rejected the premise of the plot—indeed, of almost all those nineteenth-century plots: that whom one marries is really important, where "whom" refers less to any unique individual (Mr or Miss Right) than to a social status and the conduct that is supposed to enact it in public. Their expected incredulity was in fact the starting point for the unit on *Emma* that some of my Wesleyan colleagues had developed.[1] We would work through letters of Austen, historical documents, and historically based criticism to open a vista of marriages as hugely consequential for the two parties and their families, for the social order of the village, and, beyond that, for the very future of England, which depended in part on whether the landed gentry and the aspiring commercial class would peacefully negotiate their relations and justly rule the nation and the world.

Most students could understand the historical and symbolic seriousness of marriage within and across classes, and even see how such issues got tangled up in the emotions of individual lovers. But along with this grudging acknowledgment went an almost palpable sense of condescension, and of relief that our own civilization had left such superficialities behind, that nobody could now be stigmatized or ruled out as a marriage partner because his or her family was "in trade," that we were free of class chains and class blindness. I decided, one year, to challenge the assumption:

"Well, hypothetically if you were ever to get married" (I had to put it that way to get past their quite proper unwillingness to leave lesbian and gay people out of the conversation and their perhaps less proper revulsion against marriage as an arrangement even for straight couples) "if you were to get married, would class lines be no barrier?"

"Certainly not" –general agreement "it's love that counts."

"You would be as free to marry a 7–11 clerk as a medical student?" "Of course we'd be less likely to meet and get to know the clerk, but it's the person, not the job or the money, that matters."

"What about differences in education or taste?" "No, the 7–11 worker could read the same books and like the same music that we do." (I hear strains of *My Fair Lady*.)

"And how would your parents react to news of your plans?" Hmmm: that turns out to be a quite different story. To translate their response into my own words: the parents didn't shell out $25,000 a year or otherwise support and strive, and sacrifice, in order to have their kids marry straight down and out of the professional-managerial class (PMC). The parents, though maybe nice enough, are old fashioned, bound by antique social rigidities; they are something called "classist." If only we could get rid of classism, along with sexism and heterosexism, and racism, people would be unhampered individuals at last, free to love where the heart sings, perhaps even to marry; and the ghost of Jane Austen could rest in her grave.

Now let me acknowledge the narrow reach of this anecdote. Wesleyan University is selective and expensive. Over half of the students have some kind of financial aid, but even many of those come from PMC families. The rest have, with help from parents, striven to join that class. Many of those are minorities. All have come to a college that, like many similar ones, advertises its diversity as an attraction. The ethos is liberal, respectful, what its enemies like to call "politically correct." Most students hate prejudice and inequality; they accept the goal of a small utopia in Middletown, Connecticut, at whose threshold you check all invidiousness, distinction, and privilege based on color or gender or sexuality or ethnicity. (I think that's one meaning of the disappearance of family names from social interaction, so that it's almost rude to ask "Jason what?" after an introduction).

But if this analysis is right, the anecdote may after all have something to teach about class and identity. These students have entered a college world that is supposedly without hierarchy. Living for a while in such a "diverse" world is a PMC initiation ritual; living in a classless world is, paradoxically, a manifestation of class privilege. To notice or make a fuss about class would, then, spoil the illusion; it would remind all that they came to a selective college in part to preserve or upgrade their class standing. It would call into question their individuality, uniqueness, and freedom. So, they enact class without allowing its reality—at least now, at least in this society, at least for enlightened Wesleyan students.

Granted, the students are reasonably self-aware. They can mock the ideology. Gags about "diversity" abound: "Wesleyan is so diverse that you can meet people here from almost every neighborhood in Manhattan." The students make their way through the world with sensitive compasses and gyroscopes that tell them also which neighborhoods in Brooklyn are homelike to them and which parts of Boston; which places have nothing to do with their lives (e.g. Staten Island and Paterson); where are the places to go after college (New York, San Francisco, Seattle, Boston, Washington); where they might spend summers; what styles and fashions signify how to speak in what Basil Bernstein called the "elaborated code" of the middle class[2]; how to place those who don't; how to avoid alienated labor by deploying credentials or creativity and—yes—whom to marry, should it come to such a pass. Their political causes are numerous and sincere. They know there are rich and poor people. But many are reluctant to decode all of this intuitive knowledge, and much else, in terms of class.

Is class an identity? I think yes. It is a complex and powerful identity, a script you act out daily, a bundle of habits and feelings and ways of relating lodged deep in your psyche and broadcast by your talk and conduct. It is not instantly visible like race and gender. But neither is it easy to revise or conceal—much harder than suggested by those ads for tapes you can listen to while commuting, which will soon have you speaking as well as Henry Higgins, thus shielding yourself from harsh inferences about your background.

But most people don't so readily identify themselves by class as by gender or race, and perhaps don't even feel being working class or PMC the way they feel being white or male or straight or, especially, being Latino or black or female or gay—except of course when they are way out of their usual class habitat: a mechanic plunked down in the Century Club, say, or an English Professor at the Elks. And even such misadventures are not likely to endanger the displaced person, the way women and African Americans and gay men and others risk insult or violence in many venues. Class is not so insistent, not so turbulent an identity as these others. Famously, a large majority of our fellow citizens place themselves in the vague and commodious middle class—just as our rulers would have them do, in order to preserve this supposedly classless and harmonious society. In writing courses I sometimes would ask students how they characterized their class membership. A typical set of uncomfortable replies: 18 middle or upper middle class, and two not. One of the two said she was "lower class"; the other said his family was "rich." Bold and disconcerting replies, I might add.

I have much less experience of other class locations in US education, but I wonder if these generalizations mightn't apply, at least partially, in settings very different from Wesleyan. The students I taught a couple of times at our local community college knew where they came from and where they were, and they knew it wasn't Harvard. But except for a couple of trade unionists, they were reluctant to think of the difference in terms of class. First-generation college students, they had a big stake in believing anyone could make it in this country. Class seemed an artificial barrier and a rebuke to their hopes of rising. They needed to see class as epiphenomenal.

Now, of course the ideology we take in with every breath has a lot to do with the many ways in which students at Wesleyan and at Middlesex Community College overlook or evade the hard reality of class. The U.S. is a country where every immigrant's destiny is to make good, or at least enable his and her kids to make good. A country with no hereditary ranks, where everyone is as good as everyone else. A country where all who work for a corporation are part of a big "family." A country with equal opportunity, where you end up with what you earned through talent and hard work.

So, for any teacher of composition or literature who wants to nourish critical thinking and writing, this is rich soil. The potential for demystification, for thinking through the myths we have lived, is large. In addition, class so subtly mixes the external (hood or burb, Brooklyn Tech or Exeter) and the interior (including language and love) that the possibilities for discovery through writing are exciting and endless. I used to adapt Ira Shor's classroom investigation of best and worst jobs to get students started on what they expected out of life and how they imagined the mass of people who had the worst jobs.[3] (The best imagined jobs were all professional or creative— we're a PMC institution.) Students did collaborative projects on work, taking off from Studs Terkel and interviewing people at the college and elsewhere about their jobs. A couple of times, students set off to interview others they knew to be rich or poor, discovering among many things how differently the two classes imagined social space. The kids without money talked about college as an escape hatch, a way to "get out of" rural Maine or their Korean neighborhood in Queens. The rich students had the whole world in their sights, a sense of choice as their birthright, but also, often, an ethos of obligation or even guilt, derived from their good fortune. I have written about group projects on dress and fashion that discovered class in every morning's choice of garments. Interviews were one of my favorite media for the writing class, for various reasons.[4] But my point here is not to recommend that pedagogy, just to urge a focus on class.

Those my age remember that for the more privileged college students, race, gender, and sexuality were also in hiding through the 1940s and

50s. It took Betty Friedan and James Baldwin and Paul Goodman and the movements of the 60s to make them real, put them on the educational agenda. If they sometimes reside there as frozen identities surrounded by halos of correctness, we can try to complicate that rigidity in our teaching and political work, partly by considering how these identities interact with one another and with class. In teaching about class, I think we start at a more basic level. Yet students and teachers do have deep reserves of tacit, textured knowledge about class. We can draw out and structure that knowledge, adding what social scientists know; understanding why class won't go away if people just stop being snobs; theorizing; *writing* class in the writing class.

It's a good time to be doing that. After long absence, class has once again become visible in the public arena, if crudely, as the "widening gap between rich and poor." Everywhere, global capitalism is degrading and casualizing the labor of the old, industrial working class—but also of the PMC itself. Look at what's happening to our own profession, including to most of the people who teach first-year writing courses. Students seeking class advancement face that same barrier. There's room for solidarity between students and instructors, perhaps in ways that have not been possible for a while—perhaps even in a way comparable to the solidarity that sometimes pervades and enlivens black and women's and queer studies classrooms.

Notes

1 This essay is based on a talk I gave at the 2001 convention of the College Conference on Composition and Communication. I have written about this course in "Teaching Historically," an essay included in my *Politics of Knowledge: The Commercialization of the University, the Professions, and Print Culture* (Middletown, CT: Wesleyan University Press, 2003).
2 Basil Bernstein, *Class, Codes and Control*, 3 vols. (London: Routledge & Kegan Paul, 1973).
3 Ira Shor, *Critical Teaching and Everyday Life* (Chicago, IL: University of Chicago Press, 1987).
4 See "Writing and Empowerment." In Richard Ohmann, *Politics of Letters* (Middletown, CT: Wesleyan University Press, 1987).

PART TWO

Who Gets to be in
the Classroom

2

A Dream Deferred: Undocumented Students at CUNY

Carolina Bank Muñoz

Class, in all its dimensions, deeply affects which students end up in which college (if any) and whether they are able, psychologically as well as economically, to stay. The challenges faced by undocumented students involve not only getting into college, and staying in college, but also staying in the country. Carolina Bank Muñoz describes teaching, advising, and struggling alongside these threatened, and highly motivated, students at Brooklyn College.

I first became aware of the difficulties for undocumented students at the City University of New York (CUNY) when I started teaching a course at Brooklyn College, a CUNY campus, on the sociology of immigration. On the first day of class, five students requested appointments to speak with me in private. This was extremely unusual to say the least. All five students were undocumented and had family members who were undocumented. They were hoping I could help. As one student put it, "I'm hoping you can teach me how to get my papers." I had to explain that I was not a lawyer, nor was the class about how to immigrate "legally," but about the social process of immigration. Needless to say, the students were deeply disappointed, but nevertheless stayed enrolled in the course. One student in particular made a tremendous impression on me.

Luisa came to the United States when she was 5 years old.[1] Her father was diagnosed with a rare and serious illness and they initially migrated so that he could be treated. Like many other immigrants, they obtained a visa to visit the United States. Once Luisa's father was treated and recovering, they decided to remain in the United States. They overstayed their visa, and from one night to the next became undocumented. Luisa attended public school while both of her parents worked in the garment industry. After Proposition 187 passed in California, Luisa's parents decided that it was time to leave California and move to New York, where the antiimmigrant climate was less intense.

During high school, Luisa worked after school as a seamstress in the factory where her mother worked. Her father was now a union janitor and their financial situation had stabilized substantially. In her last year of high school, Luisa started researching colleges. At that point she realized that there were very few opportunities for undocumented immigrants. She had been in this country for 12 years. She had learned English, worked hard, and made good grades. Yet, she was not going to be able to simply apply to college like many of her classmates. Despite her 3.8 GPA, Luisa would have to attend a community college because she simply could not afford to pay full tuition at a 4-year college and she was not eligible for any federal loans. After working full time and attending school part time for 3 years, Luisa had finally saved enough money to enroll at Brooklyn College. During her first year at BC, Luisa's brother was deported. She used her entire savings to bring her brother back to the United States across the US-Mexico border and was forced to drop out. She was devastated to have to delay her education, but her family was the priority. After a 2-year hiatus from school, Luisa was able to re-enroll at Brooklyn College. That very semester she enrolled in my immigration course. While Luisa's story is incredible, it is not exceptional. Hundreds of undocumented students across the country have similar stories.[2]

In fact, over 60,000 undocumented students, the vast majority of whom are people of color, graduate from high school every year (UCLA Labor Center 2007). Most of these students migrated to the United States at a young age along with parents or other family members. Yet they are subject to the same harsh immigration policies as their parents, who predominantly work in the low-wage sector. The United States is the only home that most of these students know, but they are forced to live in the shadows of American society, in fear of Immigration and Customs Enforcement (ICE), with marginal access to good jobs or a college education.

For these students, a college education is usually only a dream. In fact, only 5 to 10 percent of these students make it to college (UCLA Labor Center 2007, NILC 2006). Undocumented college students have no access to federal and state student aid, work study programs, or many scholarships. Furthermore, since the 1990s but especially since September 11, 2001, access to higher education for undocumented students has been severely curtailed. Many states passed laws that required colleges and universities to charge nonresident tuition to undocumented students (Gonzales 2007). Nonresident tuition is often two to three times more expensive than in-state tuition, making it nearly impossible for undocumented students to attend college.[3]

The half-dozen undocumented students in my class and the more than 2000 undocumented students at CUNY (according to the CUNY Immigration and Citizenship Project) have had to overcome tremendous adversity to be at the university. Over the course of the semester, several of my students saw their family members deported, one student successfully evaded a workplace raid by Immigration and Customs Enforcement, and two students had to drop out because they simply could not afford to stay in school. Since my first experience with these five students, I have run into dozens of undocumented college students across CUNY who have had to drop out of college, find work, save money, and return to college a few years later. Many never return to school because they simply do not earn enough in the low-wage sector or underground economy to afford a college education.

Undocumented students are systematically denied access to a college education by a flawed immigration system that has roots in institutionalized racism. At its root, contemporary immigration policy is inherently flawed because it seeks an individual solution to a structural problem. In the recent round of immigration reform, legislators have focused on either blocking the flow of migration through "solutions" such as a border fence or severely limiting it through guest worker programs and other means. These policies treat immigration as a faucet that can be turned on and off. In fact, immigration is far more complex. There are structural conditions and policies that force people to migrate. The North American Free Trade Agreement (NAFTA), structural adjustment policies, and war—all impact migration. NAFTA, in particular, has been instrumental in increased forced migration from Mexico. NAFTA resulted in removing tariffs that were protecting Mexican farmers without removing US subsidies to US producers. As a result, the Mexican market was flooded with underpriced agricultural goods from the United States, especially corn. Unable to compete with these underpriced goods, Mexican farmers had no choice but to leave their land and seek employment in other parts of Mexico. Many displaced farmers migrate to large cities in Mexico to work in factories. As those factory jobs disappear or are exported to other countries, these former farmers have nowhere to go but to the United States (Bank Muñoz 2008). Ironically, then, US economic and trade policies are significantly responsible for the increase in immigration from Mexico and other Latin American countries.

The ongoing backlash against immigration disproportionately affects immigrants of color (militias and vigilante groups such as the Minutemen are not for the most part violently attacking "illegal" Germans). As Ngai (2005) aptly puts it, "restrictive immigration laws produced new categories of racial difference ... The legal racialization of these ethnic groups' national origin [in the 1920s] cast them as permanently foreign and unassimilable to the nation"(7–8). A perfect example is that in the contemporary immigration debate, Latina/o immigrants are racialized as "illegal" even if they were born in the United States or otherwise hold "legal" status (Bank Muñoz 2008).[4] This blanket racialization falls on undocumented students in very particular ways.

The crisis in access to higher education for undocumented students affects not only the students who are in college or trying to get into college now, but also younger undocumented students who drop out of high school because they see that they have no opportunities for upward mobility. We are facing the possibility of a lost generation of extraordinarily bright and talented students. What can we, as radical teachers, do? In the following sections, I will discuss immigration policy at CUNY, the challenges and opportunities presented in both teaching and working with undocumented students at Brooklyn College, and some ideas for action.

Immigration policy and practice at CUNY

Since the late 1980s, educational immigration policy has been implemented at CUNY in a variety of ways. From 1989 to 2001, students who were undocumented but had lived in New York for more than 1 year were eligible to pay in-state tuition. Even in 1996, in the wake of the Oklahoma City bombing, when the federal government passed an immigration act that denied undocumented students in-state tuition, CUNY held its ground and did not change its progressive policy. However, after 9/11, in the midst of the hysteria over immigrants and terrorism, CUNY (like all colleges in New York State) immediately changed its policies and began charging undocumented students nonresident tuition. As a result of significant public pressure, New York State changed its laws again in 2002 (National Conference of State Legislatures 2006). At this writing, undocumented students need to have attended a New York State high school for 2 years and enrolled in a state college or university within 5 years of graduation to qualify for in-state tuition. This new law is significantly more restrictive than the previous law that only required that individuals live in New York for 1 year to qualify for in-state tuition.

Despite changes in the law, undocumented students who want to enter a CUNY school face serious access problems. Fischer (2004) demonstrates that even when undocumented students have access to in-state tuition, a majority do not use the benefit. Sometimes it is because they do not know about the program. More often than not, it is because they simply cannot afford a college education. This is significant in terms of life chances, because workers with BA degrees will earn on average, over a lifetime, a million dollars more than high school graduates (Day and Newburger 2002).

Furthermore, those immigrants who do access the in-state tuition programs overwhelmingly enroll in 2-year community colleges and vocational schools instead of 4-year colleges and universities. Once at CUNY students face additional barriers. There is significant misinformation about who is in fact eligible for in-state tuition and who is not. At Brooklyn College, for example, numerous students have reported to me that they were told by admissions officers that they do not qualify for in-state tuition, because they do not have social security numbers. This, of course, is not accurate, but it has the effect of turning away eligible undocumented students who often do not know their rights under the law. Only the most persistent students, who do their research, know their rights, and access the very limited support resources available, end up making it into CUNY. Even these exceptional students face serious problems once they enter the university. According to several undocumented students at Brooklyn College, even once they have made it into the university they are looked down upon by administrators, professors, and other staff who mark them as "illegal," either because they have not presented a social security card or because the last four digits of their social security number are not on the roster. Were it not for all these barriers and gatekeepers, there could potentially be far greater numbers of undocumented students at CUNY.

Teaching and working with immigrant students

Working with immigrant students, and particularly undocumented students of color, offers various opportunities and challenges. On the one hand, their life experience provides them with an intuitive sense of the global economy and of racial and class disparities. Many of them come from the Global South and have experienced poverty, racism, and exploitation. These students also tend to have a greater understanding of world politics. Needless to say, their knowledge and experiences contribute tremendously to a vibrant classroom environment. I recall a particularly intense classroom discussion over the idea of reparations. Native-born Blacks were arguing that only Black people who can prove a link to slavery in the United States should benefit from reparations, while Caribbean Blacks argued that they were also entitled to reparations because they were forced to migrate to the United States due to the devastations of globalization and colonization. All students in the class, immigrants and native-born alike, benefited tremendously from this exchange.

In my experience, undocumented students are among the most self-motivated and focused students we have, perhaps because they have the most to gain or lose. There are very few paths to obtain permanent residence and a green card. One can acquire it either through a family member (spouse, parent, etc.) who is a US citizen or through employment.[5] Employment is often the best option for undocumented students. In this case, employers have to make a case for why a foreign national (instead of a US citizen) is better suited for the position. A college degree gives undocumented students, especially in high demand fields, some hope of finding a job in which an employer will be able to help secure their immigration status. On the other hand, having to drop out of school minimizes the chances that these students will find good jobs and a road to citizenship. Therefore, college recruitment and retention of undocumented students is imperative for enhancing their life chances.

Unfortunately, undocumented students face extreme barriers to succeeding in school and completing their college education even when they overcome the barriers to getting into college. Immigrant students in general and undocumented students in particular often live in poor neighborhoods with underfunded public schools. This is also true for other students of color. However, immigrant students have the additional barriers of having had to transition from schools in their native countries to a new method of US education and to learn US English.[6] As a result, they often have weaker writing and public speaking skills than other students have. Additionally, as I have already mentioned, many of these students face significant barriers outside the classroom which limit their prospects for campus-based activism.

What can we do? *Support the Dream Act*

It is not good enough to rely on states to change their policies regarding undocumented students. We need a federal policy that would affect all states so that all undocumented students have access to higher education in the United States. To this end, lawmakers have been trying to pass the Dream Act, which would give undocumented students a road to citizenship. Several variations of the Dream Act have been introduced in Congress since 2001. While no form of the legislation has passed, as of this writing, it has gained significant momentum. The Dream Act would make two major changes to current law. It would "permit certain immigrant students who have grown up in the U.S. to apply for temporary legal status and eventually obtain permanent status and become eligible for citizenship if they go to college or serve in the U.S. military" (NILC 2007). It would also "eliminate a federal provision that penalizes states that provide in-state tuition without regard to immigration status" (NILC 2007).

Under the Dream Act, students of "good moral character" who came to the United States at age 15 or younger would obtain conditional permanent resident status (6 years) upon acceptance to college, graduation from a US high school, or achievement of a General Educational Development (GED) certificate. Students would also be able to qualify for the federal work-study program and for student loans. At the end of the 6-year conditional period, students would be granted unrestricted lawful permanent resident status if "during the conditional period the immigrant has maintained good moral character, avoided lengthy trips abroad, and either (1) graduated from a 2-year college or studied for at least 2 years toward a B.A. or higher degree, or (2) served in the U.S. Military for 2 years" (NILC 2007).

The Dream Act is far from perfect. The condition of "good moral character," for example, is troubling. How is moral character defined? How would gay students, activist students, students who have been arrested for acts of civil disobedience, and students in left organizations fare under this condition? What kind of invasive investigations into their moral character would they be subjected to? These are all important questions, and as a result of the vagueness of the concept, a significant layer of students would not be eligible to reap the benefits of the Dream Act. Furthermore, the option of participating in military service to obtain permanent resident status is deeply problematic. It gives military recruiters who already prey on communities of color further ammunition to convince these students to participate in military service instead of going to college. States would have an incentive to encourage young undocumented immigrants to go into the military since it would save them the costs of granting in-state tuition and save federal government Pell grant money. Moreover, given that recruiters use free college tuition as a carrot for potential recruits, joining the military might look especially attractive to young undocumented immigrants.

In addition, the Dream Act would not require (or prohibit) states to provide in-state tuition, nor would students qualify for federal Pell grants. They would, however, be eligible for federal work study and student loans. In short, the Dream Act has many problems. However, it would offer undocumented students a path to citizenship. Most importantly, states would not be restricted from providing their own financial aid to students. Given that we are unlikely to see progressive immigration reform in the near future, it is important to support the Dream Act as a first step toward change.

Organizing at the state level

Because of the limitations of the Dream Act (if it eventually becomes law), it is important to keep organizing at the State level. As I have mentioned, as of this writing, only ten states provide undocumented students with in-state tuition, and only two of those (Oklahoma and Texas) offer such students state financial aid (Krueger 2006). As radical teachers, we can make this a key legislative issue and work with our unions and the community to change state policy.

Activists in California provide an excellent example of mobilizing around this issue. In May 2007, the UCLA Center for Labor Research and Education held a public hearing on the state of undocumented students (UCLA Labor Center 2007). The hearing was attended by legislators, community members, and students (both documented and undocumented). Senator Gil Cedillo chaired the proceedings and provided information on the pending California Dream Act, which he had introduced into the State Senate in February 2008 (UCLA Labor Center). The introduction of the bill was followed by a teach-in at UCLA in March to bring the dire situation of undocumented students to public attention. The California Dream Act was approved by the State Senate and Assembly, but was vetoed by Governor Schwarzenegger.

Teach-ins and public hearings

Despite some public attention, the barriers facing undocumented students are still largely unknown. It is crucial to educate students, faculty, staff, legislators, and the broader community about this topic. As I mentioned above, UCLA has held both teach-ins and hearings on the subject, drawing more than 300 attendees. At Brooklyn College, Students for Direct Action (SDA) organized a teach-in in the spring semester of 2007. The purpose of the teach-in was to draw attention to the issue at CUNY, specifically at Brooklyn College. One panelist courageously shared her story of the challenges she faced as an undocumented student at CUNY. Other panelists spoke about the rise of anti-immigrant sentiment in the surrounding campus community since September 11, 2001. Over 50 students, faculty, and staff attended the event, held a week before finals. As a first step, this was a significant event in terms of bringing this issue to the attention of the campus community. We hope to organize more events on the campus this coming year.

Immigration clinics

Colleges, universities, and law schools across the country have started immigration clinics to provide legal resources to undocumented college students and to the broader community. CUNY established the CUNY Immigration and Citizenship Project in 1997 to address the needs of an increasing number of foreign-born students at the university. CUNY has "the most comprehensive immigration law service and education program of any college or university in the United States" (CUNY Immigration and Citizenship Project). The mission of the program is "to provide free, high quality, and confidential citizenship and immigration law services to help immigrants on their path to U.S. citizenship" (CUNY Immigration and Citizenship Project). Under the leadership of Prof Allan Wernick at Baruch College, the program has grown significantly. We have eight free immigration clinics on the campuses and an additional six clinics which are located in the community but affiliated with the university (CUNY Immigration and Citizenship Project). These clinics are run by law students, paralegals, professors, and students themselves. In addition to providing legal resources for students, these clinics also function as safe spaces where students can meet and share their common issues and concerns. Hundreds of CUNY immigrant students and immigrant New Yorkers in general have benefited from this project.

In the spring semester of 2007, a group of faculty, staff, and students talked about starting an immigration clinic at Brooklyn College. There was tremendous enthusiasm about the project. Given the number of immigrants on the campus, we felt that it would be a project that would inspire and activate a considerable layer of progressive students. Ironically, the very problems the clinic hopes to address have affected our ability to organize quickly: several of the students who were most enthusiastic about working with me on the project had to drop out of school in the fall semester because they simply could not afford to stay in school. These setbacks only strengthened our resolve: the next spring, we renewed efforts to start the clinic.

Conclusion

Why is higher education for undocumented immigrant students so important? It's a fundamental issue of rights. Today, we would be hard-pressed to find individuals who do not believe that women and native-born minorities should be given access to higher education. What is so different about someone who at the age of five was brought to this country by their parents? The United States is the only country that a majority of these students know. They are going to stay, work, pay taxes, and possibly raise families in this country. As I have mentioned, earning a BA degree significantly improves the life chances of all citizens. An education means access to better jobs, which means access to savings, which means access to the accumulation of wealth that is passed on from one generation to the next. A majority of these students will be contributing to our economy, culture, and collective conscience. As a nation, we should want undocumented students to be empowered through education.

Currently, our immigration policy is sending the message that undocumented students who have been raised in the United States are disposable. Undocumented students' dreams and aspirations are shattered every year, as they realize that they have few possibilities for obtaining a college degree. Many lose hope for the future and begin the slow decline into accepting their fate. Others turn to crime and violence as a method of releasing their frustrations with inequality. Undocumented students who migrated to the country with their parents should not be expected to pay the price for a flawed immigration system. As radical teachers, we can support the plight of undocumented students by working with them to win access and resources for a college education and inspire them with hope for a meaningful future.

Notes

1   All names have been changed to protect students' identities.
2   For an excellent resource on this issue, see Gabriela Madera, et al., eds, *Underground Undergrads: UCLA Undocumented Immigrant Students Speak Out* (Los Angeles: UCLA Center for Labor Research and Education, 2008).
3   As of this writing, only ten states (California, Illinois, Kansas, New York, Oklahoma, Texas, Utah, Washington, New Mexico, and Nevada) had passed laws permitting undocumented students to pay in-state tuition. (Immigration Policy Center).
4   There is a wealth of scholarly work on this issue. Notable works include: Nicholas DeGenova, *Working the Boundaries: Race, Space, and "Illegality" in Mexican Chicago* (Durham, NC: Duke University Press, 2005); Leo R. Chavez, *Shadowed Lives: Undocumented Immigrants in American Society* (Fort Worth: Harcourt Brace College Publishers, 1998).
5   There are also a variety of refugee programs. However, these are very limited in eligibility. For more information on all the roads to permanent residence, visit: www.uscis.gov.
6   I use the term "US English" because many immigrants from the Caribbean already speak English, but the writing norms and vocabulary for US English are different. So, while these students speak and write English, they often have to relearn it to reflect US norms.

References

Bank Muñoz, Carolina. (2008). *Transnational Tortillas: Race, Gender and Shop Floor Politics in Mexico and the United States*. Ithaca, NY: Cornell University Press.
CUNY Immigration and Citizenship Project., http://web.cuny.edu/about/citizenship.html.

Day, Jennifer Cheesman and Eric C. Newburger. (2002). "The Big Payoff: Educational Attainment and Synthetic Estimates of Work-Life Earnings." *Current Population Reports*. U.S. Census Bureau, 1–13.

Fischer, Karin. (2004). "Illegal Immigrants Rarely Use Hard-Won Tuition Break." *Chronicle of Higher Education*, A19–21.

Gonzales, Roberto. (2007). "Wasted Talent and Broken Dreams: The Lost Potential of Undocumented Students." *Immigration Policy in Focus*, v5(13): Immigration Policy Center, 1–11.

Krueger, Carl. (2006). "In-state Tuition for Undocumented Immigrants." Education Commission of the States, http://www.ecs.org/html/Document.asp?chouseid=6100.

National Conference of State Legislatures. (2006). "In-State Tuition and Unauthorized Immigrant Students," http://www.ncsl.org/issues-research/immig/in-state-tuition-and-unauthorized-immigrants.aspx.

National Immigration Law Center. (2006). "Basic Facts About In-State Tuition for Undocumented Immigrant Students," http://istillhaveadream.org/in_state_tuition_basicfacts_041706.pdf.

—. (2007). "DREAM Act," http://www.nilc.org/DREAMact.html.

Ngai, Mae M. (2005). *Impossible Subjects: Illegal Aliens and the Making of Modern America*. Princeton, NJ: Princeton University Press.

UCLA Labor Center. (2007). "Undocumented Students, Unfulfilled Dreams. . . ." Report. http://labor.ucla.edu/publications/reports/Undocumented-Students.pdf.

3

Last in and First out: Poor Students in Academe in Times of Fiscal Crisis

Vivyan C. Adair

Vivyan Adair, who herself started college as a welfare recipient, gives voice to poor women who faced not only cultural challenges on campus but also often outright hostility, not to mention the very punitive changes brought about by the Personal Responsibility and Work Opportunity Reconciliation Act of 1996. Today's data are different from those in the immediate wake of that "welfare reform," but the challenges poor women seeking higher education face have, if anything, intensified.

The disparity between the experiences of allegedly "deserving and normative" middle-class and wealthy students and those of low-income students in higher education is clear when we consider practices that at best discourage and at worst prohibit the poorest of the poor—welfare and former welfare recipient parents—from earning educational degrees. Despite numerous studies confirming the relationship between higher education and increased earnings (Adair and Dahlberg 2003; Greenberg et al. 1999; Strawn 1998; Wolfe and Gittell 1997; Thompson 1993), in 1996 Congress enacted the Personal Responsibility and Work Opportunity Reconciliation

Act (PRWORA) as a part of welfare reform. Composed of a broad tangle of legislation, this Act "devolved" the responsibility of assistance to the poor from the federal to the state level and, through a range of block grants, sanctions, and rewards, encouraged states to reduce their welfare rolls by developing work requirements, imposing strict time limits, discouraging "illegitimacy," and reducing the numbers of applicants eligible for services. The Act also allowed for the development of programs and requirements that had the effect of discouraging welfare recipients from enrolling in higher-education programs, mandating rather that they engage in "work first."

Specifically, the Temporary Assistance for Needy Families (TANF) work requirements, part of the 1996 PRWORA, drastically limited poor women's opportunities to participate in postsecondary education programs while receiving state support. Unlike previous provisions in Aid to Families with Dependent Children (AFDC) and JOBS education training programs in existence when I first went to college as a single-mother welfare recipient student in 1987, TANF restrictions from 1996 did not allow higher education to be counted as "work" and required a larger proportion of welfare recipients to engage in full-time recognized work activities. This work-first philosophy emphasized rapid entry into the labor force and penalized states for allowing long-term access to either education or training.

As a result of the dramatic overhaul of welfare policy in 1996, recipient students left college for low-wage jobs in record numbers. Even as we as a nation embraced the belief that access to education is the pathway to social and economic mobility, poor women were denied access to higher education that could have positively altered the course of their lives and those of their children. According to the Center on Budget and Policy Priorities, in the first year of welfare reform, tens of thousands of poor women were forced to drop out of school; across the nation, the decrease in enrollments among welfare recipients ranged from 29 percent to 82 percent (Bazie and Kayatin 1998; Greenberg et al. 1999; Pastore 1999; Strawn 1998).

In 1998, the Center for Law and Social Policy (CLASP) conducted a preliminary survey of key policy advocates in the 50 states and Washington, D.C., regarding welfare recipients' abilities to enter into and complete educational degrees. The study found that welfare recipients are "generally unable to count postsecondary education as a work activity" (Strawn 1998: 28). The CLASP study reported that, as a result, the number of families reported as participating in activities that would lead to a postsecondary degree was cut in half by 1998. In 1995, almost 649,000 students across the nation were receiving AFDC benefits while enrolled in full-time educational programs; by the 1998–99 school year, that figure had dropped by 47.6 percent, to fewer than 340,000 students. By 2004, the number was estimated to have been reduced again by over 93 percent, with a national enrollment of fewer than 35,000 students.

The prospects for students shut out are dismal. A 25-year-old former computer science major with a 10-year-old son now works earning $7.90 per hour (2004). In response to my query concerning changes in her family's quality of life as a result of the 1996 reform, she wrote:

> I call it welfare deform. Things are so much harder now. We can barely pay our rent. My son is alone all the time when I work. I just don't see a future anymore. With school there was hope. I was on my way to making a decent living for us. Now it is just impossible to survive day to day. Usually I can't pay my rent. They are hounding me to repay school loans and I don't have enough for food. Did you know that you can't even bankrupt student loans? I don't have a cent saved for emergencies. I don't know what I'm [going to] do.

Another gifted and dedicated education major returned to welfare after being forced to leave the university and then losing several minimum-wage jobs because she could not afford reliable child care and was denied child care assistance from the state for failing to name her child's abusive father. She described the nightmare of losing job after minimum-wage job in order to care for her child, emphasizing that this was a "choice no mother should be forced to make." She added:

> It came down to, if I want to keep this job at [largest retailer in the U.S.] I have to leave my three year-old daughter alone or maybe with a senile neighbor. And I couldn't even really afford that! Or we could go back to her dad who is a drunk. If I don't do that we could both end up hungry or homeless. The choice they are making me make is to either abandon or hurt my daughter, and for what?

Similarly, Tonya Mitchell, the single mother of twins and a very successful prenursing major committed to providing health care for low-income and minority populations, was forced to drop out of a nursing program and was assigned a "work first position" in a nursing home. She reminds us, "all I wanted was to be a nurse and help care for people. I had a very high grade point average and was on my way to a nursing degree with jobs that pay over $25 an hour in addition to benefits." Today, after over 6 years as an aid, Mitchell makes $8.75 per hour. She adds:

> I still need help from the state with childcare and food stamps and life is so much harder for us now than it was before. Clearly welfare reform and the Personal Responsibility Act changed our lives. I do not have the money I need to pay my rent and bills, my twins are in an awful daycare for about ten hours a day while I work in a job I hate, and we have little hope. If we survive it will be despite welfare reform! (Mitchell 2003: 163)

The experiences of students who had worked diligently to become responsible workers, taxpayers, and parents capable of providing their families with some degree of financial security, and who were forced to drop out of school to live in perpetual poverty, illustrate one startling failure of 1996 "welfare reform."

In 1997, policy analysts Leslie Wolfe and Marilyn Gittell warned that "the work requirement of the new federal welfare law is causing thousands of low-income women to drop out of college to take dead end jobs with low pay and no future. This exodus of welfare recipients from the classroom must stop" (1999: 1). The hope among committed educators and social activists was that this failure would be remedied in 2002 when the PRWORA came up for reauthorization. A record number of educators, educational administrators, students, and citizen activists lobbied for reauthorization that would include postsecondary education as an option for welfare recipients. Despite these efforts, reauthorization of welfare reform's key legislation has proven to be even more punitive for low-income women attempting to earn educational degrees in the United States.

The House of Representatives Welfare Reauthorization Bill, passed on 16 May 2003, put greater limitations on recipients by allowing a maximum of 3 months of vocational training during a 2-year period and counting only "job readiness education," and not education and training that would lead to career development and sustainable wages, as work activity. The Bill (HR 4092) also increased TANF participation rates that all states are required to meet and increased the required hours each TANF recipient must work. House Bill 4092 set unrealistic work requirements for many families without necessary support services. The new TANF work goals required almost all parent recipients to work, and increased their work from 30 to 40 hours a week regardless of the ages of the children in the household. At the same time, the Bill provided only a fraction of needed child care dollars, prohibited child care assistance for non-work-related activities (such as school), sanctioned entire families (including children) if parents failed to meet work participation requirements, and gave states the right to override protections for families under federal law with a "super-waiver" provision.

Four months after the passage of HR 4092, the Senate Finance Committee approved a reauthorization bill, dubbed the PRIDE Bill (Personal Responsibility and Individual Development for Everyone). The Senate's PRIDE Bill also increased both work hours for individual recipients and states' participation requirements, but failed to allocate sufficient child care funds, and allowed state super-waivers to take precedence over federal protections. For many, the most egregious component of both the House and the Senate reauthorization bills was a reduction in allowances for recipients to enter into education programs and in child care funding, coupled with the ground-breaking earmarking of $1.5–$2 billion dollars in federal TANF funds over the next 5 years for a narrow set of rigidly defined "marriage promotion" activities.

As many welfare analysts and recipients argue, welfare reform in 1996 and the reform reauthorization in 2003 were designed to control, regulate, and somehow "neutralize" poor women's "illegal and unruly" bodies through the institutions of marriage and work. Indeed, the first sentence in welfare reform's key legislation proclaims that "marriage and work are the foundations of a civilized nation." From the perspective of welfare students, this prohibition against both personal fulfillment and independence through education and single motherhood has dangerous implications.

While being denied support with which to feed and care for their children and prohibited from entering into educational programs, welfare recipient parents are encouraged and rewarded for attending marriage formation clinics and workshops (for which child care and lunch are provided). During the last family formation seminar that I attended with student recipients in the basement of a church in Utica, New York, we were treated to a complimentary set of artificial fingernails, as we were reminded by a very enthusiastic pastor that a good wife yields to both God and her husband, sometimes even against the perceived needs of her own children. When a student participant from our group asked the Department of Health and Human Services Director, who was observing our seminar, his thoughts about higher education for the poor, he replied, without irony: "Education is necessary in order to support and nurture your families. I strongly encourage you to support your husbands in going to college and doing whatever they can to make you and your children healthy and happy. Millions of wives – even my own mother – helped put their husbands through school on the GI bill, and they wouldn't be where they are today if it weren't for that sacrifice."

Obvious questions arise from these mandates: Who are poor women going to marry? Why would poor women want to marry? How does marrying a poor spouse and risking more children lift anyone out of poverty? More fundamentally, legislation that denies poor women the opportunity to earn educational credentials, to be fulfilled as individuals, to be able to stand on their own two feet and care for their own children, coupled with rhetoric that says that all single mothers are bad mothers and that as a nation we can only value "legitimate" married mothers and their children, is, or should be, a problem for all.

These punitive and damaging welfare restrictions are exacerbated by an educational policy that dissuades low-income, single mothers from entering into college programs and completing degrees. My colleague Sandra Dahlberg has documented financial aid practices that further disadvantage already economically disadvantaged students. In "Families First: But Not in Higher Education," she reminds us that financial aid offers that count child and welfare income as resources but fail to offset them with child-related costs of living, grant and aid offers that result in a zero-sum game for low-income students, and minimum wage work-study programs that subsidize the profitability of US colleges and universities while penalizing low-income students, all create institutions that increasingly "penalize and facilitate the failure of low-income aid recipients" (Adair and Dahlberg 2003). The combination of lack of access to higher education, stringent work and parenting requirements, financial penalty for poor students, and lack of support for low-income student parents results in devastating drops in enrollment and college completion that are then used to justify further cuts in support and access.

PRWORA welfare reform policy has also dramatically impacted educational policy in state equal opportunity programs around the nation. Higher Education Opportunity Programs (HEOP) and Equal Opportunity Programs (EOP) are charged with recruiting and supporting underrepresented students of color and economically disadvantaged students. In the United States today, the vast majority of those living below the poverty line live in single-mother-headed households, with mothers who themselves have little or no experience with higher education. Throughout the 1980s and early 1990s, the EOP programs served about 58 percent students of color; the majority (over 90 percent) of those students were traditional age, dependent, childless students, and about 70 percent of those students were from low-income families. Thirty three percent of the students served in that same period were white, but economically disadvantaged students. In total, EOP and HEOP programs supported welfare student populations that made up about 12–15 percent of their total student population. EOP programs that supported these nontraditional, low-income student parents offered limited support to their students, but were able to calculate some nontraditional needs—such as child care and the cost of raising children—into their students' need equations.

In the postwelfare reform and reauthorization era, these figures are dramatically altered. In 2004, less than 0.5 percent of EOP and HEOP populations around the nation were low-income, single parents, and thus nontraditional students of any race. That 0.5 percent of students were no longer entitled to have family need calculated into their support packages and must fulfill all state and county work and reporting requirements, even if enrolled as full-time students, and of course as full-time parents.

All of these damaging material practices are exacerbated by pedagogical strategies that hurt poor students. An absence of comprehensive social, academic, personal, family, and career services in the academy means that poor single mothers often face insurmountable barriers to their education. A study my colleagues and I conducted in 1999 and 2000, at Hamilton College, provides additional analysis regarding some of these obstacles. Analyzing survey responses from over 85 former welfare recipient, postsecondary students in the Central New York area, we found that poor single mothers had indeed often left school even when they had been successful with their studies, because they could not manage child care, transportation, and work responsibilities. Respondents to our survey—who had attended a range of public community colleges, and public and private colleges and universities—made it clear that they also often ended their studies because they felt demoralized, misunderstood, and misrepresented in the classroom. When asked to cite the primary reasons that these students left school, only 20 percent noted that they had ever received a failing grade. A far greater number reported that they left school due to lack of sufficient social services, financial aid, and family support. And a startling number—almost 60 percent—also indicated that they left school because they had been made to feel "shamed," "worthless," and "invisible" in their classrooms and throughout their educational experiences.

One student said that the most important lesson she learned in a class on the sociology of poverty was that "my people, my family and I, and our culture are problems" and that "poor people in general, but welfare recipients specifically, are stupid and immoral drains on the country." Another student in our interviews spoke of attending a class on American literature with a professor who failed to interrogate pat, stereotypical depictions of poor women in Erskine Caldwell's *Tobacco Road*, or John Steinbeck's *In Dubious Battle*. She claimed: "I was so humiliated by what the professor found charming and amusing, that I left the class never to return to school."

In "Not by Myself Alone: Upward Bound with Family and Friends," Deborah Megivern similarly reflects on her experience in a political science class where "students expressed extremely negative and stereotypical views of poor people, and I was too afraid to challenge their thinking," and where her "shame and vulnerability about [her] background prevented [Megivern] from discussing [her] history or even sharing [her] perspective." For Megivern, classes focusing on poverty were especially challenging. As she recalls: "It felt as though people who had never gone hungry were essentially discussing my family, my friends, even me, as though we were all objects. When I attempted to share my first-hand knowledge of poverty, I did not have the credibility to be heard in class. At any rate, personal experience often is not a legitimate basis for disagreement in school, whereas it is a form of truth for poor people" (2002: 125).

My own experiences as a welfare recipient student certainly support these perspectives. My sense of dislocation and fragmentation was particularly acute in classes where I often became both the subject and the object of investigation. Experiencing an overwhelming sense of liminality, I recall one particularly painful experience in a graduate English classroom, in which students and teacher alike were lamenting and laughing at the inability of the poor to come to "political consciousness." One student—the daughter of a doctor and a lawyer, as I recall—joked that welfare women were "too busy bowling and breeding, too busy eating Cheetoes, and too numb with complacency" to fight for political equity. As the class chuckled in amused agreement, I felt ripped in two. I was laughing with those I hoped would be my new colleagues, about my own existence, my own people, and those I loved and valued. In the bitterness of that moment I knew that I was homeless. It took more courage for me to return to that class the following week than I have ever had to muster in my life.

For many poor single mothers, the academy becomes a place of fear and diminished value rather than a site of empowerment. For it is here that a culture that often "others" poor single mothers is represented and legitimized by those who profess authority over our lives. Low-income single-mother students often experience profound and debilitating terror, shame, humiliation, and objectification, even in classrooms meant to foster independent scholarship and critical thinking. Students feel alienated and inferior because of their poverty and social class, in ways that reflect the language and sentiments found in the PRWORA and in pejorative educational policy. As one former welfare recipient and honor student astutely reflected:

> With the passage of welfare reform, and the belief in the academy that poor women are stupid and undeserving, layers of citizens from welfare officials to teachers and students question why we are in school. Through their actions and in class they represent us as unworthy and imply that by attending college we are somehow wasting our and their time and money. One professor told me exactly what I had just heard the day before from my caseworker when he said "Why don't you get off your [behind] and quit playing here. Get a job or get married so you can take care of your kids. No one will allow you to waste your time in school."

And this is where it all comes together. Welfare reform, supported by voters, posits that poor women should either work or marry and that they are neither able nor entitled to go to school. Educational policy reifies this belief by financially punishing and failing to support this increasingly underrepresented population; and classroom pedagogy is the final nail in the casket, driving poor student parents away from the educations they so desperately need and want.

A small but growing number of colleges and universities have responded to the needs of this struggling population by implementing mechanisms designed to assist—rather than to thwart—poor single-mother students in their efforts to negotiate punitive TANF restrictions and gain access to higher education. In addition to designing, implementing, and advocating for programs and pedagogies that support these students, educators can have a significant impact on the lives of poor single mothers by working with state legislators and local welfare offices to create policies that support and enable low-income student parents to earn educational degrees; by lobbying to extend the amount of time recipients can receive educational training beyond states' enrollment limits; by encouraging colleges to work with state and local officials to provide employment opportunities that are aligned with academic and family schedules; and by working for economic parity by attempting to amend PROWRA reauthorizations. Educators can also be a force in reshaping the Higher Education Act, so that poor women can go to college, so that financial aid offices can count the costs associated with dependent children in the needs analysis for federal student aid, so that student financial aid can be exempted as income when calculating welfare eligibility, and so that increased Pell Grants will cover dependent care allowances.

There is much work to be done. As educators we stand at a critical junction. If we challenge ourselves to champion and support this vulnerable population in their attempts to negotiate punitive contemporary welfare and college restrictions and prohibitions against earning college degrees, rather than participating in their disenfranchisement and removal from the academy, we will take a step toward positioning education as a truly democratic project with the potential to enact social change and foster economic opportunity. As an educator who believes in and works to enact the radical potential of higher education, and as a generationally poor woman whose life was transformed through education, I not only accept but embrace this challenge.

References

Adair, Vivyan. (2001). "Poverty and the (Broken) Promise of Higher Education." *Harvard Educational Review* 71(2): 217–39.

Adair, Vivyan and Sandra Dahlberg. (2003). *Reclaiming Class: Women, Poverty, and the Promise of Higher Education in America*. Philadelphia: Temple University Press.

Adair, Vivyan, Eroi Balkan, and Sharon Gormley. (1999–2000). Clinton, New York: Hamilton College. Unpublished survey.

Bazie, Michelle and Toni Kayatin. (1998). *Average Incomes of Very Poor Families Fell during Early Years of Welfare Reform*. Washington, D.C.: Center on Budget and Policy Priorities.

Dahlberg, Sandra. (2003). "Families First, But Not in Higher Education." In *Reclaiming Class: Women, Poverty, and the Promise of Higher Education in America*. Ed. Adair and Dahlberg. Philadelphia: Temple University Press, 169–95.

Greenberg, Mark, Julie Strawn, and Lisa Plimpton. (1999). *How State Welfare Laws Treat Post-secondary Education*. Washington, D.C.: Center for Law and Social Policy.

Megivern, Deborah. (2003). "Not By Myself Alone: Upward Bound with Family and Friends." In *Reclaiming Class: Women, Poverty, and the Promise of Higher Education in America*. Ed. Adair and Dahlberg. Philadelphia: Temple University Press, 119–30.

Mitchell, Tonya. (2003). "If I Survive, It Will Be Despite Welfare Reform: Reflections of a Former Welfare Student." In *Reclaiming Class: Women, Poverty, and the Promise of Higher Education in America*. Ed. Adair and Dahlberg. Philadelphia: Temple University Press, 113–8.

Pastore, Claire. (11 August 1999). "Threatened with Lawsuit, State Overhauls Policies for Student Welfare Recipients." *Equal Rights Advocates*. On line at http://www.equalrights.org.

Strawn, Julie. (1998). "Beyond Job Search or Basic Education: Rethinking the Role of Skills in Welfare Reform." Washington, DC: Center for the Law and Social Policy.

Thompson, Joanne. (1993). "Women, Welfare, and College: The Impact of Higher Education on Economic Well Being." *Affilia* 8: 425–41.

Wolfe, Leslie and Marilyn Gittell. (1997). *College Education Is A Route out of Poverty for Women on Welfare*. Washington, DC: Center for Women's Policy Studies.

4

Welfare "Reform" and One Community College

Susan Jhirad

Picking up, in a sense, where Vivyan Adair left off in the previous essay, Susan Jhirad explores the lives of poor women determined to stay in college in an era of rapidly eroding social support; the focus here, though, is on organized political attempts to fight back. The challenges today are somewhat different from those of the late 1990s that she describes, but the efforts she documents provide a valuable model of faculty involvement with students in their individual and organized struggles.

I tend to think of community colleges in general, and my own in particular, as a "Last Chance Saloon," a bastion of equal opportunity in a society that increasingly rewards those born rich and powerful. Community colleges serve not only women on welfare, but also the laid-off worker, the disabled, the poor, the returning veteran, the immigrant, the "displaced homemaker," people of all ages, ethnic, and economic backgrounds. Even Republicans claim to want people to "pull themselves up by their bootstraps," which may be why President Bush felt obliged to pay lip service to our nation's community colleges all the while underfunding and defunding their programs.

In a burst of ideological fervor, I once viewed my own college as "the salvation of the working class," much as I had previously viewed revolution as bringing that salvation. Through my years as a political activist—starting with the Civil Rights movement in 1962 and on through the antiwar and women's liberation struggles, and then 9 years of working and organizing in factories—I had pretty well burned out with trying to change the whole world. By the time I began teaching in a community college, I thought maybe I could change just a little piece of it. Even working there on what seemed like a limited, winnable reform—helping welfare recipients gain access to education and training, and allowing those activities to count as work—proved to be a daunting, 6-year-long task, as the political climate deteriorated and funding for all sorts of services disappeared.

Even so, some truth remains in the idealized image I originally brought to my teaching job at North Shore Community College. We continued to serve immigrants, laid-off workers, and displaced homemakers. We still offered an education at far lower cost than public 4-year colleges. We still were the place where students who never dreamed of going to college could find an open door to college life, from English as a Second Language and basic language courses, to upper-level college courses that transfer to prestige colleges. We still provided a welcoming, supportive environment for students who faced the greatest obstacles, both psychological and economic.

However, my rose-colored glasses became somewhat clouded with the years, as my college (like others) took serious hits: antiaffirmative action at the federal level resulted in the elimination of our excellent Minority Engineering Program, Project Interlock; cuts in state funding and increases in tuition and fees left many of our poorest students shut out; immigration reforms made it ever more difficult for immigrants to attend college; and, finally, welfare reform (termed "welfare deform" by women who have experienced its effects), bringing with it a work first, antieducation philosophy, disastrously reduced the number of welfare recipients we serve. From a high of nearly 900 before welfare reform, time limits and work requirements brought us to a welfare population of around 100–120 in 2005. As one recipient activist put it, "How are we supposed to pull ourselves up by our bootstraps when we don't have any boots and they don't have any straps?"

A short history of state and federal welfare reform[1]

In 1995, the state of Massachusetts passed its own welfare reform plan, bringing a 2-year time limit (24 months, down from 60) and work requirements that explicitly excluded education and training. How such a restrictive plan came about in a relatively liberal state is a cautionary tale for progressive activists. Briefly, after years of legislative work on a moderate welfare reform plan that would have allowed education to count as work, our Republican Governor, the wily William Weld (who once touted his "successful welfare reform" plan in his failed attempt to run for Governor of New York), managed to persuade two of our most liberal, but tragically naive, state senators, Dianne Wilkerson and Lois Pines, both of whom opposed welfare reform, to cast decisive votes against the legislative package, promising that he would improve the plan. Why they believed the word of a millionaire Republican, who had long proven hostile to any sort of social program, remains a mystery to this writer. However, their votes effectively killed the more moderate plan. Incensed legislators, who had worked for years to craft the compromise, simply threw up their hands and allowed Weld to substitute his own, far harsher proposal.

The result: a plan that placed a 2-year time limit on the receiving of welfare (the federal plan had a 5-year time limit), and the imposition of 15–20 hours a week of work requirements, which was later pushed to 24 or 28, depending on the age of the youngest child, and was later raised even more. These requirements could be met by paid work or community service, but not by education or job training. In response to this, I, along with Erika Kates, long-time researcher and advocate for welfare and education, together with a group of welfare recipient students (mainly from our state's community colleges), legal advocates, teachers, researchers, and activists, founded an organization called Welfare Education and Training Coalition (WETAC). In conjunction with many other state-wide organizations, we struggled for years to pass legislation that would allow education and training to count as work. In 2004, as I had all but given up hope, such a measure did pass, surviving a veto by yet another Republican Governor, Mitt Romney. Job training, basic education, and community college could count. Four-year college, however, would no longer be permitted, thus cutting off the welfare recipients who attended the University of Massachusetts, some of whom became welfare activists in WETAC and in the excellent campus-based organization Survivors Inc. Although community college now can count, the 2-year time limit remained daunting for community college students, few of whom complete programs in 2 years (the average among our students was 3.5 years for a 2-year degree).

After Massachusetts implemented the plan, Republican Governors Cellucci and Swift, along with their appointed directors of the Department of Transitional Assistance (DTA), continued the harsh, work-first philosophy. "Get a job, any job" was their mantra. In short, our students (most of whom had worked minimum wage jobs during their lives) were now to be taught the value of hard work. The major flaws in this argument are as follows: 1. Raising children is hard and worthwhile work. 2. Education is necessary if poor women and men are ever to rise out of poverty. (Endless research data affirms the obvious: education leads to better jobs, higher return in taxes, and better lives for the women and their children—for example, the children of women who go to college are more likely to go to college themselves). 3.

Minimum wage jobs will never pay for quality (or any) child care, which, in our state, is in short supply. One of my students said, "It's pretty ironic, isn't it. They'll pay to put my kids in day care during the summer so I can work. But they won't pay me to spend time with my own kids!"

Just as we advocates were making headway, especially with our mainly Democratic state legislature, we received a crushing blow. In 1996, Democratic President Bill Clinton announced with pride his own federal welfare reform plan, including a 5-year, lifetime, limit on assistance (the state plan at least allowed people to return to welfare if necessary after 2 years off) and a mere 12 months of vocational training that could count as work. Over 40 states applied for waivers from the plan, including Massachusetts, though some did allow more education and training. In 2003, the Republican Congress and President Bush passed further restrictions, allowing only 3 months of vocational training and specifically excluding any higher education. In short, both in the nation and in the state of Massachusetts, the message was out. Go to work; forget school. The impact on the political climate and on my own community college was dramatic. Now, welfare deform was bipartisan, and welfare recipients were on their own.

North Shore Community College

North Shore Community College is based in Lynn, Beverly, and Danvers. It serves a diverse population, especially in Lynn, historically the home to many immigrants. It was once the center of the world-wide shoe industry, and has had a long, proud working-class tradition. It still has one of the few large factories left in Massachusetts, GE Lynn. Our immigrant students come from Southeast Asia, Haiti, Latin America, Africa (especially Nigeria), and Russia, among other countries. Some of our students are political refugees. I have taught a Tutsi student who was jailed and tortured, a Haitian student whose father was shot in front of him by the military dictatorship, and many Cambodian students who served time in forced labor camps, as well as Vietnamese "boat people."

We serve approximately 7,000 full-time students a year in a variety of academic and career programs, as well as thousands of students taking noncredit courses. Many of our students take 2 years of Liberal Arts courses that apply for transfer into 4-year college (provided the student maintains a C average). While most of our low-income students transfer to state colleges such as Salem State and the University of Massachusetts, some, especially from our Honors Program (which has always included a number of welfare recipients), have gone on to prestigious 4-year colleges—Smith, Wellesley, Mt. Holyoke, Brandeis, Tufts, and Boston University among many—on full 4-year scholarships.

Our career programs—including Nursing (rated the best nursing program in the area), Engineering, Legal Administrative Assistant, Early Childhood Development, and Criminal Justice—have sent out students who have almost immediately found relatively well-paying jobs with benefits, and sometimes even with child care. When more liberal state and federal welfare laws still permitted women to go to school, receiving paid child care and transportation (their college tuition was never paid for—they received Pell grants and student loans, just like other students), they flourished.

In addition, our college offers three separate programs—Challenges, Choices, and Change; Women in Transition; and Motivation to Education—that provide special support systems, including counseling and tutoring, to low-income women both on and off welfare. One program is state funded, one funded by our own college, the third by a federal grant. Some of the women teaching and counseling in these programs are themselves former welfare recipients. Toni Hatfield in CCC and Carellen Brown in Motivation to Education not only supported the women in their programs, but also became advocates for WETAC. Finally, thanks to the activism of one of our former recipient students (she went on to get her MA in English at Simmons), who 10 years earlier organized a sit-in in our college president's office to highlight the need for on-site child care, we now have a Head Start Center right in our Lynn campus building.

The results of this are hundreds, if not thousands of success stories. To name but a few: D., a single mother living in a homeless shelter, graduated from North Shore Community College's Honors program with a 4.0 grade point average, received her 4-year college degree at Wellesley, went on to get her PhD in engineering at the University of Michigan, and now does cancer research. Last year, she was the inspiring Commencement speaker at our college. L., abandoned by her cocaine-addicted husband with five children under the age of five (he stole the car and cleaned out the bank account), graduated from NSCC and went on to get her MA in History from Suffolk University. When last I heard from her, she had a good job in the Suffolk administration. N. graduated from our legal administrative assistant program and immediately got a well-paying job with benefits and child care. Many have graduated from our nursing and other health professions programs and immediately found jobs. C, abandoned by her husband, went through our college, became active on our school newspaper, *The Pennon*, and went on to become a full-time staff writer for a Beverly newspaper. She helped found a student club that provided support for single mothers receiving welfare. Another student, M., is now a successful businesswoman who gives public talks about the critical importance of her NSCC education.

In short, North Shore Community College offers a warm, supportive environment for women who are poor, abused by both the men in their lives and the welfare system itself, and lacking in self-confidence. It is not a cliché to say that they have been empowered by these programs to continue their educations and become successful.

Effects of "welfare reform" in our college

Although the effects of state welfare reform on our student population were dramatic, they were not uniform, or immediate. At first, confusion and fear reigned. Women literally cried in the hallways at the specter of losing their hopes. Students who had gone onto welfare before a certain date (January 1995) were technically able to be grandfathered in, permitted to pursue their education until completion. Some students were aware of this; others were not. Massive confusion at our local welfare offices continued throughout the years of other changes wrought by welfare reform. Welfare workers often did not know the rights of the women or, sometimes poorly educated themselves, resented their clients' getting an education. They were also under pressure from Claire McIntire, director of the DTA under Weld and subsequent Republican governors, who had considerable leeway in her interpretation of the state law. She was explicitly hostile to the cause of education and training, and added her own restrictive regulations to the system. It did not help matters that in the next couple of years, cutbacks caused the layoff of welfare workers and the shutting down of the Lynn welfare office. Student recipients from Lynn were forced to go to Salem (a hardship for those without cars) to face overworked, ill-informed, and often grouchy welfare workers.

Advocates had to inform students of their rights, because welfare offices did not. The case of our student L. is particularly sad. The law explicitly stated that a mother caring for a handicapped child is exempt from both time limits and work requirements (at this writing, Governor Romney was trying to change this humane provision). L., young mother of three children, had been encouraged to enter NSCC under our Women in Transition program. She had already enjoyed a year of school and was very happy, fulfilling a long held "dream." She had one severely disabled 5-year-old child, who could not walk or talk, and was in a special school. This child was disabled because his father had beaten L. within an inch of her life while she was pregnant. Obvious case for an exemption, right? Wrong. Her welfare worker insisted that since her child was 5 years old (then the point at which the work requirement went into effect; later it was when the child is three) and "in school," she needed to go to work. With the aid of a sympathetic attorney, she could have fought the case. I encouraged her to do so, but this was a woman who had been beaten. She was afraid to take on her abuser. So, she decided to drop out of school and take a job at

Boston Market. Unfortunately, although her employers were sympathetic, she was too often late to her job because she had to take her disabled son to his special school. So she had to quit, and was therefore cut off welfare for "noncompliance." "What will you do?" I asked her. "I'll be all right," she told me. "We grow vegetables in the back yard for food, and I'll give quilting classes. Besides, when I was little, my family lived in a school bus. I know how to survive." Her enduring spirit moved me, but I was terribly sad that she had to give up on "her dream." Her story was so poignant that when Ann Withorn, activist-professor at the University of Massachusetts Boston, asked if I had any recipient students who could attend her class that was meeting with a *Boston Globe* reporter, I asked L. if she would come with me, suggesting that it would help other women if she could tell her story to the public. Though very shy, she finally agreed and we drove together to U. Mass. However, the reporter insisted that she be allowed to use the woman's real name in the article. Fearing her abuser's retribution, she refused.

Another young student attended one of our campus WE-CARE meetings. She was facing homelessness and needed advice. She also was pregnant, but about to be penalized under the "family cap" provision of state welfare reform. That is, if a woman has more than two children, the third child will be denied any benefits. (This measure passed under the faulty premise that women were having lots of children simply to obtain the munificent sum of $90 a month per extra child. In fact, statistics show that the average number of children of women on welfare was two, like that of the general population.) The young woman whispered in our meeting that the child was a result of rape, but she didn't believe in having an abortion. When we asked why she didn't tell her welfare worker about the rape, she said, "Because I was raped by a cop." This young woman did drop out. Heaven only knows what happened to her.

Another of my students was living in a homeless shelter, where new regulations required her to drop out of school and spend her time in "structured job search" instead. This new DTA policy made women without jobs spend 30 hours a week looking for minimum wage jobs and learning things like "how to dress for success," rather than obtaining education or real job skills.

Some of our students did fight back. One was told that with only a month to go before she obtained her nursing diploma (and a virtually guaranteed nursing job), she should drop out and work for minimum wage. The insanity of this proposition was obvious to virtually every legislator I lobbied, including Republicans. But the student said, "I'm staying in school. I don't care what they do. I've worked too hard for this. I'm not going to give up." And she didn't. She worked, went to school, took care of her kids, and got her degree.

K., for a time the student head of our WE-CARE club, was informed by her caseworker that she owed the DTA thousands of dollars, because they had "overpaid" her. I still believe that this was the result of harassment, because K's photo and her comments against welfare reform had appeared in the *Lynn Item*. Luckily, she had saved all her receipts, proving that she owed them nothing. She also brought me to the Salem welfare office to back her up. I believe that both these factors forced the officials to back down. In many cases, either I, or our sympathetic Dean of Students Cheryl Finklestein, a strong supporter of women on welfare, called the DTA and made them back down when they unfairly tried to deny child care or transportation to our students. Caring legal advocates from Neighborhood Legal Services in Lynn (Laura Gallant), Greater Boston Legal Services (Melanie Malherbe), and Mass Law Reform in Boston (Pat Baker, Deborah Harris) also helped our students (and me) with crucial legal advice. Some came to our college to give workshops on the complex ins and outs of Welfare Reform law. Our WE-CARE newsletter also tried to inform women of their rights to an education. Some of our students attended hearings, and visited legislators at the State House to testify for our cause, even though they were scared to death. Generally, they were well received, although when one unsympathetic legislator implied that poverty was my student T's own fault, I thought she was going to punch him out.

Some women do manage to juggle work, school, and children. But it is very hard. When M., an outreach worker for WETAC, testified at the State House about the difficulties of her life, and she proudly stated that she was managing to raise five children, attend University of Massachusetts Boston, and work as a social worker, this testimony was used against her. Some said, well, if she can do it, why can't all of them? Activism can be a double-edged sword for women on welfare.

One NSCC student, excited at a sympathetic interview she had been given by *The Christian Science Monitor*, decided she would offer another interview to *The North Shore Weekly*. Unfortunately, this newspaper was hostile to welfare recipients. After she had given the interview, she called me, sobbing, "they came to my house, and all they did was trash me." The reporter looked around her house suspiciously, then said, "Well if you're on welfare, how come you have a car?" She wanted to rescind her interview, but it was too late. The article managed to smear not only her, but also me, suggesting that the only reason I was helping welfare recipients stay in school was so I could keep my own job. To a tenured English professor, this argument was ludicrous, but it shows how the media can twist the stories of those who are brave enough to speak out.

Where we are now

As stated above, in 2004 the Massachusetts legislature did pass an amendment allowing education and training to count as work. This positive measure was offset, however, by a dramatic increase in work requirements. Now, under pressure from more stringent federal laws, there was a push to increase this to 40 hours, and to increase the mandatory participation rate to 70 percent (mothers with handicaps and those caring for handicapped children were required to participate). The increased pressures of life, work, and education have brought a definite decline in activism among students on welfare. Our club WE-CARE eventually died for lack of attendance. There were simply too few hours in the week for women to attend meetings. WETAC, too, ultimately collapsed, due to lack of funding, internal conflicts, and, I believe, the difficulty of involving overextended welfare recipients as activists. The Family Economic Initiative, a coalition in which we worked, continued to advocate at the State House for the cause of welfare recipients. Mainly, they tried to block ever harsher measures from being passed.

It is obvious that for most single mothers, responsible for their households, their children, work, and education, welfare reform has been daunting. We do still have some welfare recipients at North Shore Community College, though far fewer; we still have our wonderful Challenges, Choices, and Change and Women in Transition Programs (I have had the privilege of teaching the English classes in CCC), but the obstacles for women getting that all-important education are enormous. Cleaning, cooking, working, driving their children to doctors' appointments, all the while studying for tests and trying to keep up the high standards they have set for themselves academically: this is the life of women who, according to those in power, "need to be taught the value of hard work." Maybe they should tell it to our nation's President. Oh, I forgot. He's on vacation.

Note

1 For a detailed overview of federal welfare reform, see Vivyan Adair, "Last In and First Out: Poor Students in Academe in Times of Fiscal Crisis" in *Radical Teacher* 73(2005), reprinted in this volume.

5

Teaching Freire and CUNY Open Admissions

Kristen Gallagher

The connections between social class, race, and college success can themselves be made the subject of classroom discussion. Here, Kristen Gallagher describes a course in which she asks students to explore campus archives and to analyze the implications for their own lives of what they discover. Her approach has something to offer any teacher who wishes to engage and empower students in new ways.

"Open admission – college for anyone who wants it – has long seemed to many educators the natural extension of the American ideal of equal opportunity for all."

—Fred Hechinger, "The Problem of Open Admission to College"

"Our next subject is equity and the equitable ... and their respective relations to justice and the just ... [The] equitable is just, but not the legally just but a correction of legal justice ... And this is the nature of the equitable, a correction of law where it is defective."

—Aristotle, Nicomachean Ethics

At LaGuardia Community College of the City University of New York (CUNY), we are lucky to have two things: the most ethnically and linguistically diverse group of students in the United States, and the LaGuardia and Wagner Archives, an archive of the mayoral papers of every New York City mayor, beginning with Fiorello LaGuardia. Faculty from a variety of disciplines use the archive to teach New York City issues, from the history of graffiti or community gardens to the garbage strikes of the 1970s or the development of the Meals on Wheels program. A wealth of personal letters, recorded speeches, letters of complaint, memos, photographs, and artifacts is available to anyone who wishes to use it. This archive is where I first came across the compelling list of "Eighteen Demands" for open admission to City College of New York made by Black and Puerto Rican students in 1969. I had been teaching Paulo Freire's chapter "The Banking Concept of Education"[1] to my English 101 composition students for years, but I hoped supplementing Freire's ideas with this document and some further history of open admissions would provide new insights into what Freire meant by "the scope of action allowed to students."

Previously, reading Freire had been enlightening to students, but we rarely got past talking about personal bad experiences with school. Students would recount stories of bad, sometimes abusive, teachers who cut down students' own patterns of thought and response. They were often shocked that one could conceive of education in any way other than to treat students as "empty 'containers' waiting to be 'filled' by the teacher." Our conversations allowed students, often for the first time, to dream about what a school could be and to think about what they really wanted to learn for themselves. It opened up an opportunity to imagine taking control of their own educational goals beyond financial gain. But I often felt we were not making the connection to the social and political ramifications of education systems and policies. In the end, adding the archival resource on open admissions inspired more concrete and wide-ranging questions and helped move the discussion beyond the personal into the social.

Beginning with Freire

Beginning with students' personal experience still felt useful as a way into this discourse, so I began by having them write about their previous education in terms of key ideas from Freire. I asked them to quote at least one key idea from Freire and pair it with an experience—positive or negative—that served as an example of the concept. As usual, many students discussed how much of their previous education had served only to "obviate thinking," to stop them from expressing themselves or asking necessary questions. One student, Karen, a young woman who had emigrated from Columbia 5 years earlier, described a particularly oppressive teacher who made her write and rewrite her papers until not only her English grammar, but also her ideas, matched perfectly the ideals of the teacher. She put it well: "her personality threatened to eclipse my own." Writing about past educational experiences seemed cathartic to the students. Story after story indicated students were realizing as they wrote how often they had simply been told what to do and followed orders—or did not, to their own academic peril. One student wrote, "I think this is why I never cared to do so good in school. I am in nature a resistant person. I don't like to do what I'm told. I have my own ideas." He went on to describe one teacher who differed from that pattern and how that had been the one time he enjoyed school and did well.

Though this was a great bonding experience for the class and a much-needed catharsis, I hoped that studying the history of open admissions would expand students' awareness beyond the personal, "partial view"—the sense that educational experience is simply an individual one whose critique should center on personal freedoms and insecurities—toward a realization of the role education plays in forming (or deforming) the connections of all humans to one another, and that it would work against the idea of school as a place to consolidate power over others. The idea of a college education in the United States is woven throughout with assumptions about competition and "getting ahead." Many colleges even sell themselves as places where graduates can increase their earning potential and compete for better jobs—to be the manager instead of the managed. While it is important to acknowledge the desire for class mobility that draws many students to college, we know that for every one of the students from a background of poverty or recent immigrant status who gets ahead, there are many more who stay poor. I want to help students see college as a place to explore all the varieties of thought and action available to them, instead of simply a place to accrue financial power. Furthermore, I wanted them to see how their education could help them challenge the forces that make college into a place that simply reproduces a workforce. It is my experience that, as students begin to understand how their positions connect to and participate in the creation of others' positions, the mythology around college as a place to get ahead starts to dissipate.

The history of CUNY open admissions

CUNY, the nation's largest urban university, was founded in 1847 as the Free Academy of the City of New York. Its goal was "to give poor and working class students a chance for a first-rate college education" (Crain 2001: 37). By 1969, you could say the university had succeeded, but its student body was largely white, in spite of the fact that the college's surrounding community was not. On 22 April 1969, a group of mostly Black and Latino students, influenced by educational initiatives of the Black Panthers, Young Lords, and Students for a Democratic Society, took over part of the City College campus and "demanded that the student body better reflect the ethnic and racial makeup of the surrounding Harlem community" (Crain 2001: 37). During the takeover, students made a sign reading "Harlem University" and hung it at the main gates of the campus.

This is where the "Eighteen Demands" were delivered. A bit lengthy in their original written form, essentially they ask for the following provisions: to accept all Black and Puerto Rican students regardless of scholastic record; to provide free tutorial and basic skills courses; to abolish course requirements and attendance policies; to make the existing Black and Puerto Rican Institutes autonomous; to end biological and chemical warfare research and cooperation with the CIA; to establish a student resource center and lounge exclusively for Black and Puerto Rican students; to implement a yearly increase of financial assistance to needy students; to never raise fees or tuition without student consensus; to hire 50 Black and Puerto Rican faculty; to allow students a direct say in the hiring and firing of faculty; to fire all white teachers who have shown racist tendencies; to provide special tutoring for Black and Puerto Rican students by Black and Puerto Rican faculty; to establish a six-credit course where students work with a community organization and are graded by that organization; to guarantee that no student, worker, or faculty member experience disciplinary action for attempting to implement these demands; to make all faculty take Latin American Spanish and courses pertaining to Black and Puerto Rican neighborhoods; to develop an exchange program, controlled by Black and Puerto Rican faculty and students, to bring Black and Puerto Rican scholars to the college; to re-hire the recently fired campus bookstore employee who initiated a fundraising program to provide books for poor students; and to "free the 21 Panthers framed-up by D.A Hogan and the City of New York."

We spent a great deal of time discussing these demands and doing problem-posing exercises (described later in this essay) when students disagreed with one another. Among the toughest issues for students were these: Can students really take part in hiring and firing faculty? Should faculty be required to learn Spanish? Can a college exist without course requirements?[2] More than anything, students were very curious about the emphasis on "Black and Puerto Rican students," and some were concerned that the demands excluded students who weren't Black or Puerto Rican. So in order to fully grasp this aspect of the history, it became important for students to investigate race and education in 1969. One assigned article that helped address race and open admissions describes the conditions of living in 1969 Harlem: "Evidence indicates that objective admission standards are working against black applicants. A combination of poor schooling, a past history of deprivation and the continuing impact of ghetto life keeps out a disproportionate number of blacks" (Hechinger 1969a, "A Growing Conflict," E11). We turned to this passage to discuss how "past history" affects present "success" in school. We discussed how a poorly funded, overcrowded New York City public school can affect students' chances at college, and linked poverty and racism to problems with academic standards. We went on to address how the stresses of poverty, violence, and racism create different kinds of questions and ideas in the minds of certain students—and how these differences, expressed in the classroom, are perceived by banking concept educators as outright hostility. Many students were satisfied with the insight gained from discussing this article in light of their own experiences,[3] but a few students remained disturbed by the repetition of "Black and Puerto Rican students."

Because English 101 involves not only work on essay writing, but also introductory research skills, I had students work in groups searching Lexis-Nexis and ProQuest Historical *New York Times* to see if they could find some further explanation for this emphasis on race. The results were fascinating. One group found a source describing how after World War I, when Ivy League universities such as Yale discriminated against Jews, CUNY became a haven for Jewish youth who wanted a chance at college (Oren 1985), and argued, "Race is nothing new to CUNY. If CUNY was the place for people of Jewish descent who were discriminated against in the 30s, then why not for Black and Puerto Rican people in the 60s?" Another group, influenced by a class member who was a middle-aged, white, native New Yorker and National Guardsman, reported that in 1969, one of the ways to get out of going to war in Vietnam was by enrolling in college. Their report included the statement that "not going to college in 1969 meant dying – literally." The student reports impressed everyone and much of the tension over race began to dissipate.

The students' success at solving their own problems with this history is further proof that Freireian student-centered education works. In pairing Freire with the study of open admissions, not only are we talking about the link between students' educational backgrounds and their scholastic preparation for college, but we are also talking about creating an experience of college as a place where students' diverse thought processes can be expressed, heard, and developed through discourse with one another. This moment in the class allowed students the experience of gaining for themselves, through their own processes, insight into the historical struggles of 1969. It also happened because students who felt disconnected from Black and Puerto Rican history felt free to admit their discomfort and get informed through a combination of research and discussion. Not only that, but this issue was not something I had planned to emphasize—here the students directed their own learning.

Equal educational opportunity for all in 1969 meant young people had to take enormous personal risks to correct City College where it was defective in meeting its own stated goal to give oppressed citizens a chance at the college experience. One article tells of Representative Adam Clayton Powell of Harlem showing up to support protestors after the City Controller Mario Procaccino procured a court order to take action against the occupation of the school. "Don't give up the struggle," Powell said. "I have fought the courts for eight years. I fought 100 judges. They said I was wrong but I won" (quoted in Brady 1969: 23). Powell's words played a central role for students in imagining the fight for open admissions. He adeptly called attention to the difficulty of fighting against common practices and unjust laws—the "law" in this case works against what seems fair, so the law itself must be confronted. Eventually, the City's political leaders agreed to an open admissions policy that guaranteed every New York high school graduate entry to the university. As David Lavin and David Hyllegard point out, CUNY open admissions was radical because it included not only the community colleges, but also the 4-year colleges (Crain 2001: 37).

Students were deeply affected by the realization that student struggle can change things at a college. Several students remarked verbally and in writing that learning about this made them feel "lazy" about taking on authorities— teachers and political leaders alike. Many realized they had developed a habit of "going with the flow," "just getting by," and "dealing with whatever happens." One student concluded her final paper for the course stating, "the battle for open admissions at CUNY has made me appreciate my education so much more deeply. People fought and put themselves on the line, risking jail or worse, so that I could go to school here. It makes me want to do more to improve my school."[4] However, every time the class seemed to feel satisfied with sentiments such as this one, someone else in class would remind us of a way in which access was still a problem. At one point, a student exclaimed in class, "Yeah but my mother went here in the 70s and it was FREE. But this semester I paid like two thousand dollars for my classes. So doesn't that pretty much cancel out the 'we're doing this for the poor' part?" In addition to the increasing demands of tuition since the 70s, there have also been regular impositions of testing and new policies that stratify the different colleges of CUNY into a tiered system where some colleges are "honors" or "flagship," while some at the bottom tier are primarily seen as remedial. So, the next phase of the course turned to the moment when these new policies began.

From 1969 to 1999, all CUNY colleges were open to anyone with a high school diploma or GED. But in 1999, Chancellor Matthew Goldstein, facing pressure from Mayor Rudolph Giuliani[5] and his negative media campaign about "standards at CUNY," ended CUNY's open admissions policy to the University's 4-year colleges. This story largely involves a discussion that began in 1997 over whether to mandate standardized testing. While some testing was imposed after the onset of open admissions, the tests were nonbinding. Passing them was not officially required for exit from remediation or for graduation, and most colleges chose their own methods of implementing these measures (Gonzalez 1997, "ABCowards," 8). To investigate this round of attacks on open admissions, I had the students again search online databases, but this time I gave them key phrases to search for: "standards at CUNY," "CUNY writing test," and "CUNY ACT exam."

I assigned the reading this way because the whole of the debate had to be taken in to appreciate the incredible volume of writing, yet serious lack of data or definition of terms. The class read extensively in this debate and what we discovered was an overwhelming, obstreperous insistence on objective standards, yet no definition of the term "standards." Furthermore, journalists and editorialists regularly claimed that CUNY degrees were worthless without citing evidence. There was only occasionally an article from Juan Gonzalez fighting against the mainstream. Students appreciated his article "Facts Don't Matter Much in CUNY's Quest for Hostos Prez' Head." Among other things, it chronicled the many awards won by Hostos and its President, whose besmirching went largely unchallenged in the media. Literally the only data cited throughout the media coverage of the discussion was Hostos's low pass rate on the nonbinding standardized test in 1997, and an unsubstantiated claim that some Hostos students once tried to steal a copy of the test. Countless articles expounded on how there were no standards at CUNY, no boundaries whatsoever, and characterized faculty and students alike as lazy.

One inflammatory highlight for the students was an article, "The War on CUNY Excellence," whose title students, laughing and rolling their eyes, exclaimed, "just went too far." As one student responded, "A war on excellence? Are they saying I paid over $1200 this semester to ride the subway for two hours each way so I could resist goodness? How does that work?" Another student put it this way: "When they put this whole argument in terms of 'excellence' it's like they're saying the students here now, and those about to graduate, are not capable of greatness. If they worry about CUNY having a bad reputation, maybe they should look first at the way they talk about it in the media." Students felt angry about the way CUNY students and faculty were portrayed in the New York media. One student counted it as an example of Freire's claim that banking concept education "project[s] an absolute ignorance onto others." These students felt they were seen as having no intelligence simply because they had not gone to the best high schools or did not have perfect English. Through the students' response to the portrayal of CUNY students and faculty, this became an exercise in critical reading.

Students were disturbed to realize that they themselves might have fallen for these arguments if they had not learned in college how to read critically and to search for proof of claims made. They grew more and more upset as we read on and realized how the journalists' assertions lacked evidence and presented flimsy arguments. One student surmised, "The whole thing is circular. The argument is made to keep the poor and poorly educated out of college, and the argument is made on a level that wouldn't pass the CUNY ACT exam because there is no fact or example to back it up." Looking over the entirety of the media coverage for this issue was truly enlightening for students. They learned a valuable lesson in media literacy.

Students also identified a covert racism throughout the "debate." One piece that raised discussion was a 9 January 2007 *New York Sun* article entitled "Brave Badillo," which looked back and celebrated former chair of CUNY Herman Badillo, 10 years after he led the call for standardized testing and attacked several CUNY community colleges.[6] The article celebrated Badillo for taking "his fellow Hispanics to task for not stressing the importance of education to their children"(Wolf 2007: 6). In our searches, Badillo's name came up repeatedly. In 1997, he led an attack on Hostos Community College, CUNY's bilingual education college, whose pass rate on the nonbinding standardized test was quite low. Hostos became the emblem for an argument that said, first, CUNY could no longer limit its entrance requirements to the possession of a high school diploma or GED because this gave CUNY a reputation for having "no standards," and, second, that mandating standardized tests in reading, writing, and math would be the only way to restore the standards that had supposedly deteriorated under open admissions. Many students expressed frustration that a Puerto Rican political leader led this charge by making Puerto Ricans the main example of what was wrong with CUNY. One Puerto Rican student wrote in her paper, titled "Bad Badillo," that he "made himself a tool for all the racists in New York. Now instead of admitting they are racist, they can just cheer for him." I can only characterize the racism in the "debate" as metonymic. Overt racist statements were not made, but the regular appearance of "Puerto Ricans," "fail," and "no standards" in close succession was much like the Bush administration's proximate usage of "Iraq," "Saddam Hussein," and "WMDs": argument through repeated association. The whole episode made for further critical reading experience.

In this phase of the course, students got exposed to arguments about standardized and high-stakes testing. Over the past few years, mostly beginning in 2001, coverage of the issue has been more nuanced in the media, possibly due to discussion across the nation about No Child Left Behind and its impetus to "teach to the test." Some students were already suspicious of the CUNY ACT writing test because they had to pass it to place into English 101. Students who failed it upon entrance to the college and as a result went to English 099, Basic Writing, were dismayed to read so much evidence against the value of these tests, and to see that the evidence appeared regularly in newspapers. "Why do they make us do this if they know it isn't good?" they asked. And that remains an open question as long as testing is still pushed as the only way to guarantee "standards." One student noted that our practice in class of focusing on the word "standards" helped achieve the Freireian goal of "restor[ing] the vitality of words" in linking intellectual life to civic action. He said, "the use of a single word has impact on many students' financial and everyday life."

Praxis

1   *Reading Primary Sources*. Using the LaGuardia and Wagner Archive, our class looked at images from the 1969 campus occupation, including a photo of the top portion of the original, handwritten "Eighteen Demands" and a typed transcription of those demands from a local newspaper. Using online databases, we read articles from the *New York Times*, *New York Sun*, *Daily News*, and *New York Post* covering the debate past and present. The use of primary sources helps students to "see history as an ongoing process of constructing the past, rather than a fixed body of knowledge" (Tsao 2005: 470). Unlike what one typically finds in a textbook, archival materials tend not to summarize or tell the reader which side is correct. This work immediately challenged the banking concept of education in that the materials provided complex situations with no answers. Within the realm of deductive risk-taking in the classroom, it expanded "the scope of action allowed to students." Students had to experiment and take intellectual risks to make sense of the materials. They also came to see reading as an active political process. Especially as a result of our discussion of the word "standards," they came to see that the ways certain reporters and public figures represent an issue, the language they choose, is symbolic action with real repercussions. The use of language like "standards" creates a false perception about who is fit to read, write, think, speak, question, and deduce. These encounters showed students something they already knew but had been encouraged to forget in banking education—the right to one's own educational purposes. Why can't students and teachers be trusted to work together to decide when learning is complete or sufficient, as these students did in working out the question of why the 1969 struggle was framed in terms of race? How is a standardized test grader—someone we have never met—the best judge of who we are and what we are capable of?

2   *Comparing Quotations When Writing*. Because this is a college essay writing class, I encouraged students to base their writing on links between pieces of evidence in the form of quotations from Freire and from news articles. Throughout the process, I asked students

to do short writing experiments relating particular Freire quotes to particular quotes from articles on open admissions. One student noted how a 1984 retrospective on open admissions written by two SEEK Program[7] professors quoted a professor from the opposition saying the students let in by open admissions "didn't really belong" in college (Quinn and Kriegel 1984: 414). The student found this an example of how the banking concept "project[s] an absolute ignorance onto others." Instead of seeing the new admittees as taking part in a needed correction to an unjust system, or as people who might have new and interesting perspectives, some professors saw open admissions as opening the door to proven failures who would drag down the entire university. "But this 'projecting an absolute ignorance onto' underprivileged students," said this student, "just goes to show how professors often use their own standards to keep other people out." But the ultimate realization of the class was that you cannot keep other people out—it is impossible. As Freire reminds us, "the oppressed are not 'marginals,' are not people living 'outside' society. They have always been 'inside' – inside the structure which made them 'beings for others'."

3   *The Problem Posing Method.* Because many of the concepts in the class were difficult, and problems arose such as the question of race in the "Eighteen Demands," this method provided a student-centered way to approach difficulty and to solve problems without the teacher "taking over" or imposing her own answers or politics on the situation.

I created a variation on the problem-posing method developed by Elsa Auerbach:

a   *Define the Problem.* For each reading we do, and whenever a problem comes up in discussion, students are asked to describe the specific problem that they see as meriting discussion. In this course, the problems that students brought up included the emphasis on race instead of class in the 1969 takeover, the difficulty of Freire's writing and the question of whether this writing was or was not truly "for the people," and the issue of whether students should protest standardized testing at CUNY.

b   *Identify a Quotation to Support Your Definition of the Problem.* This is not something Auerbach suggests, but I find it helpful in the discussion process and in building students' confidence in articulating the problem if we strive as a group to keep things textual. This is the equivalent of asking students: "What in the text gives you the impression this needs further discussion?" or "What in the text seems to account for the problem?"

c *Personalize the Problem.* This step provides students the opportunity to share their experiences, to relate the issue to their own backgrounds and cultures, and to share stories. It helps affirm students' personal experiences and often forges bonds between classmates. There is also great opportunity for laughter—much needed after a long day of reading about oppression. In this course, students wrote about their own problems passing the CUNY ACT, their experience of banking-concept education in other contexts and other countries,[8] and the difficulty of paying tuition (this, in light of information that, until 1976, the university had been free). One student in the class, who had expressed frustration over the emphasis on race in 1969, divulged at this stage that she was upset because she felt the origin of open admissions was "racist against white people." Her statement started a long, uncomfortable discussion, but by that time trust had been built up in the class, and this white student was able to talk to her classmates respectfully about her feelings of alienation at a virtually all-black high school, which she still carried with her. Her classmates were primarily not white, but also primarily immigrants, who, through this conversation, were able to ask some naïve questions about race history in New York—questions they admitted they had been a little embarrassed to ask before. This all led to the research exercises described above.

d *Note Possible Responses to the Problem.* This step is where students quickly run down a list of possible responses to the problem, no matter how silly or ridiculous. This is also a chance to discuss what alternatives have been tried and failed, or tried and discontinued. Just as in Auerbach's formulation, it is of vital importance that the facilitator not expound on his/her personal or political beliefs so that students who have disagreements feel comfortable openly sharing their ideas. Students are encouraged to just "throw ideas out there," mainly to get the juices flowing for the next step.

e *Discuss Alternatives and Solutions to the Problem.* As in Auerbach, this last step is about imagining new possibilities for solving the problem. It asks students to have a vision, to imagine. The only rule is to avoid thinking anything is impossible. Through this exercise students hopefully discover it is possible to approach any problem, to try things out. Ultimately, discussing alternatives to the problem creates an opening for action, an opportunity, as one student put it, "to stop being for others (those in power), and be for myself, my family, my friends and my community." One student imagined what it would be like if "the whole University stopped all activity and said we would not start up again until the ACT exam is abolished." Yes, what if?

Conclusions

In spite of the many successes of open admissions, the arguments about academic standards and standardized testing slowly chipped away at the resolve of the administration and the public alike. The rhetoric of standards had become so pervasive since the Reagan era that even students who were frustrated with their own lack of success in passing standardized tests began the semester mechanically repeating that rhetoric: "others don't pass because they're lazy," "college isn't for everyone," etc. Ting Man Tsao writes of this as his impetus to teach open admissions:

> As a professor at LaGuardia Community College of CUNY, what worries me most about this large institutional shift is not only the narrowing of access to higher education for New York's diverse populations, but also the general ignorance and nonchalance among students about open admissions as a social policy that over the years has made a difference in the lives of countless people. The majority of my students have not heard about this policy. (470)

Thanks to professors like Tsao, and the generous librarians at the LaGuardia and Wagner Archives, we developed a curriculum to counter this lack of access to, and nonchalance about, CUNY history.

Providing students the raw materials to investigate the history and conditions of their own education and its connection to the social justice issues of poverty and racism changed a number of them. Six months after the class, one student wrote to me saying, "I attended a city council hearing at City Hall recently to dispute budget cuts to the CUNY system. I was interviewed by a local radio program about CUNY on the perspective of a LaGuardia student and was able to articulate the history of open admissions and what it originally stood for." And one of the middle-aged students wrote to me 1 year later, "That class made me decide to stay in school. I figured if that's what school is about, then I'm in the right place. I wanna stay on top of the issues and share my experience with these kids." Having the students pose and solve their own problems set the wheels in motion to reverse the tide of years of schooling that served to "obviate thinking." Years of banking education repress thought and action in people, often forcing them to succumb to a kind of obedience training and a sense that nothing else is possible. I believe that this class not only brought a realization that students have power, but also invigorated them with the power and thrill of thinking.

Even without such an archive, this kind of lesson can be implemented in other institutions. The upheavals in the University of California (UC) system spawned a huge amount of documentation in the form of student manifestos, newspaper editorials and articles, and statements from California officials. Not only could a similar class be taught at UC on its long history of struggle for public education, but the UC materials, like the CUNY materials, could be used to augment such a course anywhere. In particular, the next time I teach this course, I plan to use the student manifesto "Communiqué from an Absent Future," which links the UC struggle to struggles in New York, France, and Greece. Likewise, activists at the State University of New York (SUNY) system fought successfully against the imposition of standardized testing; it might be useful for all SUNY students to understand more about this issue and its history and what it would mean if more tests were imposed on them. It might be equally interesting for my future students at CUNY to learn how SUNY successfully fought off this imposition. Similar connections could be made to historical critiques of the American university system, including Henry Adams's critique of Harvard as a center of networking rather than a seat of learning.

The rhetoric of "standards" has been around so long that it has become difficult these days to see it as anything but inevitable common sense. Taking students back to the root of this construction, giving them the opportunity to think of college as a space for the exercise of their own educational purposes rather than a place to compete with one's fellow humans for money, may seem like an idealist's fantasy. But we must keep educating to liberate people in this regard, for otherwise, as Freire tells us, "it is the people themselves who are filed away through the lack of creativity, transformation, and knowledge." Pairing Freire with arguments about CUNY open admissions—or any college's particular history—can help people to rescue themselves from the file-cabinet life that current education policy promotes—and to resist language and policies that file away others.

Notes

1   All quotations without in-text citation are from Freire's Banking Concept essay, which is Chapter 2 of *Pedagogy of the Oppressed* (New York: Seabury, 1970).

2   For this last question, I directed students toward Goddard College and the Free School Movement, which surprised all of the students tremendously; a few showed continued interest and pursued their own outside reading on the topic.

3   It is worthy of note that neither of the two middle-aged students in the class had trouble understanding this; it was the youngest in the class who remained suspicious of the emphasis on race. I suspect, as our current society appears less racist to our younger students, that many of them may have a hard time believing what it was like in the 1960s. Obama was elected after this class, so this kind of reaction from some youth may be on the increase.

4 This student has gone on to attend forums on open admissions and discussions led by its advocates. She emails me to report on these events as they occur.

5 Giuliani is the only mayor since Fiorello LaGuardia to decline to house his papers in the LaGuardia and Wagner Archive. So far, Giuliani has also declined all archive requests from other archives. Mayor Bloomberg, however, was working with the LaGuardia archive and indicated he will deposit his mayoral papers there when his term is finished.

6 Just days before graduation in 1997, under pressure from Giuliani and Badillo, the CUNY board made the university exam a condition of graduation at six CUNY community colleges. More than 500 prospective community college graduates were suddenly denied diplomas (Arenson 1998).

7 SEEK stands for Search for Education, Elevation, and Knowledge. It is an education opportunity program at CUNY 4-year colleges, established to provide comprehensive academic support to students who would experience barriers to attending college due to their educational and financial circumstances. SEEK began in 1965 and was signed into law by the New York legislature in 1966, to provide access to CUNY for poor students who graduated from high schools that had not prepared them for the rigors of college. Today (2010), there are 11 SEEK Programs across CUNY.

8 A student from Brazil discussed his high school experience with the Socratic method which he believed to be less of a "banking concept" education than what seemed to happen in his classmates' American high schools, while a student from Bangladesh wrote about how her entire school experience there was based on rote memorization, and a student from Haiti had similar stories of memorization—but supplemented with severe corporal punishment for failure to memorize.

References

Arenson, Karen. (10 December 1998). "CUNY Wins Ruling in a Dispute Over Graduation Requirements." *New York Times*.

Auerbach, Elsa R. (1990). *Making Meaning, Making Change: Participatory Curriculum Development for Adult ESL and Family Literacy*. Boston, MA: University of Massachusetts.

Brady, Thomas F. (3 May 1969). "City College Agreement Reached," *New York Times*.

Crain, William. (2001). "The Battle for Social Justice at the City University of New York." *Encounter* 14(4): 36–41.

Gonzalez, Juan. (29 December 1997). "Facts Don't Matter Much in CUNY's Quest for Hostos Prez' Head." *Daily News*.

—. (29 May 1997). "ABCowards of the CUNY Writing Plan. *Daily News*.

Hechinger, Fred M. (1 May1969a). "The Problem of Open Admission to College." *New York Times*.

—. (12 October 1969b). "A Growing Conflict over the Effect of Open Admissions." *New York Times*.

Oren, Dan A. (1985). *Joining the Club: A History of Jews at Yale*. New Haven, CT: Yale University Press.

Quinn, Ed and Leonard Kriegel. (7 April 1984). "Open Admissions Revisited: How the Dream Was Deferred." *The Nation*.

"The War on CUNY Excellence." (10 December 1998). *The New York Post*. Editorial.

Tsao, Ting Man. (August 2005). "Open Admissions, Controversies and CUNY: Digging into Social History through a First-Year Composition Course." *The History Teacher* 38(4): 469–482.

Wolf, Andrew. (9 January 2007). "Brave Badillo." *The New York Sun*.

PART THREE

Class and the Working Teacher

6

A Teaching Temp Talks Back[1]

Michelle LaPlace

The dreams many a graduate student cherishes of living "the life of the mind" as a professor bring the most pleasure when they soar to the top of, or else simply ignore, the class structure within and between institutions of higher learning. Michelle LaPlace's eye-opening cri de coeur *from the bottom ranks of the teaching profession is even more relevant now, two decades after it was written, as the proletarianization of college teaching has continued, even intensified.*

I work as a part-time instructor at a San Francisco Bay Area community college. The California public university system, which includes universities, state universities, and community colleges, was designed in the 1960s (when there was lots of money kicking around) to enable any young Californian who wanted one to get a college degree, regardless of economic level. I myself was a product of the education boom. Thanks to the largesse of financial aid, I armed myself (along with the rest of the hordes) with my liberal arts degree, ready to tackle the world. I'm still tethered to the public university system, but now I'm looking at it from the inside as an employee, and, along with my fellow part-time instructors, watching it disintegrate.

Nowhere do you see the insidious undoing of the promise of equal opportunity as in the current California community college system. With the passage of the tax-cutting Proposition 13 and the election of a short-sighted, "bottom-line" governor, the California community colleges had begun their slow decline. Government funds have been reduced to a trickle over the last few years. Administrators moan and groan over the restrictions imposed on them. Classes have been cut. Tuition is raised yearly. Attendance is down. Low-income teenagers have proven to be a completely expendable commodity in the highly competitive, high-tech job market, and the California system of education has remorselessly abandoned them.

The university system is also abandoning the very graduates it spawned—the new crop of mainly extraneous teachers in the arts, humanities, and social sciences. In the community colleges, the teaching profession is slowly but surely going the route of two-tiered polarization, just as with the thousands of traditional, skilled jobs that are currently being degraded. On the top, you have the 20-year veterans protected by the American Federation of Teachers and an antiquated tenure system in which incompetence, egotism, and banality unfortunately run rampant. On the bottom, you have people like me—people who want to teach and therefore accept low-rung jobs working as temporaries in the colleges.

Budget-minded administrators knew it would be impossible to disturb the sanctity of the "ivory tower," so they found a way to screw the new teachers—by simply not letting them in. Increasingly, when a college-level teacher retires, he or she is replaced by one or more disposable, cheap, part-time teachers. More than half of the faculty at the college where I work is part time and temporary. The ratio is even higher at other schools. The "teaching temp" is paid an hourly wage for classroom time only. There is no vacation pay, holiday pay, or health or retirement benefits. Months like December and April are total hell. While the old-timers bask in the luxury of periodic paid weeks off, part-timers get stuck with paychecks about half their normally miserable size. Nor is there compensation for classroom preparation time or "office hours," the customary time in which the teacher and the student can talk one-on-one. At the end of the semester, they "let you go"—unless, that is, they keep you on for the next semester . . . and keep you on for the next semester . . . and the next . . . and the next.

The result is that at the college level these days, half the faculty are walking zombies who are disillusioned, insecure . . . and tired. Part-timers spend their off hours scrambling for other part-time jobs that can support their teaching habit. I work as a part-time word processor; an acquaintance of mine tutors high school kids. Many part-timers have families that rely on their income. It's not unusual for them to dash off after class, in a mad race to make a decent living. Most likely they jump in the car, get on the freeway, and drive 45 minutes or an hour to their next class at another school, or else they run home to grade piles of exams and papers, a grueling activity for which they don't get paid.

As a consequence, part-timers hardly ever see one another. I only know two other part-timers at my school, and I see them very infrequently. The implications are obvious: we are too alienated, isolated, and enervated to develop the camaraderie required for serious job organization. The American Federation of Teachers reps encourage us to attend their meetings, but we know they don't really represent us. We know we're going to have to organize ourselves if we want change, yet we're overcome with a paralyzing malaise, underneath which rage battles burn-out. But from day to day we mainly accept things, silently praying that enough of the old-timers will die so that we can get their jobs.

It's not just the part-timers who are suffering here; it's the whole system of education that's going down the tubes. Part-timers, generally speaking, do not participate in departmental affairs. Curriculum and policy are decided by the 20-year veterans (the full-timers) who have generally given in to their apathy. A more cynical and beaten bunch you'd be hard-pressed to find. For the most part, they're appalled at the degradation of education, yet they're overcome by inertia. They shrug apologetically when they see you in the halls, stopping to chat about "how the teaching's going," yet their primary goal is to reduce the amount of work they have to do themselves. Decision-making by the discouraged is a dreary business. Policy is either nondescript or totally inconsistent. Passing the buck has been elevated to an art.

In addition, many full-timers strike me as having completely lost touch with student needs. Wracked by insecurity at being low-level professoriate, and despairing at the shrinking level of esteem society affords them, community college faculty members unconsciously vent their frustration on their students. I've been appalled at the disparaging words exchanged among teachers in reference to the declining abilities of the students. That the students try their best, given inadequate intellectual preparation in high school and at home, isn't much considered. Nor does it strike the full-timers that perhaps building intellectual skills in the classroom first requires recognizing the validity of ignorance and understanding some of its origins.

It's funny; the community college teachers seem to think that the professors at the university level have it made because students there are "so much more intellectually motivated." But having just arrived at the community college from the university, I know better. Faculty alienation from students—and vice versa—is omnipresent in the university system. Students arrive at college less trained for critical analysis than for stifling obedience from which they understandably long to escape. Oversized classrooms and psychologically insensitive teaching methods have made instruction in the public schools a matter of power and submission. Professors at the college level interpret the younger students' indifference as "lack of academic ability and interest" rather than a healthy response to bullshit drudgery. Professional egos get bruised ("why should I have to teach incompetents?"), and students are punished for it.

The academy gets its steam from intellectual self-hatred. Professors rush to the library in their off-hours for research, to convince scrutinizing administrators and fellow academicians that they are worthy of tenure. The competition is fierce, the work ethic unbounded. Professors then carry this weak-kneed egotism into the classroom, where they try to impress their poor students with what scholarly hot shit they are. Students are then blamed for not being smart enough to understand abstruse, self-obsessive, disorganized academic mumbo jumbo. If they give up trying, as so many students do, then they're totally ignored by the education system. Many students have become "bottom-line" thinkers—the value of intellectual effort is measured by its cost-effectiveness ("what'll this effort get me?").

The whole milieu for mind expansion and personal growth has become warped beyond belief. Used to be, a professor would hang out during office hours and students would drift in to discuss intellectual issues, learning problems, or personal dilemmas. A good teacher could really make a difference in somebody's life. Students often looked to a teacher for encouragement and advice and attention, stuff the student probably wasn't getting a lot of at home. But today, neither the full-time nor part-time teachers have the psychic energy required to reach out and inspire. And students often seem more interested in their economic futures than in ideas or abstractions.

Nevertheless, many of my students strike me as starved for positive feedback, kind words, and strong role models. They're also hungry for something interesting that they can relate to. I myself am torn between my desire to provide them sympathetic guidance and adult friendship, which is so lacking for young people these days, and my unwillingness to donate too many hours of my already busy week. I usually volunteer 3 or 4 hours to office time, and I'm glad I do it, but it's not really enough. The sad truth is, with the majority of teachers on the run, the student who is slower or less confident will probably get overlooked. Students with learning disabilities or family problems often drop out.

Something pretty tragic's going on here: with a few minor exceptions, the personal relationship between student and teacher is becoming a thing of the past. Enrollments are declining as a result, creating more cutbacks, more substandard teaching, and less intellectually capable students. It's a bureaucratic vicious circle that's completely out of control, and virtually paralyzing education. And it's the kind of organizational dysfunction you see everywhere these days.

The decline of education in America offends me to the core for a couple of different reasons. First of all, it represents the arrival of a new socioeconomic lineup here in the richest country in the world. Today, even the myth of America as a "nation of middle-class people" is dying a rapid death. Social classes are polarized and the growing numbers of poor, without access to better opportunities, are mercilessly shut out of the system. Life has become a survival-of-the-fittest aerobic scramble to the top, in order to join the closing ranks of the "boomoisie." The majority is undeniably being left behind.

But the decline of education has other ramifications that I find equally frightening. Critical thinking and the thirst for knowledge are becoming rare. Mass media have chipped away at intelligent reasoning by offering fluff packages as "information." People are increasingly rendered passive by their ignorance. The old myths have made a comeback. Americans today are accepting responsibility for their own "failure," instead of lashing out at the appropriate instigators who value money over lives. We're at a dangerous crossroads. It'd be easy at this point to give in to fear or despair. I sense that tendency in me on the one hand—but I'm also too fucking *angry* to give up.

Note

1   A version of this article first appeared in *Processed World* 19.

7

Instruction

Kat Meads

Adjuncts and other part-time college teachers at the bottom of the academic hierarchy can be exploited emotionally as well as economically by the institutions they work for, especially, as Kat Meads illustrates in this essay, when confronted with the burden of reading, listening to, and trying to respond meaningfully to students' painful personal stories—stories that themselves are rooted in deep class inequality.

When I received my graduate degree, there was an implication that "of course I would teach somewhere." Yet, even at the onset, I was wary of the assignment. My grade school memories were full of brave teachers who struggled against snakes let loose in the classroom, oblivious teachers who recited "Blessings on thee, little man" as spit balls flew past their cheek bones, desperate teachers who screamed themselves hoarse to impose an order that never came about. By and large, my high school teachers were jocks in disguise, and then came college, where I sat before erudite, often brilliant scholars so clearly unsuited to rough and tumble reality I feared for their safety. In my estimation, I possessed none of the qualities necessary to teach at any level. Still, there came a time when I tried. The experience was an eye-opener. I was hired to teach freshman composition on an adjunct basis at a university whose administration imagined the institution up and coming in the small, liberal arts category. Before the semester officially began, my colleagues and I attended several meetings that emphasized the department's commitment to fine writing and the writing program. We were encouraged to adhere strictly to the policy that forbade a D student from progressing to the next course level; to "grade tough," in other words.

There were 17 adjuncts among a core faculty of 10. Adjuncts were only allowed to teach two courses maximum at 1,300 dollars a course. The chair, as a kindness, offered me an additional 1-hour workshop in which I might, "for example," lecture on Sylvia Plath's "Ariel," discussing the finished poem, examining its many revisions, and discussing in depth the effects of each one; sixteen researched, composed, delivered, hour-long lectures for one third of 1,300 dollars. I declined. Nonetheless, a shockingly high percentage of those 17 adjuncts were supremely dedicated people: true teachers who loved their work and who worked unstintingly at that miserable pay scale for four, five, even seven consecutive years, moonlighting to pay the rent. Full-time appointments consistently went to outsiders to enhance the department's regional reputation. Adjuncts tended to remain adjuncts. During my one semester, a representative delegation launched a protest against such treatment and met with the dean. The dean lamented conditions, called the problem "very grave indeed," and hid behind budgetary restrictions. The university's ledgers could not accommodate a pay increase for part-time employees. His hands were tied, he said within spitting distance of a new, multi-million-dollar gym.

Although we remained a nameless, faceless majority to the administration for the most part, within the department I gained fleeting recognition for reneging on spring semester commitments 2 weeks into the fall semester. I apologized in writing to the chair; I could make more money in fewer hours waitressing. For a week or so, colleagues stopped me in the hall to exclaim variations of "I hear you'd rather be a waitress." I adjusted my reply to match their supportive or sarcastic tones but, either way, after I removed myself from the war, no one went out of his or her way to bond.

Office space for both instructors and professors in the humanities was severely limited. The office assigned to me was partitioned off into three sections, a desk in each. Four adjuncts shared my chair in rotating shifts. In the cubicle ahead, a philosophy professor labored to overcome the resistance of his logic students. ("But I have to know what a rule means before I can plug it into an equation. That's just the way my mind works.")

I liked Tom, the philosophy professor; he was a wry, generous man, but listening to that daily tug of war exhausted me. No doubt my student conferences exhausted him. Jammed together without sound proofing, we were forced to hear every frustrated sigh by default.

A professor of Chinese occupied the cubicle ahead of Tom's, the one nearest the door. Throughout the semester, her book shelves remained absolutely bare. A tiny woman, she kept her chair snug against the far wall, the only one of us who seemed to have more space than she cared to inhabit. She and I spoke our "good mornings" without mishap, but after that, our respective language barriers kicked in. Once, when two of us from the English Department were attempting to hold simultaneous mid-semester conferences in the same cubicle, she very kindly offered me the use of her desk. "Lunch," she said repeatedly, although the hour was nowhere near noon. I was indebted to her for the sacrifice, but there was something utterly deflating about teachers rushing about, routing other teachers from their work spaces, squeezing in here and there, dragging a line of bewildered students behind them.

Despite the overcrowding of offices and classrooms, the department expected its composition teachers to take students with rudimentary if not inadequate writing skills and turn them into critically astute persons capable of organizing and clearly communicating their chaotic and underdeveloped thoughts 16 weeks later. The expectations on the student side of the fense I found equally daunting. They arrived in the classroom convinced they were geniuses, in need of no instruction, or they arrived convinced they would become geniuses after a tap from the magic teacher wand. No one took into account the amount of collaboration involved, nor the inevitable fallout from that unequal and unsatisfying partnership.

Departmental policy required at least one teacher-student conference per student per semester to discuss ongoing papers, revisions, difficulties, gripes. I met with Carmen between papers one and two. She trembled in my presence and seemed eager to please the "teacher" if only she could discover how. Her proposed topic of "a trip somewhere North—Connecticut, maybe" didn't do the trick. Together we tried to brainstorm an alternative.

She went blank-eyed.

How about her childhood? Secret retreats? A favorite aunt? An eccentric pet? Something that meant more to her than anything else? A scary incident? A happy one?

"Well, we did live in a bad neighborhood in Johnson City," she whispered finally.

Helping a student find a topic with enough punch and emotional resonance to be worth writing about can be a risky undertaking. After 30 minutes of probing, Carmen came up with a topic large and painful enough to fill 3 or 30 or 300 typed pages. But was the remembrance worth any grade?

Every day she lived in Johnson City she cried. Teenage gangs terrorized her block. Burglars broke into her house while she hid under a bed. Her brother's drugged out buddy, like some specter, knocked on their door by the hour, continuing to knock even after someone agreed to let him in. Her mother carried a gun. Her dog was shot; her cat run over. Had I been able to grade her on the telling, she would have fared better, grade-wise. Her deadpan tone worked well against the dog and cat carcasses, the gutted cars, her adventures in living at a tender age of five.

"Do you think you can write about that experience?" I asked at the end of her recitation as gently as I could.

She meekly nodded.

After that session with Carmen, I canceled the rest of my conferences for the day. When I got home, I climbed in bed and slept for 15 hours straight.

Classes canceled less easily. Twenty-two students at 10 o'clock, 24 at noon congregated, waiting for instruction or simply braced to endure another 50-minute waste of time. Every Monday, Wednesday, and Friday I appeared before an audience who looked intrigued or plainly bored; who yawned or smirked or occasionally frowned in the effort to concentrate. I began to dream of students piling into my bedroom while I slept, students crowding my typewriter, students winding around the legs of my desk.

Brad proudly informed me of his "royal Scottish" heritage in paper one. He had served in the Navy, was older than the majority of his classmates—"different," as he constantly pointed out. He already had a story published. He already knew how to write, and not the choppy sentences I liked, either. Sentences that flowed.

"And what makes you think I prefer choppy sentences?" I asked.

"Because the paragraph you picked to read aloud, the one out of the whole class . . . *Choppy!*" he declared. "I can tell you aren't going to understand a thing I write."

Laura, another older student, was Brad's character foil. Trusting, eager, earnest, a front-row sitter, she was the type of student who makes a teacher hesitate to issue all those thundering composition commands: Active not passive voice! Show, don't tell! She took your every word as law, and she treated laws with far too much reverence.

I noticed her Monday absence because she attended every class without fail, the first one seated, the last to depart. The next Wednesday she came up behind me at the blackboard. When I turned, she said only "I can't stay." She didn't need to say more. I had seen that awful expression on the faces of women before. Over the weekend, on a date, Laura had been raped.

I gave her my home phone number, a rarity for me. With students invading my dreams, once off campus I strived to keep my distance. She called me when she needed to talk between sessions with her school advisor and therapist. Sometimes she asked to meet at the local Pizza Hut, where I drank coffee and she drank nothing, ate nothing. In the best of times there was a child-like quality about Laura, but after the rape, the child lost the joy of discovery and twirled in confusion.

"His eyes were so . . . "she began, but never could fully describe the terribleness of his eyes. She remembered hearing her dress tear, feeling as if what was happening couldn't possibly be happening. Not to her.

She might have been talking to any woman, but she was talking to me, her female English teacher. I listened as I have listened to other horrid, enraging accounts of women being raped in their homes, in their beds, with their children watching; women going about their business, going about their lives, and then one morning, one afternoon, one black night, being taken cruelly by surprise. In Laura's case, it happened on a seemingly harmless date, her first in 5 years. The man was a friend of a friend. They had met and talked over coffee and donuts. She liked him, trusted her instincts about liking him. Now she relied on the trained instincts of a therapist, the staff of the Rape Crisis Center, the police, her school advisor, the Dean of Student Affairs, and assorted others. She didn't need to hear another opinion and I didn't give it. Whatever I thought, ultimately, the decision to prosecute or not rested with her. So she talked and I listened, but as we sat at that fake wood table in the red-curtained Pizza Hut, I could feel her disappointment with my silent support. I was her teacher. Teachers were supposed to tell people what to do.

As the semester wore on and I read more and more pages describing girlfriend/boyfriend troubles, stories of parental conflict, accounts of first drunks, testimonials to Jesus Christ, evaluations of cafeteria food, of on-campus parking, of registration procedures, what all 46 wanted to be and do when they grew up, I began to feel as if I, personally, toted the weight of all those experiences and expectations. However poorly or wonderfully that information had been conveyed, I became its repository, data-banking the intimacies of 46 lives. I began to feel as if I should be responding to the issues that drove the prose: parental abuse, alcoholism, depression, home sickness—although I was not remotely qualified to undertake that counseling role. Eventually, I began to wonder what qualified me or gave me the right to red-mark their sentences. In a dangerous slide from the educator's viewpoint, I became unable to believe that niceties of style took precedence over the purge of rawer communication.

Mark enrolled late in my class. Computer error. As a consequence, he missed the first meeting at which other freshmen introduced themselves to me in a one page, in-class exercise. He wrote his introduction at the end of the semester. *My full name is,* he wrote. *I was born on my oldest brother's birthday,* he wrote. *It was my brother that named me.*

I came from an unusual family. My siblings and I grew up in a "hellraising" atmosphere. My mother and father came from illiterate families. It was not unusual for our "father" (again, his quotes) to get drunk and slap Mom around and target shoot inside the house with a pistol. Luckily my dad died when I was small. My family and I came to North Carolina from Illinois. It was tuff but everyone made it ok. My brothers and sisters moved out and started their own life when I was about nine or ten. Things were cool until my mom remarried. We moved several times about the country. Moving to a new place was frightening, but the worst part about it was dealing with my stepfather. He drank a lot. He was a small man with an oversized mouth. I use to listen to him for hours talk down on everyone under the sun. He would put down my mother, myself and especially my brother. I hated hearing that about my brother and there was nothing I could do about it. I never understood what my mother saw in that bum, but love is strange.

After listening to him I would get so sad and depressed, I would slip off to make collect calls to my brother. He wanted to help me so bad but there was nothing he could do. The conversations would always make me cry. One day my mom and stepfather were going to South Carolina to visit relatives. They were going on a weekday, and I was told they would be back before I got home from school. Well I beat them home by a great deal. I stayed at the house for about two weeks wondering about them. I didn't call the police or nothing because I suspected something in the first place. I finally called my brother and I've lived a somewhat normal life ever since.

I had been hired to correct Mark's comma splices, his dangling participles, his run-on sentences—that was my job, the duties for which I was being paid. But after reading *Luckily my dad died when I was small*, I could only set aside my pen.

8

Contingent Teaching, Corporate Universities, and the Academic Labor Movement[1]

Joseph Entin

*Graduate student and teaching assistant organizing have
accompanied what Joseph Entin calls the increasing
"casualization" of academic labor. The kinds of intense efforts
from the previous decade that he describes here have ebbed
and flowed in the years since, but corporate thinking, whose
impact on academia he analyzes, has only intensified, and the
question he poses to progressive teachers at the end of his essay
still needs answering.*

The movement to unionize teaching assistants and adjuncts has come a long way since I first joined the organizing committee of the Graduate Employees and Students Organization (GESO) at Yale in 1994. Since then, over 15 graduate student unions, at both private and public universities, have won or begun efforts to win recognition, bringing the total number of Teaching Assistant (TA) labor organizations to over 30. Adjuncts, too, have held union elections at several campuses and formed a nation-wide coalition, the Coalition of Contingent Academic Labor (COCAL), to coordinate their efforts. In a landmark decision in 2000, the National Labor Relations Board

(NLRB) ruled unanimously that graduate students at New York University (NYU) are employees under federal labor law and thus eligible for a federally certified union election. In 2002, NYU's TA union became the first at a private institution to win recognition and sign a contract.

Yet these advances have been met with growing resistance, both at local institutions and in global arenas of politics and economics. Graduate students at a handful of campuses have voted against unionization and in July 2004, the Republican-controlled NLRB overturned the 2000 decision that facilitated the victory at NYU, ruling along party lines, 3–2, that graduate student teachers and researchers at Brown University are not employees. As Nelson Lichtenstein suggested, this ruling represents another salvo in the long and largely successful fight that conservatives have waged to diminish and marginalize the labor movement.[2] Indeed, it suggests that as local organizing drives have begun to gain traction, national political opposition is coming together in an increasingly determined effort to undercut the larger significance of specific campaigns. And perhaps most discouraging, because most systemic, the casualization of academic labor—the transformation, begun in the 1970s, of full time, tenure-track jobs into contingent and temporary jobs—shows no signs of slowing. In fact, a 2004 Modern Languages Association (MLA) newsletter reported that the number of assistant professor positions posted in the Association's job list had decreased steadily over the previous 3 years.

Although the notion of a job market "crisis" suggests a short-term problem, it is in fact the product of deeply rooted, long-term changes in the economic structure of the university and of global capital more generally. And it's worth stepping back briefly to look at the bigger picture. In the 1970s, in response to the economic downturn and calls for smaller government and lower taxes, public spending on higher education plummeted, inaugurating an era of divestment that continues today.[3] In an effort to compensate for reduced federal and state funding, universities began shifting part of the burden to students (by raising tuition rates) and, especially, to academic workers by initiating a massive replacement of full time, tenure-track jobs with temporary and part-time positions. The transformation of academic labor has been dramatic: the proportion of academic adjuncts rose from 22 percent in 1970 to 46 percent in the late 1990s. Non-tenure-track appointments now (2005) account for about 70 percent of all faculty positions across all institutions. In effect, universities have created a two-tier labor system, with a shrinking pool of tenure-stream positions at the top and a massive sea of contingent, low- or no-benefit jobs at the bottom.

The accelerating use of flexible academic labor mirrors the downsizing and outsourcing occurring across economic sectors and is more directly the result of an elemental trend: the corporatization of universities. By this I mean the tendency of universities to behave like, and make closer ties with, multinational, for-profit businesses. Increasingly, universities are using the profit-driven strategies of globalizing corporations, creating revenue by cutting labor costs and commodifying their products and resources—education and research. Within this new, "managed" university, "the goals of higher education are increasingly fashioned in the language of debits and credits, cost analyzes, and the bottom line," in the words of Henry Giroux.[4] Key features of the new academic capitalism include the privatization and outsourcing of university functions and institutions, including food service, maintenance, and bookstores; the growing presence of corporate CEOs on university trustee boards; the rapid expansion of industry financing and control over scientific research, ideas, and technologies; the promotion of a consumer attitude toward education (in which students become "customers"); the movement of resources away from the liberal arts and other areas of knowledge that are not potential income generators; and rising tuition costs and debt loads for students.[5]

The corporate transformation of universities and the casualization of academic labor have devastating implications for higher education. Perhaps most significant, the widespread rise of contingent teaching is undermining three fundamental benefits of academic work won by professionals early in the twentieth century and consolidated during the post-World War II period of university expansion: tenure, academic freedom, and faculty governance. As Cary Nelson, editor of *Will Teach For Food* (1996), observes: "The gradual shift to part-time teachers has accompanied a gradual reduction in the percentage of tenured or tenure-track faculty, the only faculty with reasonable guarantees of free speech and with a significant role in institutional governance."[6] The numbers tell a shocking story of tenure's demise. In 1969, only 3.3 percent of faculty appointments were off the tenure track; by the 1990s, over half of new, full-time appointments were to non-tenure-track positions. In the first years of the new century, only 25 percent of all new appointments were to full-time, tenure-track jobs.[7] We work, increasingly, in a posttenure academy. Rather than a right or even an expectation, tenure is now a privilege, available only to a select few whose privileges are, increasingly, predicated upon the exploitation of the vast majority of university teachers. As in many other industrial sectors, in which the job security and benefits won by skilled and unionized workers during the post-War period are falling victim to post-Fordist dictates of "flexibility," outsourcing, and "lean production," the academic workplace is witnessing a full-scale assault on what were, for a generation, the basic terms of life on the job. Moreover, as the number of faculty members who have bona fide institutional power decreases, the void in governance is being filled by administrators and corporate board members.[8] Thus, in addition to undermining academic freedom, the casualization of pedagogical labor is also silently, but steadily, undermining the viability of a faculty-centered university.

This assault on faculty control is part of a full-scale de-professionalization—indeed a proletarianization—of academic work, a process that has grave consequences not only for those with PhDs, but also for those in "training" to become academics. The dramatic shrinkage of full-time teaching positions has decreased the number of jobs for PhDs and yet has caused many universities to maintain large graduate programs in order to staff their courses. In the most brutal of paradoxes, then, universities are using graduate teachers to eliminate the very jobs those students hoped to obtain upon graduation. Marc Bousquet, one of the most trenchant and incisive critics of the new academic labor regime, has suggested that, in such an environment, the PhD "degree holder is really the 'waste product' of a labor system that primarily makes use of graduate schools to maintain a pool of cheap labor."[9]

The widespread use and exploitation of contingent teachers also has serious pedagogical implications. The conditions of flex teaching—low pay, high job turnover, institutional invisibility, little or no funding for research and professional development—discourage scholarly growth, pedagogical innovation, and individual attention to students. What's growing in the new, corporate university is on-line, flexible, consumer-oriented education that is short on face-to-face teacher-student contact and long on "delivery" of information. Moreover, because contingent faculty members, typically working on semester-by semester contracts, are vulnerable to both student complaint and the slightest administrative disapproval, they do not have the same freedom as ladder faculty to teach controversial subjects or risk the resistance that might accompany heavy reading assignments and rigorous grading.[10]

If the casualization of academic labor degrades the teaching conditions of virtually an entire generation of teachers, it also compounds the historic disadvantages of women and persons of color, who occupy a disproportionate number of temporary and contingent teaching positions. Scholars of color, for instance, accounted for only 9.6 percent of senior faculty, but 17.6 percent of nonladder faculty, according to a 2003 report.[11] In 2000, women represented 55 percent of lecturers and 58 percent of instructors, but only 36 percent of associate professors and 21 percent of full professors.[12] In a cruel, but perhaps not coincidental twist, the participation of women and persons of color in academe is increasing just as the opportunities for tenure are disappearing.

Finally, the massive shift to low-cost, contingent labor has devalued not only the work of those in casual positions, but also academic labor as a whole. Contingent faculty—including graduate student teaching assistants, instructors, lecturers, adjuncts, teachers on short-term "fellowships"—teach the same students and many of the same classes as tenure-track faculty. Yet they are, as we know, paid a pittance to do it: a 2002 survey by the Organization of American Historians (OAH) and the American Historical

Association (AHA) found that only 25 percent of adjuncts earned over $20,000 a year, and the vast majority received no health care.[13] From the point of view of university administrators, these teachers are effectively "disposable faculty." These developments are not only reprehensible in and of themselves, but also send a message that academic work in general isn't valuable. Indeed, what does it say to students and to the public when a university deems the faculty who teach many of its (core) courses to be unworthy of a living wage or steady work? By effectively allowing the casualization of academic labor, tenured, and tenure-track faculty are thus participating in the devaluation of their own work, too.

Having briefly sketched the contours of the recent academic labor regime, I want to return to the story of contingent organizing, understood as resistance to both local and global forces. While the massive replacement of faculty with non- and sub-faculty labor has radically altered the academic landscape, it has been met with some creative and, at times, forceful opposition. Since 1980, graduate students have launched over 25 unionization drives at both public and private universities across the United States and Canada. Several of these campaigns have won inspiring and historic victories. In the late 1990s, for instance, graduate student teachers in the University of California staged a massive, system-wide strike. The Campaign to Organize Graduate Students, the TA union at the University of Iowa, won a dramatic representation election in 1996 despite having lost an election 2 years earlier. Graduate teachers at the University of Illinois staged sit-ins and occupied buildings to establish the right to a union election, which the union won, 1188–347, in 2002.[14] The emergence in the last 3 years of campaigns at Columbia, the University of Pennsylvania, Brown, and Tufts suggests that the TA union movement is spreading.

Adjuncts have also made significant strides. Faculty unions at the University of Massachusetts, Boston University, Western Michigan University, and the City University of New York have bargained to win important gains for contingent faculty members. Adjuncts at Emerson College, the New School University, and NYU all voted in favor of collective bargaining. COCAL, the national network of adjunct unions, worked to coordinate organizing activities around the country such as Campus Equity Week, an annual, nation-wide event that draws attention to the plight of contingent university workers.

In addition to winning several local, institutional victories, adjunct and TA organizing helped to build an emerging network of progressive full-time faculty members, intellectuals, and activists. The American Association of University Professors (AAUP) made the casualization of academic labor one of its primary concerns and issued several studies and policy papers urging departments to limit their reliance on part-timers and to increase compensation and benefits for adjunct teachers. Several major academic professional associations, including the MLA, the AHA, and the OAH, also issued statements supporting the right of contingent teachers to unionize. In 1999, the MLA membership endorsed "the right of all academic employees – full- and part-time faculty members, graduate employees, and support staff – to engage in collective bargaining if they choose to do so." Scholars from across the academic spectrum have collaborated on conferences, teach-ins, books (beginning with the landmark *Will Teach for Food* and including later books such as *Steal This University: The Rise of the Corporate University and the Academic Labor Movement* and *Cogs in the Classroom Factory: The Changing Identity of Academic Labor*), and on-line journals (most notably *Workplace*) that constitute an expanding forum within which progressives can communicate and strategize.[15]

In my most optimistic moments, I feel that recent struggles have given birth to a nascent movement culture. Door-to-door, lab-to-lab organizing has, in many places, sparked new forms of intellectual discourse and forms of sociability founded on a sense of collective purpose and common interests. My own experience suggests that, despite the fact that GESO was not formally recognized by Yale, it created—in federation with the other university unions—a dynamic culture of democratic engagement and struggle that reaches beyond the university's walls, linking graduate students to the city's wider civic culture and to the national labor movement. Indeed, the most significant counter-trend to the corporate influence on university life has been the formation of creative, previously untapped cross-class and interunion alliances that have fought to improve working conditions for university workers of all kinds and to connect their struggles to other segments of the labor movement. These coalitions not only won significant material gains for contingent teachers at schools across the country, but also made the casualization of university labor a national issue by linking it to the patterns of downsizing in other industries and by launching a thoroughgoing labor-based critique of the political economy of American higher education. This critique, and the creative organizing out of which it grew, gave a new generation of academic workers a deeply political perspective on the university system and a crucial message about the need to forge new lines of solidarity with other workers, intellectuals, and activists.

However, in the face of the systemic economic, political, and institutional forces that are driving the corporatization of universities and the proletarianization of academic labor, the gains made by teachers and their allies feel frustratingly small and tenuous. Despite the growth of TA and adjunct unions, the vast majority of contingent workers are not protected by collective bargaining agreements. Moreover, among many academic workers, the ideology of intellectual exceptionalism—the idea that, as creative brain-workers, academics are not suited to unions—remains pervasive.

This ideology underpins the Supreme Court's 1980 Yeshiva ruling, which asserted that faculty members at private universities are managers, not workers, and thus don't have the right to organize. Despite the dramatic transformations of academic labor since it was issued, Yeshiva remains intact. And, as universities shrink full-time faculties, full-timers are forced to take on more administrative responsibilities, managing the contingent workers—from adjuncts to graduate employees—who are doing the very teaching which, in the 1960s, 70s, and 80s, those tenured and tenure-track faculty performed.[16] To make matters worse, recession has only placed more pressure on universities, especially public ones, to reduce costs, which they have in recent years accomplished by cutting labor costs and inviting corporations to take a greater role in shaping research. This, combined with the re-election of George W. Bush in 2004, suggests that the economic and political contexts in which organizing takes place will be more adversarial than ever. Our hopes lie in forging a movement that can fight on multiple fronts simultaneously. Such a movement must place labor struggles at its center, but it must do more than that. It must imagine itself as what Michael Denning calls a "social movement unionism"—a labor movement that is also a campaign for social and cultural justice.[17] Such a movement will take different forms in different settings. It must foster ongoing and emerging local struggles at individual institutions, such as TA and adjunct organizing drives, living wage and antisweat shop campaigns, ethnic studies, and minority student support initiatives. But these local struggles must also think and act globally, connecting themselves to new and established large-scale organizations, including sympathetic union internationals (such as, among others, the UAW, the AFT, the Service Employees International Union, and the Hotel and Restaurant Employees' International Union) as well as progressive academic and intellectual networks such as COCAL, the AAUP, the Coalition of Graduate Employee Unions, United Students Against Sweatshops, and the MLA Radical Caucus.

Progressive faculty members can contribute to this work in several ways. If we teach in unionized schools, we can insist that our bargaining units work vigorously on behalf of adjuncts and teaching assistants. Faculties at nonunionized schools can also play an important role. In particular, as labor historian and former OAH President David Montgomery asserted, ladder faculty must take responsibility, within their own departments, for the conditions under which adjuncts and teaching assistants work: "There will be little progress made . . . until history [and, by implication, all] departments around the country address their own use and treatment of part-time and adjunct teachers."[18] In addition, concerned faculty can organize themselves and their colleagues in a range of forms—from department-based labor support committees, to AAUP chapters, to student-faculty antisweatshop alliances. As Brenda Carter, a GESO staff member suggests, "Even if [faculty] can't imagine immediately organizing themselves into unions, they should develop some organizing structure on their campuses, whether through faculty senate-type organizations, the AAUP, or [other venues] in order to talk about the crisis of casualization, corporate influence, and academic freedom in universities, and to figure out ways to exert some influence over their own administrations . . . [W]hat we really need is to secure more power for academics over all at universities, and faculty need to figure out a way to start doing that, whether through unions or not."[19]

Let me conclude with a question: given the transformation of university work and research in recent decades, what premises should our movement build on? Specifically, do we fight to preserve the idea of the university as a special institution and a fortress of professional arrangements? Or should we forge a new vision of the university based on the notion that teachers are subject to the same historical pressures as workers in other sectors? The university has never been an innocent institution; indeed, it has always served dominant state and economic forces. Yet the massive assault on the professional protections and benefits that is underway does, I think, signal a new era, one in which the university is now part of the global assembly line. At the same time, the status of the university (public or private) as a not-for-profit institution chartered to operate in the public interest offers a point of leverage to contest the growing dominance of for-profit interests in higher education. Should we fight to preserve this traditional vision of the university as a model institution, committed to fostering critical thinking relatively free of the demands of the marketplace? I find this vision compelling, but its fate seems unclear. What is clear is that progressives need to take a lead both in imagining a utopian yet viable future for the university and in fighting in alliance with other workers, intellectuals, and activists to bring that vision into being.

Notes

1   I'd like to thank Marjorie Feld, Louis Kampf, and Brenda Carter for their support and suggestions. I owe a special debt to Richard Ohmann, who encouraged me to write this piece in the first place and whose editorial guidance has greatly improved what I've written.

2   Nelson Lichtenstein, "Graduate Education Is a Seamless Web of Learning and Work, Not Class Warfare," *The Chronicle of Higher Education* (6 August 2004).

3   For more on this trend, see the July-August 2004 issue of *Academe*.

4   Henry A. Giroux, "The Corporate War Against Higher Education." *Workplace* 5(1): (October 2002).

5   See Richard Moser, "The New Academic Labor System, Corporatization, and the Renewal of Academic Citizenship," http://www.aaup.org/AAUP/issues/contingent/moserlabor.htm; Richard Ohmann, "Academic Freedom, 2000 and After." *Radical Teacher* 62 (Winter 2001–2002); and "The Politics of Teaching." *Radical Teacher* 69 (2004); Stanley Aronowitz, "The New Corporate University: Higher Education Becomes Higher Training." *Dollars and Sense* (March/April 1998); Jeffrey Williams, "Brave New University." *College English* 61(6): (July 1999).

6 Cary Nelson, "Introduction: Between Crisis and Opportunity: The Future of the Academic Workplace." In *Will Teach for Food: Academic Labor in Crisis*, Ed. Nelson (Minneapolis: University of Minnesota Press, 1996), 4.

7 Gwendolyn Bradley, "Contingent Faculty and the New Academic Labor System." *Academe* 90(1) (January-February 2004), http://www.aaup.org/AAUP/pubsres/academe/2004/JF/Feat/brad.htm.

8 Jeffrey Williams, citing data from Paul Lauter, notes that nonteaching professional staff expanded by 61 percent between 1975 and 1985, a period of deep retrenchment in full-time faculty employment. Williams, "Brave New University," 747.

9 Marc Bousquet, "Tenured Bosses and Disposable Teachers," *minnesota review* nos. 58–60 (2003), which is available on-line at: http://www.theminnesotareview.org/journal/ns58/bousquet.htm.

10 See GESO, *Blackboard Blues: Yale Teachers on Teaching* (September 2003).

11 CGEU, *Casual Nation: A Report by the Coalition of Graduate Employee Unions* (2003), 4.

12 AAUP, "Policy Statement: Contingent Appointments and the Academic Profession," adopted 9 November 2003, http://www.aaup.org/AAUP/pubsres/policydocs/contents/conting-stmt.htm.

13 Jacquelyn Dowd Hall, "Part-Time Employment Hurts the Entire Profession." *OAH Newsletter* (August 2003), http://www.oah.org/pubs/nl/2003aug/hall.html.

14 David Scott Kamper, Review of *Cogs in the Classroom Factory: The Changing Identity of Academic Labor*, edited by Deborah M. Herman and Julie M. Schmid (New York: Praeger, 2003). In *Workplace* 6, no. 1, (February 2004).

15 Benjamin Johnson, Patrick Kavanagh, and Kevin Mattson, eds, *Steal This University: The Rise of the Corporate University and the Academic Labor Movement* (New York: Routledge, 2003); Deborah M. Herman and Julie M. Schmid, eds, *Cogs in the Classroom Factory: The Changing Identity of Academic Labor* (Westport, CT: Praeger, 2003). *Workplace: A Journal for Academic Labor* can be found at: http://ojs.library.ubc.ca/index.php/workplace.

16 For a discussion of the growing managerial role of tenured and tenure-track faculty in the new university, see Bousquet, "Tenured Bosses and Disposable Teachers."

17 See Michael Denning, *Culture in the Age of Three Worlds* (New York: Verso, 2004), especially Chapter 11.

18 David Montgomery, "Colleagues On and Off the Tenure Track." *OAH Newsletter* (August 2003), http://www.oah.org/pubs/nl/2003aug/montgomery.html.

19 Email from Brenda Carter to the author, September 2004.

9

Anti-Intellectualism, Homophobia, and the Working-Class Gay/ Lesbian Academic

Carlos L. Dews and Carolyn Leste Law

Some things have gotten easier in higher education, at least for some faculty. In this essay from the late 1990s, Carlos L. Dews and Carolyn Leste Law describe their complicated experiences growing up as a gay man and as a lesbian looking to college for an escape from the alienation they felt from home-town and family—only to encounter a new form of alienation as faculty from working-class backgrounds teaching in middle-class institutions. Though homophobia may have declined in the decades since, class alienation surely has not, and their analysis is as relevant today as ever.

One afternoon, while Carlos and I were drafting a letter to publishers to sell the idea for our book on the experiences of working-class people in higher education (the book that was to become *This Fine Place So Far From Home: Voices of Academics from the Working Class*), I blurted out that I had always felt more comfortable being out as a lesbian in the academy than being "out" as a person with blue-collar roots. Until that moment, I hadn't really considered that there might be an intersection of these two axes of my identity. I had not considered that in both of my coming out stories "going away to college" was the defining moment—as a lesbian at age 20, as a working-class academic at age 30. Not only did I realize that my sexuality and class axes do intersect, but also that they do so, significantly, on campus.

Several months later, when responses to our call for papers for the book began coming in, we were surprised (naively, we now know) by the number of essays and inquiries we received from gay men and lesbians. As we started to speculate on what these responses might reflect or say about sexuality, class, and higher education, we looked into our own experiences and listened to the stories of other gay and lesbian working-class academics and found that coming out for lesbian and gay young people from the working class is in some important features very different from coming out for lesbian and gay young people from professional/managerial-class families because of the conspicuous role that higher education plays in almost every coming out story we know. The unique conflicts that cluster around higher education for all people of the working class contribute, in many instances, to a dual crisis of identity for those gays and lesbians from the working class who, like us, choose higher education as their careers. We wish to explain here the kinds of attractions universities hold for working-class gay men and lesbians seeking greater social and sexual freedoms, while also considering the ways in which the intolerance of higher education to working-class experience and values constructs for them a new closet—a class closet.

In our families, our forays into higher education are blamed for nearly everything "awful" that we now are or believe; high on that list is our queer sexuality. Professional/managerial-class families may be unsupportive of or hostile to their lesbian and gay children, but in such families, where more adults are college educated, college isn't likely to be seen as the cause of homosexuality. In my family, however, while we now enjoy a kind of detente, it is firmly believed that had I not gone to college, this lesbian thing would not have happened to me. What is at work in such a belief seems to be a complex relationship between two prejudices often attributed to the working class: antiintellectualism and homophobia. Carlos and I speculate that this relationship is perhaps peculiar to the working class, though anti intellectualism and homophobia certainly are not, because education and gender nonconformity are equated in many working-class homes.

The anti intellectualism of working-class people is used against them as evidence of their intractableness, often assumed to be a manifestation of low-brow hostility. However, working-class anti intellectualism is not indicative of an absence of working-class intellect. It is, rather, an expression of an extreme ambivalence toward higher education and other social institutions designed, maintained, and enforced by and for the benefit of the American owning classes. We see the anti intellectualism of our families as a complex system of responses to American intellectualism and higher education, which our families see as denigrating of labor and working-class values. American intellectuals are surely as antiworking class as the working class is anti intellectual.

The result of the ambivalence created by a society that holds up college education as a fulfillment of the American dream is that working-class families often aspire to participate in a system of education they neither understand nor trust and which they ultimately fear. Anti intellectualism is the fear of encountering ideas that might disturb one's way of living in the world; homophobia is the fear of dissolving gender roles and collapsing heterosocial conformity.

Carlos and I, however, did not aspire to a life of the mind in order to find intellectual freedom; our higher education promised college dorms and university campuses where we could find young men and women openly defying the gender norms and compulsory heterosexuality of our working-class upbringing. Rather than fleeing the anti intellectualism of our homes and hometowns, we were fleeing their homophobia. For us and for many gay and lesbian academics from working-class families of origin, college offered an opportunity to fly not only with our minds but also with our bodies; going to college was an escape to a highly idealized place we believed was more tolerant of sexual exploration and emerging identities than our highly demonized working-class homes.

We are aware of the misimpression we might create when we detail our experiences of homophobia in our working-class pasts. We do not want to give the impression that working-class families are necessarily more homophobic than middle- or upper-class families. What we can say is that our own experience of the homophobia of our families and communities is what propelled us toward the academy, which we perceived as simultaneously of a different class and less homophobic.

University campuses are full of young people like Carlos and I were—sexual refugees from working-class life. Carlos was conscious at the time that his primary motive in leaving home—to go to school only a few hours away—was to escape the difficult future he saw before him as a gay boy in his hometown. The academy seemed a much safer prospect than hauling logs in the piney woods of East Texas. For me, I simply couldn't imagine a future before me at all.

Of course, many working-class gay men and lesbians do not go to college and many narrate coming out stories very different from ours. Our experiences growing up in working-class families were and are informed by the regions in which we grew up: Carlos in the Deep South, I in a southern-identified family in Missouri. Our southern working-class upbringings probably further complicate the nexus of class, region, and sexuality we are describing. Our stories also differ from one another in the kinds of communities in which we lived—rural and small-town/suburban. We also need to acknowledge that our own experiences of coming out were/are informed by the period during which we grew up and came out. Young working-class queers might experience things very differently today, in light of the fact that adolescents are coming out and finding support at younger ages than when we were teens and because working-class issues are being discussed more frequently in the academy. We can only imagine what a positive impact seeing one of the gay/lesbian-themed episodes of "Roseanne" or Ellen DeGeneres's coming out episode might have had on us as working-class, queer adolescents. To see a working-class family dealing with sexuality in a positive way on television, we are sure, would have altered the trajectory of our lives immeasurably.

As it was, we grew up imagining that only middle- and upper-class people were allowed the luxury of being gay: famous artists, rich eccentrics, writers, and poets. It shouldn't surprise us, then, that for many working-class adolescents, to be lesbian or gay means to also leave the working class—through education. In the early 80s, our college days, the Bronski Beat had a hit song, "Hometown Boy," about a gay boy leaving his British working-class family for gay life in London, with the refrain: "run away, turn away. . . ." Interestingly, also in the early 1980s, Joseph Harry was publishing extensive research on gay sexuality and social class. Harry (1983) finds that gay men "may be found to be disproportionately better high school students and have more education than heterosexual males relative to their classes of origin" (9). Harry hypothesizes that adolescent heterosexual activity reduces educational attainment and achievement in males, and further, that the correlation between precocious heterosexual experience and reduced educational achievement is higher for boys and young men of lower socioeconomic strata—suggesting that poor and working-class boys have more heterosexual experiences than their professional/managerial-class cohorts. Harry concludes that boys and young men who are not interested in heterosexual activity find fewer opportunities for same-sex adolescent sexual experiences overall and are less interested in "male-typed" activities, thus increasing their likelihood of success in school. Again, these correlates strengthen at lower socioeconomic strata, determined largely by level of father's education.

While the focus of Harry's work is limited to gay male experience, his study is intriguing for what it suggests about gender roles and heterosocial expectations and advanced education for all gay and lesbian people. Harry, more than any other social researcher in gay studies, tracks the effects of anti intellectualism and homophobia on higher education among working-class gay or lesbian youth. He found that gay men "coming from middle- and upper-income families expressed less guilt than those with working-class backgrounds" and that "blue-collar respondents who were more troubled as adolescents by their emerging homosexual feelings were more likely to attend college than their non guilt-ridden counterparts" (Sears 1991: 108).

Harry's finding is consistent with our experience in that we feel that our flight to higher education was fueled by lack of support and the homophobia of our working-class neighborhoods and families.

The homophobia of working-class communities is often spectacular in its visibility and violence. Leslie Feinberg in *Stone Butch Blues* draws this picture in disturbing and realistic detail, but we should make clear, too, that higher education is rife with homophobic and sexist persons and policies, which any gay person or woman on any American campus knows first-hand (see McNaron 1997). Still, the relative freedom to test gender and sexuality norms within communities of gay and lesbian people found on college campuses affords children of the working class a place to come out away from family and the scrutiny of small towns, tight neighborhoods, or ubiquitous extended families. Still, it is important to acknowledge the signal difference between the oppression we face as gay men and lesbians, within and outside the academy, and the oppression we describe within the academy because of our class. There is a tremendous difference between our experiences of the oppression regarding our class of origin and that regarding our sexuality. The bias against class feels like shame with the aim of erasing our origins (something the academy and the "American Dream" are confident is accomplishable), while the homophobia feels violent and tangibly destructive in its intent. We don't wish to confuse the two or indicate that these two distinct types of oppression are identical. Neither of us has ever felt physically threatened by anyone because of our working-class origins. The pressure within the academy is not the same as that which drove us away from home and to the academy in the first place.

As I suggested at the beginning of this paper, though, the tolerance which I felt as a lesbian on campus did not extend to my working-class sense of identity, and I found myself having to negotiate the class closet in higher education just as I was emerging from the queer closet. Carlos and I assert—and the work of Harry corroborates our experience—that the college campus attracts young people from the working class who feel extraordinary tension between themselves and their families, such as results from developing gay consciousness in a working-class culture that abhors it. Yet the culture of the college campus abhors working-class experience and precipitates another extraordinary tension, driving the working-class student to closet her or his class identification and to assimilate the middle-class values privileged in higher education.

I was a secondary English education major, self-conscious but sincere in my studies and my desire to do well, but of all my education my most enduring memory is of my developmental reading coursework. There I encountered explicitly the source of much of the tension I had been feeling in my English coursework: a curriculum premised on contempt for parents who either could not or did not read to their children. I arrived at college without having read the children's literature and young adult fiction upon which so many of the classroom assumptions of middle-class literacy depended. My professors and other students in the class created an atmosphere that silenced my experiences of school and reading that I now know would have been valuable to the class. But I could not tell these people that in fact there were no books or library cards in my house, that I had never seen my mother read anything other than a newspaper, or that print was not a privileged medium of communication in my family. I felt constantly vulnerable and somehow implicated in the demise of American society by the hostility toward blue-collar experience and values I confronted throughout my university career. As a result, I retreated to a class closet constructed from my own silence and shame.

In our families of origin, education is believed to make men effeminate and women masculine. Educated men, like male academics, especially in areas other than the sciences or engineering, grow softer and softer with education. This attitude extends to straight-identified men, too, of course. We know of numerous expressions by straight men about "breaking the news" of their career choices to their fathers and high school pals that reveal trepidation similar to that felt by gays when coming out to family. Oddly, though, what makes men effeminate makes women less feminine. The educated woman is too intellectually aggressive and politically demanding to readily accept the gendered roles of many working-class homes and communities.

The coming out/going in/coming out again of lesbian and gay academics from the working class is a puzzling and poorly researched area of both working-class studies and gay/lesbian studies, so perhaps we can begin the work best by asking questions to elicit further discussion of these concerns: What are the characteristics—real or imagined—which make the academy a relatively congenial place for gays and lesbians from the working class, while simultaneously a relatively hostile place for working-class people? Does awareness of sexuality and its difficulties precede awareness of class difficulties within the academy? Can we see a pattern whereby gay and lesbian academics first deal with their sexuality and then turn to deal with the perhaps more subtle issues of class in the academy? Are people queer first and classed second? Or are they classed then queer? Are these even askable questions? If homophobia is responsible for our presence in the academy, should we then be thankful for it?

John Champagne, in "Seven Speculations on Queers and Class," complicates the consideration of the experiences of queer academics when he speculates that the construction of homosexual culture is contaminated by upper middle-class biases. Champagne quotes Jeffrey Weeks: "The common interest among many early twentieth-century middle-class, self-defined homosexuals with the male working class, conceived of as relatively indifferent to homosexual behavior, is a highly significant element in the homosexual subculture" (Weeks 1981: 105, quoted in Champagne 1993: 160). Champagne goes on to argue that "the discursive traces of these upper-middle-class values can be found in a number of different cultural texts circulating within the urban gay male community in particular – so much so that these values often appear to be 'natural', part and parcel of being gay" (160).

We would offer, then, that part of the difficulty of being gay and working class in the academy is not only the result of the tension that exists between the academy, with its supposed classlessness, and the working-class queer, but also of the middle-class definition of queer that the working-class queer confronts in the academy. The academy's problem with class permeates and transcends sexuality. Perhaps the discomfort we experience in the academy is in fact our lack of comfort at the class and sexuality junction. The working-class queer is asked to effect being a middle-class queer, which in the class-hostile milieu of higher education means a classless queer.

* * *

In the 2 years after Carolyn and I finished work on *This Fine Place* So *Far from Home*, I settled into a tenure-track faculty position and felt another change in my perception about the nexus formed by my career, sexuality, and class of origin. The three pivotal moments in my life so far have been: (1) my deciding to go to college to escape home during my late teens; (2) my "return" home by acknowledging a concern for social class in examining my life in the academy and my origins during my late twenties; and (3) my job as a professor, which has brought me what seems like full circle, where sexuality suddenly becomes a concern again. There is also irony in the fact that our writing and research about class and sexuality is helping me gain a life-time appointment within the institution which we indict with our work. When I left for college, getting to a safe place where I could come out as a gay man was the most important thing on my mind. Yes, I did well in school, but I think to a great extent that was due to the guilt I felt about coming out. I wanted to prove to everyone around me, as I was coming out, that as a gay man I could be "the best little boy in the world" and that being gay was good. I was convincing myself and those around me of this. I think guilt over sexuality has produced more 4.0 grade point averages than we can imagine. Midway through graduate school, after I had worked through the more difficult issues around sexuality, I began to miss my home, a home I felt I had to abandon to be able to come out. As Carolyn and I explored what our families meant to us and how the people around us in the academy had very different experiences growing up, we came to call our heritage "working class." Suddenly, class became at least as important to me in my self-definition as my sexuality. I used the words "white trash" as a badge of honor rather than as an insult in the same way I had embraced "queer." However, now that our work on class and my consideration of my class origin have gained substantial acceptance in the academy (I see the publication of our book and the great interest expressed in the topic by so many people as a sign of this), I see concern about sexuality returning to the forefront.

Given where I teach, at a relatively small regional state university in a poor, racially diverse, and traditionally very conservative part of Florida, I find my working-class background a tremendous advantage. My students, the majority of whom are first-generation college students like me, respond well to my working-class way of knowing and teaching. Retired military members, a large percentage of our student body, seem especially understanding of class issues, given their own experience in the military, its imposition of a false classlessness and its promise that one can "rise above" one's class of origin. However, the conservative Christian fundamentalist background of many of my students and fellow faculty members makes the topic of homosexuality much riskier than it was at the University of Minnesota during my graduate school days.

When I come out as having come from a working-class background, I feel a tremendous two-way identification with my students. I see more heads nodding in agreement when I talk about my background and my experience of higher education than I get from any discussion of any literature. It's as if my students (at least those from working-class backgrounds) have waited all their educational careers for a professor to admit being white trash. The book I coedited with Carolyn comes up in class fairly often, either because a student has seen it or because something about the book is relevant to the work we are doing in class. When I talk about having experienced a "blue-collar background" and the difficulty in "going away to college," I feel they think of me as one of them, to be trusted, seen as a model in some way. Many students tell me that they are experiencing people in college for the first time who tell them that it is okay to want to learn and that they shouldn't be ashamed of their intelligence. I certainly identify with this experience. My father often proudly announced that he had lived his life without having read a single book in its entirety.

However, when I come out to my students as a gay man (when I announce meetings of the gay/lesbian/bisexual student organization, when I am interviewed by the student newspapers and out myself in print, or when students see some of my published work in which I come out), I am concerned that I lose them in some way, that knowing my sexuality distances them from me and me from them, just like coming out as a gay man distanced me from my family. I know this is the case when some students immediately stop coming to me for advice about how to negotiate the difficulties in adjustment to college coming from a working-class background. I fear that when I come out to students who already identify with me because of similar class background, they immediately read me as "other," as if to say, "He may be from a similar background, but he must have become a professor to distance himself from us (our common background) or because he sees himself as ultimately different from us (perhaps better than us)." Obviously, there is a considerable amount of projection on my part in this reaction. I am also here thinking of my students as primarily heterosexual. I can only imagine how strong my reaction would have been if one of my college professors had come out as both working class and queer. As an undergraduate student I did have working-class professors and queer professors but never one who was both, no one I could identify with in both ways. I now find myself freely discussing class and shying away from discussions of sexuality.

I imagine the trajectory of my concern over class and sexuality over the time period beginning when I left home for college traced in two bell curves. The first plots the importance of sexuality: starts high, drops to little concern during graduate school, only to be rising again. The second, overlying the first, begins low with little concern over class, growing to a peak during graduate school, and then beginning to drop. Coming out to colleagues about my working-class roots is easy now especially where I teach. I am seen as representing the attainment of the American Dream and am a good example for our working-class students. However, coming out as a gay faculty member/colleague, I represent a threat. There is strong irony here given that I originally came to the academy because it seemed to be beckoning me as a queer undergraduate and graduate student.

I remember clearly how I decided to use college as an escape from home. I also remember my father telling me when I told him I wanted to be a music major to watch out for the queers at college. He of course didn't know that I was going away to college precisely to find those queers and to get away from men like him. I was running away from the working-class homophobia to what I perceived as the accepting university. I have come full circle now, having realized in my late 20s that to some extent I had thrown out the working-class baby with the homophobic bath water. There were valuable lessons to be found where I grew up—lessons that are often times counter to those I had so readily embraced in the academy. I learned that I can pick and choose what to accept as part of my working-class origins and what I want to reject because I know better (e.g. my rejection of the homophobia, racism, and sexism of my home). Of course, I use the words "know better" to emphasize the importance of education to this understanding.

In an important way, the title of our book, *This Fine Place So Far from Home*, captures some of the nuances of the difficulty we face in reconciling our simultaneous positions as queers and working-class folk in the academy. The academy is in many ways a fine place. It certainly was when we needed it as a refuge from the homophobia of our families. Unfortunately, part of the price we had to pay for that acceptance was the knowledge which would prevent us from ever seeing our homes in the same way again.

There is a double irony and a beautiful yet dangerous symmetry in the fact that we feel we were pushed away from home by homophobia to a place where we found intellectual acceptance. I enjoy the irony in the fact that the lessons I learned about justice, lessons learned because of my class, now inform my fight for justice in matters of race, gender, and sexuality. Because of my class experience, a background whose racism and homophobia I now recognize because of the education I received by running away, I am more sensitive to injustice than I would be had I grown up in more privileged surroundings. Carolyn and I have used our adopted intellectualism to look back and gain a new respect for our place of origin. We were pushed away to a place that allows for a fuller understanding of where we came from. Our place of origin in the working class also provides us with a unique tool with which to dissect the academy while the academy provides us with the insight to separate the wheat from the chaff in our working-class heritage. Anti intellectualism, homophobia, and classism form a tangle of fear which working-class gay and lesbian academics are uniquely positioned to untangle.

References

Champagne, John. (1993). "Seven Speculations on Queers and Class." *Journal of Homosexuality* 26(1): 159–74.

Dews, Carlos L. and Carolyn Leste Law. (1995). *This Fine Place So Far From Home: Voices of Academics from the Working Class*. Philadelphia: Temple University Press.

Feinberg, Leslie. (1993). *Stone Butch Blues*. Ithaca, NY: Firebrand.

Harry, Joseph. (1983). "Adolescent Sexuality, Masculinity-Femininity, and Educational Attainment." Education Resources Information Center (ERIC), record ED237395, http://www.eric.ed.gov/ERICWebPortal/detail?accno=ED237395.

—. (1982). *Gay Children Grown Up*. New York: Praeger.

McNaron, Toni A. H. (1997). *Poisoned Ivy: Lesbian and Gay Academics Confronting Homophobia*. Philadelphia: Temple University Press.

Sears, James T. (1991). *Growing Up Gay in the South: Race, Gender, and Journeys of the Spirit*. Binghamton, NY: Harrington Park.

Weeks, Jeffrey. (1981). "Discourse, Desire and Sexual Deviance: Some Problems in a History of Homosexuality." In *The Making of the Modern Homosexual*. Ed. Kenner Plummer. Totowa, NJ: Barnes & Noble, 76–111.

PART FOUR

Students' Class and Classroom Dynamics

10

Stories out of School: Poor and Working-Class Students at a Small Liberal Arts College

Laurie Nisonoff, Susan J. Tracy, and Stanley Warner

Class differences that play out in the classroom can be fueled by student experience elsewhere on campus. Nisonoff, Tracy, and Warner document the ways cultural clashes in student living areas, condescension and resentments around financial aid and related employment, and class insensitivity and blindness among student activists threaten the egalitarian goals of Hampshire College. The $20,000 per year tuition that the authors mention will seem quite low today (they were writing two decades ago), but their descriptions, their analysis, and their recommendations could have been written last week.

Introduction

Issues of class difference and bias in education are no more sharply drawn than in small, privileged, private colleges. Not only are differences in income of greater range, but implicit assumptions about background, lifestyle, and daily living also place a special strain on students of working-class origins.

Hampshire College, known for its progressive, alternative approach to education, is, at the same time, among that small cadre of private institutions charging more than $20,000 per year in tuition, room, and board—a figure that rises about $1,500 annually. In this essay, we consider a number of ways in which class issues arise in private higher education and suggest a framework for exploring possible responses.

Two reminders should temper our discussion of class bias. First, social class is not simply a matter of income stratification. Class distinctions derive from differences in social origins and relationships, with income inequality as a consequence rather than first cause. Students arrive at college with class backgrounds that have been shaped by the experiences of family roots, community setting, parental work, and neighborhood culture. In many instances, they also carry with them the ideological message that education, rather than rewarding class privilege, rewards meritorious achievement. In college they find that the class deck has been reshuffled and that the mixture of class experiences has become more immediate, more personal, and more compressed into a college "community." The college itself—through curricula, reward structures, work expectations, and the separation of "academic life" from social life—subtly and usually unconsciously accommodates and supports a framework of class-based differences.

Second, working-class status is not a handicap to be transcended. The life experience, values, and abilities of working-class students are no less valuable than those of more privileged students in providing a foundation for becoming educated. It is more useful to speak of the barriers, both economic and social, that impede equal access to educational resources. By the same token, financial aid is not a form of charity, but a mechanism for balancing the costs of access, with the added advantage that the college reaps the benefits of diversity.

Hampshire College

Hampshire College, a small liberal arts college in western Massachusetts, was founded in 1970 as an experiment in higher education by its sister institutions within the Five College Consortium (Hampshire, Smith, Mount Holyoke, and Amherst Colleges, and the University of Massachusetts/ Amherst). There are approximately 1,200 students and 90 full-time faculty, one-half women and 16 percent from minority or international backgrounds. Faculty teach within four Schools rather than traditional departments: Humanities & Arts, Natural Science, Social Science, and Communication & Cognitive Science.

Each student advances through the College with an individually designed field of study rather than a traditional disciplinary major. Officially, progress is measured by a series of portfolio examinations, which generally include a full set of courses taken at Hampshire and the sister institutions. Each student must formulate ideas for these examinations and create a committee of faculty interested in supervising and evaluating them. Successful Hampshire students set their own academic goals, work independently, and eventually work to satisfy their intellectual curiosity rather than for the traditional "payoff" of a grade. This places expectations of professional (read "middle class") behavior which is initially difficult for students of low-income or working-class backgrounds to absorb. For instance, these students don't want to "bother" anyone and thus find it hard to ask for guidance from faculty who appear to be of privileged backgrounds and "too busy" to talk with them. Ironically, a significant minority of the faculty who are attracted to Hampshire come from poor or working-class backgrounds, but as intellectuals appear to have always been middle or upper class. They identify with the struggles of their working-class students and resent being treated as "hired help" by economically elite students.

Generally, students reside on campus in one of five living groups—two traditional brick dormitories and three clusters of low-rise modular apartments referred to as the "mods." Many of the students in the "mods" do their own shopping and cooking, and all are responsible for the housework and upkeep. The academic programs, social services, and physical facilities are designed for able-bodied 18-year olds without dependents.

Class and financial aid

When the college began in 1970, the students, faculty, and staff were heavily influenced by the 1960s social movements, and it wears upon its sleeve a progressive pride. It was the first private institution to divest from companies doing business in South Africa. Almost from its inception, the college hired women to teach an explicitly feminist curriculum and has nearly 50 percent women as faculty and more than 40 percent women in senior administrative positions. Like many colleges in the 1980s, it struggled to create a multicultural curriculum. The individualized major explicitly expects "each student to present tangible evidence of an intellectually substantial engagement with the experiences of the peoples of Asia, Africa, Latin America, or North America's own domestic 'Third World'." Students must also complete a significant unpaid service to the campus or wider community. Yet, despite the social agenda reflected in these efforts, class contradictions as an internal campus issue are seldom examined.

This limited understanding of diversity was notable even before the College officially opened. By design, the original plan sought students from among the most privileged families in the country. It was assumed that although private contributions and foundation and government support would help, the operating budget would be 80 percent tuition-dependent. When the College first opened, only 30 students, representing 10 percent of the entering class, were given financial aid. That proportion slowly climbed to 20 percent of the student body by 1979. In the decade of the 1980s, the College realized that most aid students contribute more to revenue than they add to cost. Financial aid is, in effect, a form of college price discounting, in which students pay differing proportions of the full cost of room, board, and tuition. Moving to full need-blind admissions[1] became a strategy for both reducing the operating deficit and sustaining the College's size. Moreover, because the size and quality of the applicant pool was increased, the College was able to maintain academic standards through a difficult period. Approximately 47 percent of the student body receives financial aid, with the average grant covering just under 50 percent of room, board, and tuition.

The amount of financial aid is determined by four variables: contributions from parents; at least $1200 in savings from summer jobs; work-study employment throughout the academic year (officially 10 hours per week, although some students have worked as much as 26 hours per week when there was an unexpected shortfall from other sources); and all possible loans. Many of the students also work substantial hours at off-campus jobs as waitpersons or retail clerks, where they often serve their fellow students. Extensive loan obligations create a system we have come to call "debt peonage"—students afraid to leave school to accumulate savings, because their debts will come due, yet unable because of their work obligations to maintain academic progress.

But the College does widely distribute significant grants-in-aid. Grants ranging up to nearly $20,000 have been awarded, with over half receiving more than $10,000 in direct grant aid. Men and women, on average, tend to receive equivalent awards, but there are significant differences by ethnic groups. African-American and foreign students consistently receive the largest grant awards (averaging $12,630 and $12,085 in 1989–90), followed by Hispanic students ($11,480), and then Asian, Native American, and finally Caucasian students. However, Caucasian students have made up the overwhelming majority of aid recipients. Approximately 100 financial aid students from all other ethnic groups have been enrolled throughout this period. The relative ethnic proportions and different needs have led to tension among the faculty and administration. At times, those seeking an internationally more diverse student body have been positioned against those interested in domestic class and ethnic diversity.

Student experience

Working-class and poor students have reported a series of stories which reflect their alternative consciousness and alienation from classmates and the College. One Hispanic student, from New York City, who was living in the "mods," confided:

> All these students do is complain. They complain about the food. They complain about the housing. They complain about the services. Since I've been here I've had more food, heat, hot water, electricity, and space than I ever had in my whole life. I feel guilty being here knowing how my family suffers.

Since the American college is the primary vehicle for class mobility, and itself assumes a particular class character, students arriving from working-class communities often have a sense of unreality about living under comparatively lush circumstances. While for a middle-class student, being expected to share space and facilities with others is experienced as a hardship, for other students, even having access to those comforts that the middle-class student takes for granted is experienced on two levels. On the one hand, the student quoted above is grateful for the comfort and is annoyed by his classmates' sense of privilege and ingratitude. On the other, he feels guilty not only for "abandoning" his family, but also for living better than they do.

Class-based incidents often arise in daily life within the mods. For instance, food buying and preparation is a reflection of a person's class and culture and may become an arena of conflict. Differences around food seem to symbolize the interaction between rich and poor. Students argue over what food, which brands, and how much food to buy at a time. How to prepare meals, when to eat, and who will clean up after meals are also at issue. These are not unfamiliar problems to anyone who has negotiated them with a partner. While Neil Simon has successfully turned such conflict to humor in *The Odd Couple*, if you are 19 and living away from your community for the first time, it is hard to laugh at what you perceive as a constant attack on your culture.

Patterns of consumption are geared to available cash on hand and the availability of transportation. Because Amherst is a small town with outlying shopping malls, students not eating at the dining common must drive several miles to shop. Middle- and upper-class students favor an expensive health food supermarket where meat and fish prices are 30 to 50 percent higher than at the multiservice supermarkets in town. In contrast, their working-class peers choose from one of the two chain supermarkets in town. If middle-class students go to one of the bigger supermarkets, they often buy brand names, not the store chain brands or generic items. They also buy in larger quantities to save time and money. However, when they present their working-class mod-mates with a large food bill, a tense discussion inevitably ensues, with neither side really hearing the other.

Again, all of these differences are familiar to anyone who has tried to live with others, but they become damaging when the character of working-class students comes under attack. Students have been told it is "tacky" to raise money issues, or to be anxious about sharing food with uninvited "guests." They are told they are endangering themselves and their mod-mates' lives, first by eating beef and chicken which hasn't been organically grown, and then by frying it in deep fat instead of preparing it "the healthy way." Perhaps most damaging, middle-class students make fun of working-class students' food choices. One couple reported that after they had done the shopping for their mod, their mod-mates thought they were being funny by bringing back store brands and generic products. The couple was subjected to jokes about working-class eating habits as the students got into the fun of "slumming it." When the couple explained that that was how they were brought up, they were met with disbelief. Until that moment, the class differences among these students had been submerged by the assumption of a common social background. Several weeks later, the couple moved back into the dorms.

The attitude of privilege is nowhere more apparent than in the differences among students on the subject of vandalism. Many students don't even seem to recognize their petty destruction of College property as wrong. They assume anything casually damaged will be repaired and that it's "no big deal." These students seem to think that the custodial staff is there to serve them, in addition to providing routine maintenance. Flooding bathrooms with water, punching holes in walls, dumping tar down a stairwell, writing on walls, throwing trash around, breaking bottles—these are just "boys will be boys" fun. Even more distressing to working-class students, their privileged peers often express disrespect for the custodial staff, stereotyping them as unambitious, stupid, or lazy. Sometimes student pranks are directed against the staff with whom working-class students feel most comfortable and who remind them of relatives and friends at home.

Class prejudice in the mods has its direct analog in student discussion of academic work. As faculty, we were disturbed and saddened by reports of such deeply entrenched class prejudice. It suggests that there are two cultures at Hampshire: a liberal if not radical "public" culture, where students do and say "the right thing," and a more conservative, less tolerant "private" culture, where off-handed statements may be cutting and offensive.[2] In letters written to the college newspaper last year, students noted "a few of the more common statements" they hear regularly:

I can't believe you have a typewriter and not a computer. Everyone needs a computer.

My parents pay for you to be here. Education is my right, your privilege. You should be happy with what you have and quit complaining. (In response to student workers who were demanding minimum wage.)

Doesn't it make you mad when a financial aid student gets a faculty member on their committee that they wanted and you don't?

Ironically, in the latter two statements, privileged students who are supported financially by their families see themselves as "paying" for their college education even though they haven't worked to pay their college expenses. In contrast, their working- and middle-class peers are contributing directly from their own labor to their own education.

In addition, working-class students are coping with a range of difficulties in their academic life. The exceptional rise in the cost of higher education and the disappearance of the federal government as a funding source have meant that many students are working more than 20 hours a week to meet their basic expenses. By definition, then, they have less money to spend on books and supplies and less time to complete assignments. Yet some faculty pay little attention to book prices, deem it "a hassle" to put readings on library reserve, and assume that all students have ready access to computers. Additionally, in a school where many students do buy all their books and supplies and do arrive with computers, working- and middle-class students whose families can't afford these items feel deprived. While sympathetic to the plight of poorer students, faculty on the whole are relatively unsophisticated about class as an issue. Casual or misinformed student comments about working-class experience may go unchallenged.

Hampshire College has attempted to balance its institutionalized class structure by admitting older, working adults with children. At this writing, there are 41 matriculated students ranging in age from 25 to 45. Audrey Smith, Director of Admissions, has noted: "We are committed to a need-blind admissions policy, but these students usually have a greater financial need than any other group. If we recruit a large number of nontraditional students, we have to be ready to meet their particular needs. At this point Hampshire's small endowment can't sustain that."[3] Those older students who do come encounter a variety of hurdles. For instance, a recent graduate who received a research fellowship to study abroad was told that in order to reserve a place for her daughter in the College day care program when she returned, she would have to pay for that space while she was on leave. Other older students have been told they must live in the dormitories their first semester. Still others have been discouraged from applying for food stamps because it "makes the College look bad."

Perhaps no event in recent years has illuminated class differences on campus as much as the Gulf War. The prevailing sentiment on campus was that the Gulf War represented another in a series of US military adventures.

Many Hampshire College faculty, staff, and students demonstrated against the war at Westover Air Force Base in nearby Chicopee, a primary deployment area for US troops and equipment. Our campus, like the other two colleges in town and the Town of Amherst itself, was decidedly "dovish."

As the January 15th deadline for Sadaam Hussein to withdraw from Kuwait approached, emotions ran high. President Gregory Prince convened an all-community meeting. Sitting there trying to deal with our own mixed feelings, we were suddenly confronted by the realization that the students we worked with from the class issues group we'd formed experienced this war in a fundamentally different way than other students. First, out of 20 or so students with whom we worked, almost everyone either had a parent, sibling, or friend who was in the armed forces or else had been suddenly mobilized from civilian life to be shipped to a theater of war, where some "experts" had predicted casualties of between 20,000 and 30,000. Although students, faculty, and staff who opposed the war were careful to separate their opposition to the war from their concern for the troops, that was a tricky maneuver at best, and mostly fell on the deaf ears of students who felt isolated in their concerns. One student rose in the open meeting to explain that her brother was in the army because her family didn't have enough money to send him to college. "Whatever happens," she emotionally explained, "I don't want to have to defend my brother or my friends from high school who are over there now. They aren't killers; they are victims of the poverty draft. This was the only way they could get an education."[4] In further confirmation of the public/private split, this student was applauded for her statement by an auditorium filled to capacity with students, staff, and faculty. Later, she told us that in the privacy of the student community, she received criticism from her peers.

Perhaps the essence of class and race difference in the United States is that the overwhelming number of upper-middle and upper-class white students regard whites in the armed forces and by extension African Americans and Hispanics as "losers." They see soldiers as people who "aren't smart" and who "goofed off" in high school, unlike themselves, for they had worked hard and "earned" good grades and test scores, which in turn "earned" them a seat in a college classroom instead of in a Bradley tank.

We should note before we close that our poor and working-class students have not been passive sufferers of discrimination. First of all, they found each other. Second, they have been active in writing to the campus paper and keeping class issues before the Hampshire community through lectures and discussions. Finally, they are seeing some results from their efforts. The administration and faculty have responded more to class issues, incorporating them into public discussions and courses.

Suggestions for action

What can colleges do? Hampshire College is certainly not a mirror of the full spectrum of challenges. Possible actions divide along several lines. First, students, faculty, and staff may negotiate individual exceptions or accommodations that recognize the personal hardship stemming from differences in class background. This approach helps the particular student, but it simultaneously obscures the larger institutional problem.

A second approach is to confront class discrimination in the same college arenas that have brought pressure to bear on such issues as racism, sexism, and homophobia. One method we have tried is to form a working group of students and faculty for the purpose of heightening community awareness of class bias. This group has begun to identify specific areas of concern, to seek the support and endorsement of top administrators, and to utilize the regular channels of student and faculty governance. A further understanding of the issues can be achieved by organizing an open, ongoing forum or seminar. Two of the authors (Tracy and Nisonoff) have conducted a year-long forum centered on evening speakers and student support meetings. One outcome of this effort has been a letter to the larger community calling attention to the high cost of course materials, the need to place required books on library reserve, the advantages of a clothing exchange, and the need to avoid class bias by assuming that vacations are easily available for study abroad or other non-income-earning internships and activities. Several members of our group were motivated to write about their experiences in the campus newspaper. Those articles created a flurry of responses in the paper and generated a series of discussions afterward. Last year, a Hispanic student wrote a one-act play which dealt with ethnic and race relations and received considerable comment and praise for his work.

A third approach, following upon the second, is to focus more structurally upon the terms of admission, the terms of financial aid and work, and the internal social fabric that replicate or sustain class inequality. In the area of financial aid, the costs of supporting a need-blind admissions policy are rising disproportionately faster than the rest of college budgets. Financial aid thus becomes a target for curtailment, jeopardizing whatever gains in class diversity have been achieved. Agreement not to compromise financial aid must be won through an articulate analysis of both budget numbers and the social issues at stake. Another example of structural change is a proposed work program for all students—a plan that has been advanced several times in the history of Hampshire College and that is again under active consideration. All students would be expected to work equally, thus reducing significantly the hours worked by financial aid students. Work study funds, however, would continue to be allocated unequally, according to financial need. This proposal—a legal use of work-study funds—is perhaps more suited for elite private colleges than for institutions where a high proportion of students have outside work demands of their own.

A fourth course of action requires a collective agenda that is coordinated beyond our institutional fenses. The cost of higher education, both private and public, continues to increase differentially faster than average levels of personal or family income. The class gap in ability to pay progressively widens, while politicians continue to mouth the old maxim of self-advancement through education. At the state, national, and foundation-funding levels, the concept of the right to education must be extended and the growing disparities in access recognized.

These suggested approaches certainly do not exhaust the possibilities for creative action. But no action will be forthcoming until the question of class bias in higher education is more directly acknowledged to be an issue in its own right.

Notes

1 "Need-blind admissions" mean that students are judged solely on the basis of their academic ability. The college is then committed to offering all qualified students the financial difference between full cost and the amount each student is able to contribute. Given financial realities, private colleges are backing away from this policy.

2 For instance, Jewish, African-American, and gay students report the same kinds of prejudicial statements outside the classroom and unknown to the faculty and staff.

3 Cheryl Wilson, "Older and Wiser," *Hampshire College Reports* (Spring 1991), 5.

4 Ellen LaFleche, "An Uncertain Term," *Hampshire College Reports* (Spring 1991), 6.

11

Class Privilege, Oppression, and the World in the Classroom

Erin Smith

*At the University of Texas at Dallas, Erin Smith's students had
an easy time theorizing about class issues in education in her
Gender and Education course, but they had great trouble critically
examining the power dynamics that informed their own in-class
interactions with their teacher. Smith's dissection of the challenge
of examining present experience—of questioning behavior that
just seems "natural"—as opposed to the safety and ease of abstract
social analysis offers important lessons for teachers.*

Lately, I have been thinking about the place of experience in a student-centered classroom. The personal histories and current preoccupations of students are a powerful motivator of learning, but they also limit and constrain what kinds of knowledge are possible.

For 5 years, I have been teaching an upper-level undergraduate course called Gender and Education at night at the University of Texas at Dallas. The course examines the ways educational institutions both empower individuals and reproduce social hierarchies based on class, race, gender, and sexuality. The University of Texas at Dallas is a public school emphasizing its science and technology programs, and almost half its students attend part time while they are working and/or raising families. The average age of undergraduates is 26.

I teach in the School of General Studies, which houses interdisciplinary programs and majors. It was founded in 1975 by a visionary dean, who imagined it as a safe, supportive space for women returning to college after raising families. Its programs were flexible—allowing students to count credits accumulated from the institutions they had attended in the past—and it offered special counseling and support to students who were facing a unique set of challenges.

From the beginning, the School of General Studies enrolled nontraditional students from all sorts of life situations—men and women, paid workers and homemakers, students from 18 to 65 and over. Although the School now more closely resembles the other academic units at UT-Dallas, its unique origins still mark the education it offers students. For example, UT-Dallas, like most science and engineering institutions, is majority male (in an era when women make up the majority of undergraduates nation-wide). The graduates of the School of General Studies, however, are roughly two-thirds women.

Like most courses on gender, this class is typically 75–90 percent women, some returning to school after many years. Some have come because a divorce or the death of a spouse has left them primary breadwinners for their families at mid-life, a role for which their education had not prepared them.

Increasingly, classrooms like this are representative; nationwide, more and more college students attend part time, and the college population has been majority female for a number of years. Still, UT-D's classrooms are more racially diverse and include more international students than most. The diversity of the student body and the number of people who return to school repeatedly over their life course to facilitate job or career changes bring a wealth of life experience to the classroom that makes radical teaching about class, gender, and race much easier to do. The experiences of these students are some of the most effective tools I have found for teaching about education, identity, and power.

Students come to my Gender and Education class with their own educational histories, concerns about their children's educations, and heads full of rhetoric from the education President (and former Texas Governor) George Bush. They bring these concerns and experiences into dialogue with the theories, terms, and conceptual frameworks offered by class readings and discussion. As returning students frequently making great sacrifices to be in school, they care passionately about education and what it can do for them (if they do not always have a great deal of time to do the reading!). My goals are to enable students to reflect critically about their own educational histories and to give them the tools they need to debate educational policy issues related to class, gender, and race intelligently. If all goes well, students can make connections between the world of school and the world outside, translating the codes of homes and workplaces into the discourse of scholars and vice versa in the ways advocated by the critical pedagogues who appear on my syllabus.[1]

Sometimes we succeed.

I start the class with Barbara Solomon's *In the Company of Educated Women*, a readable one-volume history of women's entrance into and transformation of higher education in America, in hopes of placing ourselves as part of a larger history of debates about education and power.[2] Before discussing the historic tensions between a liberal arts and a vocational approach to education, I ask students to write about why they are in college, and place their answers in the historical spectrum of ideas. We pair a look at pictures from women's colleges in the late nineteenth century (fine China in the dining hall, groups of sober young women reading, closely supervised by a motherly woman) with UT-D's most recent brochure (from which my 40-something students are completely absent, replaced by happy 18-year olds in UT-D sweatshirts). As a final project, students interview someone who is different from them about his/her educational experiences, analyzing them in light of class readings and discussion. Many students find that their lives and class readings are mutually informing, thereby achieving my ideal for a liberal arts education.

One of my white, female students made a connection between her life situation and the nineteenth-century college women Solomon discusses, women who frequently had to choose between family and career in a way men of their generation (or our own) almost never did. A homemaker, part-time student, and volunteer at her church, she was hoping for full-time work with the Methodist Church after she finished her degree. Her anger at the ways these women compromised their own vocational/professional dreams for their families again and again led her to realize that she really wanted a different kind of job—one that would require relocating her family to wherever the governing body of the Church chose to place her. She talked with her husband, who agreed that after 15 years of promoting his career, it was probably her turn. She was off to Divinity School the next year. An amazingly generous student, she was honest about how uncomfortable it was to see herself in this material and to let her education transform/make a mess out of her life.

Other students found different points of contact. One white, male student was a parent volunteer in his daughter's kindergarten class the week we read Karin Martin's "Becoming a Gendered Body," a study of the way children's bodies are disciplined and gendered through the practices of preschool.[3] He reported with great intensity and passion the next class meeting about how patterns in his daughter's class replicated those in the study—boys allowed to be more active and louder, to get more of the teacher's attention, to be dressed in more practical clothes, to have less attention paid to their appearance, to control more space in the classroom, etc. He shared the article with his daughter's teacher and was planning to bring up the issue at the next PTA meeting.

There is a section of the syllabus called "Race and Class in the Classroom" which works on models for thinking about gender, class, and race as interactive systems. We read several articles by Wendy Luttrell, whose work focuses on women dropouts who return to school later to increase their literacy.[4] A talented ethnographer, Luttrell uses the language of her working-class informants to talk about the interaction of "book knowledge" (that sanctioned by teachers and other middle-class professionals) and the "common sense" knowledge working-class men and women learn at home or on the job. This work discusses how a discourse about "teacher's pets," who most often embodied middle-class ideals about white womanhood, made learning appear to be an issue of personal affinities rather than a political question about access to social power.

One of my students, who had introduced herself to the class on the first day by saying that she was here—in part—because she wanted an education to put her on a more equal footing with her husband, connected with the white, working-class women in Luttrell's studies. Because working-class men learned their jobs through apprenticeship or some other official, credential-granting process, women typically saw their husbands as "smarter" than they were, since their own child-raising and homemaking skills were seen not as skills, but as caring or "just instinct." This student was able to locate her family in a larger social space. She and her husband emerged not as (smarter or dumber) autonomous individuals (how most Americans talk about themselves), but as inhabitants of unequal social institutions that constrain and enable their lives in specific ways.

Sometimes we don't succeed.

One class period, in an attempt to illustrate race and gender privilege in the classroom, I told my UT-Dallas students a story about my experiences teaching writing at Duke University in the early 1990s. Like many humanities graduate students, I supported myself for a number of years teaching the first-year writing course to undergraduates. One year, I supervised six first-time instructors who were teaching the same material, observing their classes several times during the semester and serving as a resource person for them. As writing teachers, we were charged with introducing undergraduates to the use of "inclusive language," a daunting undertaking at Duke in the early 1990s, since *Newsweek* (among others) had told them that the "politically correct" faculty on campus were ready to indoctrinate them.

Though I am a committed user and proselytizer for inclusive language, this was nonetheless my least favorite part of the semester. It took up an entire week of class time. The first day involved venting/processing all of the outrage about political correctness and discussing (aided by a chapter in our textbook and the guidelines mailed to me by various university presses) why it might be rhetorically wise to choose inclusive language. The second day was actual practice at using inclusive language—the nuts and bolts of the process, so to speak—based on specific examples. The whole week lacked the customary generosity of spirit I had become accustomed to from everyone in class.

I was amazed, I told my students at UT-D, to observe how differently this lesson played in different classrooms. White, male instructors had to spend very little time on it, and rarely encountered much resistance. Nonwhite instructors, all women, and those who were marked as gay or lesbian, had a much more difficult time. Inclusive language was contentious, I explained, if the person charged with presenting it was perceived to have an axe to grind. The neutral, objective, unmarked "human being" in this scenario was white, male, and heterosexual. The rest of us just played like "special interest groups." Guidelines for using inclusive language seemed rational and authoritative from white men, but political and intellectually suspect from the rest of us.

The UT-Dallas students were baffled by this story. They got the point about gender and race privilege, but they could not imagine the classroom scenario I had just described.

"Your students *argued* with you?" one student asked, stunned.

I assured them that this was the case, and added that one student at the end of class asserted that "he" meant everyone, always had, and always would, regardless what anyone said. He continued by announcing that when he was out in the real world, he would make all of those women and minorities working for him write the way he told them to.

"Is this kid crazy?" one student wanted to know. "You're the teacher! Whether I agreed with you or not, if you told me to write some way, I'd write that way – I'm not an idiot."

Class had run over, and discussion had to stop there for the week. I was stunned by this experience. We had spent over two thirds of the semester talking about social reproduction theory, about the ways educational institutions legitimate the re-creation of social hierarchies by making differences in income and social status appear to be the result of merit. We had countless examples in class discussion and in class reading of social reproduction theories at work. We had read a wonderful article about architecture on the men's and women's campuses at Duke and the ways it transmitted gender and class privilege in its organization of social space.[5] Several students had offered great examples in class. One had volunteered that his math instructor at our community college was, in fact, a math PhD student from Harvard, home moonlighting at the community college for the summer, who used the same book for teaching in both places.

"Same book," he said, "same teacher. What else are you buying if not connections to rich, powerful people and a piece of paper testifying that you are one of them?"

Others pointed out that what got you into an elite, private college was a high SAT score (which effectively measures things elite, WASP-types learn in their homes) and a good high school background (paid for in most states by property taxes). Most of them discussed social reproduction theory quite articulately on the mid-term exam. Yet, here I was with a classroom full of students who were baffled by the class (and race and gender) privilege this particular Duke student possessed.

This incident, like most, was overdetermined. When I taught writing at Duke, I was 24 years old, had no PhD, and was teaching an obviously low-status class. At UT-Dallas, I had a PhD, was teaching less obviously low-status courses, and had more wrinkles around my eyes. The Duke student in this story was definitely more outspoken than most, but the general pattern of behavior rang true to my experience. As a general rule, I find public school kids far more docile (sometimes maddeningly so) than those at elite, private institutions, and I believe it has to do with a class- and race-based sense of entitlement.

The next week, I started off by returning to this incident. I quoted my UT-D student from the previous week ("You're the teacher! Whether I agreed with you or not, if you told me to write some way, I'd write that way."), explaining that she had an *employee's* way of being in the world ("In exchange for a grade or a paycheck, I will do what you tell me to do"). The Duke student had an *employer's* way of being in the world (he expected to tell other people—especially women and minority people—what to do). He had a great deal of help getting that way, I explained. Students at Duke are required to take a certain number of seminars, classes of 15 people or fewer that meet in one of the countless seminar rooms that dot Duke's campus. The architecture at Duke, I explained, let that student know that the world was entitled to his opinion, that what he had to say mattered, that he—in fact—had a duty to develop some educated opinions and to defend them publicly. Duke (about $25,000 a year) gave him the opportunity to practice. UT-Dallas (then about $6,000 a year), like most budget-strapped state schools, has one seminar room for the Arts and Humanities where graduate classes meet. Our classroom—50 chairs in crowded rows facing forward at me and a blackboard—told UTD students that it was their job to write down what they were told and reproduce it later. There was no call for them to say anything at all. (Or so the arrangement of their physical space suggested. I had exhausted myself suggesting otherwise).

Although individuals can resist the structures of the institutions they inhabit (we read bell hooks; we read Paulo Freire; we discuss and debate; we break up into smaller groups; we move the chairs to a more participatory arrangement), these institutions nonetheless exercise a powerful, if often invisible, shaping force on all of our lives. Making class privilege visible in institutions always already structured by it is no easy task.

I was most struck by my students' conviction that the irate Duke student in question must be crazy. Class reproduction was so complete and so invisible that my UT-D students could not explain privileged behavior (in spite of a semester of critical tools that might have helped) in any way except that this boy was just nuts. They did not see themselves as having learned a particular (working-class? middle manager? hireling?) way-of-being in the world from their schools, homes, and jobs; everyone was like them (or they were nuts).

For the record, class and class privilege were no more visible at Duke. Although Duke students, too, grasped social reproduction theory intellectually, few were aware of speaking from a position of privilege, or recognized the ways it might shape their ideas or ways of being in the world. They, too, assumed that everyone was just like them.

On some level, my students were right. Everyone they met *was* like them. The first day of class in Gender and Education, students introduce themselves with their personal educational histories. More often than not, with the exception of international students, everyone is a public school kid from Texas. Class and class privilege are so hard to make visible, because we mostly inhabit homogeneous institutions, socialize with people who share our class background, and are in no way encouraged by public discourse to think of ourselves as having class identities at all. Because our students are so effectively sorted by class before they walk through the doors of our institutions, their own experience (however great an asset in a student-centered classroom) is inadequate to make concrete the abstract theories about class reproduction that inform so much of our own scholarly lives. Further, in a global world, the "working class" is frequently elsewhere—Singapore, China—and unless there are some vocal international students in class, the sum total of the experience in the classroom will never add up to an adequate understanding of global capitalism.

I'll hand the conclusion of this meditation to Joan Scott, who published an essay called "Experience" in 1991, in which she addressed the problematic nature of experience as a foundation for knowledge, although it had been immensely productive and empowering for many outsiders in the academy by the early 1990s.[6] Scott writes:

> When experience is taken as the origin of knowledge, the vision of the individual subject (the person who had the experience or the historian who recounts it) becomes the bedrock of evidence upon which the explanation is built. Questions about the constructed nature of the experience, about how subjects are constituted in the first place, about how one's vision is structured – about language (or discourse) and history – are left aside. (25)

In other words, a reliance on experience can effectively locate individuals *in* history (especially those previously left out), but it cannot—by itself—enable individuals to see history in themselves. The challenge for me in teaching class in the classroom is to make clear how institutions and narratives construct us, even as we are engaged in the joint process of (re)creating them.

Notes

1   See, especially, Shirley Brice Heath, *Ways With Words: Language, Life, and Words in Communities and Classrooms* (New York: Cambridge University Press, 1983); bell hooks, *Teaching to Transgress: Education as the Practice of Freedom* (New York: Routledge, 1994); Lorene Cary, *Black Ice* (New York: Vintage, 1991); Peggy Orenstein, *Schoolgirls: Young Women, Self-esteem, and the Confidence Gap* (New York: Doubleday, 1994).

2   Barbara Solomon, *In the Company of Educated Women: A History of Women and Higher Education in America* (New Haven: Yale University Press, 1985).

3   Karin A. Martin, "Becoming a Gendered Body: Practices of Preschools." *American Sociological Review* 63(4) (1998): 494–511.

4   Wendy Luttrell, "'The Teachers, They All Had Their Pets': Concepts of Gender, Knowledge, and Power." *Signs* 18(1) (1993): 505–41; and "Working Class Women's Ways of Knowing: Effects of Gender, Race, and Class." In *Education and Gender Equality*, Ed. Julia Wrigley (Washington D. C.: Falmer Press, 1992): 173–92.

5   Annabel Wharton, "Gender, Architecture, and Institutional Self-Presentation: The Case of Duke University." *South Atlantic Quarterly* 90(1) (Winter 1991): 175–217.

6   Joan W. Scott, "Experience." rpt. In *Feminists Theorize the Political*, Ed. Judith Butler and Joan W. Scott (New York: Routledge, 1992), 22–40.

12

Enforcing the Rules

Taylor Stoehr

It is fitting that Paul Goodman's literary executor should end up teaching students whose growing up brought them a future even worse than that painted by Goodman in Growing Up Absurd. *When students are on probation, hoping to get their probation time reduced, and their classroom experience is largely governed by state-imposed regulations, we can see the usual class barriers between student and teacher writ large; and Taylor Stoehr's analysis of homework policy, grading criteria, and attendance rules in a program for probationers is relevant in any setting.*

For the past 10 years, I've been teaching along with other volunteers—college professors like myself, probation officers, judges, and people from the community—in a program called "Changing Lives Through Literature" serving the Dorchester District Court of the Commonwealth of Massachusetts.[1] Our students are probationers of the Court, and after completing the 10-week course, they receive 6 months off their probation time.

I work in the men's group (there is a women's group too), which averages 12 or 15 graduates each semester, the great majority of them people of color, reflecting Dorchester demographics. Our readings have been chosen with their experience in mind. The primary text is Frederick Douglass's *Narrative of the Life of an American Slave*, which serves as the starting point for a discussion of the problems faced by the students themselves—poverty and racism, family breakdown, the weakening of community bonds and thinning out of spiritual sustenance, the long struggle for social justice. Short supplementary readings by other authors—black and white, American and foreign, contemporary and classic—clarify issues Douglass raises by putting them in a broader context, and a weekly writing assignment helps us focus on their relevance today. For example, after reading what Douglass recalls of his childhood, juxtaposed against the memories of other fatherless children like Malcolm X, Richard Wright, Maxim Gorky, or Leo Tolstoy, students are asked for their own opinion of what is necessary for a "normal" childhood, and who has the responsibility to provide it. What was your childhood like? What kind of a father do you want to be? Those are the implied questions. We also ask how a man like Frederick Douglass *finds himself*. "Where do people get their courage, self-esteem, and righteousness?"

Changing Lives began as a single experiment in New Bedford in 1991, and has spread entirely by word of mouth to a dozen other jurisdictions in Massachusetts, as well as scattered courts in six other states, in each of which the curriculum and pedagogy vary considerably, though the goals are the same. As with most alternative sentencing experiments, its appeal is strongest for those who know the revolving door of the criminal justice system most intimately—judges, probation officers, and of course offenders themselves. Obviously, for all of them, the primary aim is to eliminate recidivism, and partial evidence suggests that the usual high rate of re-arrest may be greatly reduced for our graduates. A rigorous study of the results to date is under way. In what follows here, however, I want to address another kind of concern and outcome arising in such a program.

Our dilemma is one that faces all teachers in one form or another: how are we to deal with the potential collision between the constraints of format in any classroom undertaking—rules for preparation, attendance, and participation—and our desire to foster a new attitude toward reflection and conversation, in our case with men whose past schooling has never amounted to more than playing the game, or just as likely, defying the rules or refusing to play altogether? If there is potential conflict between these goals and constraints in the ordinary classroom, how much more so in a room full of certified "failures," whose report cards have both "F" and "Felony" inscribed on them!

Our Changing Lives class meets for 90 minutes, one night a week, for 10 weeks—not a rigorous schedule, but given our students and their plight, it could be called intensive. How much external structure, and on what models, will allow them to make the best of their experience? Our aim is not to encourage anyone to step back onto the educational ladder—or treadmill—though a few may want to do so. Most of these men are too deeply rooted in complicated lives for that. They would benefit more from job training, apprenticeship programs, or just a decent employment agency helping them find work despite their criminal records. In Changing Lives, our task is not really curricular then—learning a discrete body of knowledge or an academic skill—but more attitudinal, or one might say, ethical. We're trying to find the right approach for men re-entering society after accusation, trial, and chastisement for serious criminal acts.

The courts have dealt with them forcefully, and we hope justly, but crudely and with little guidance in facing the future built into their sentences—and they are now on probation, to prove themselves obedient if not otherwise changed. Accordingly, it is one of the probation officers who announces our rules at the beginning of every semester:

- attend class on time
- arrive sober and straight
- turn off all cell phones
- respect everyone in the room

Respect for others has never been in doubt in our classes, though a lively conversation sometimes has so many voices talking at once that it's hard to hear. Usually, though, people are pretty good about listening, giving the other fellow a turn. We've had a few problems with cell phones and substance abuse, have dealt with them straightforwardly, and ultimately solved them. Our guidelines for attendance and homework have been more difficult to administer.

The attendance record is kept by the probation officers, who pass around a sheet for signatures at the end of each class. We warn everyone that more than two absences will get you kicked out, and I've seen our probation officers converge on a student who had missed two classes early in the semester, urging him to shape up. A few weeks later, when an emergency came along, the absentee had to be told he wouldn't graduate. We've lost several of our best students to this automatic expulsion, including men whose presence, however irregular, had clearly been an inspiration to their classmates. We held to the rule because it was our charge from the court, and the bargain we had made with our students.

Aside from being absent, there is really no way to fail our program. In the end there is no grade, not even a pass/fail hurdle. If you attend, you graduate. But what should count as being present or absent? Suppose a man joins the class a week late, because he couldn't find the room the first night, or because he was recruited after the program had already started? Should that count against him? We wavered, but ultimately decided to enforce the eight-meeting requirement. It takes at least eight meetings to absorb what the course has to offer, we told ourselves. If a serious student misses a third class, we have sometimes offered a makeup session at the end of the semester, but this feels more like a punishment than a solution, and niggling to boot. It's better to say, "Come back next semester."

The more we wag our fingers at absentees, the more likely we are to have people at the opposite extreme, with perfect attendance for the first eight meetings, who then skip the last two, keeping careful score. This is rare, but it's happened. Once we put rules like these in place, it becomes a game for some students, just as in most schools. Recently, we've found that attendance problems seem to vanish if we begin the semester by asking the students themselves to formulate the rules. They invariably begin by insisting that every class must be attended, and then amend this by allowing for "good excuses," rather than establishing a precise limit. Since we moved to this method of setting the guidelines, many men have never missed a class, and no one has missed more than two.

What about tardiness? For the most part we ignore it, having realized that the 10 minutes we spend waiting for latecomers buys us 10 minutes of free and easy conversation, leavening in our recipe for the communal loaf. This is a good example of how an old problem can be turned to advantage simply by asking what's really at stake. It's all a matter of attitude. If we made a fuss about it, everyone would end up feeling pissy. Again, recent classes setting their own standards have almost always started on time.

If someone is always 20 minutes late, we look into it. Sometimes there's a good excuse—a job and a long commute—but our probation officers don't like making exceptions. I do remember a night when one of the more dutiful students came rushing into the room at the end of class, 5 minutes before the attendance sheet went around. He'd been required to work late, knew he couldn't make class, but wanted us to see his face and hear his story. He had his homework with him, and we let him sign in as "present."

Policing homework is much more likely to backfire than any of these other attempts to keep everyone on track, and in my opinion something to be dealt with case by case. Of course, teachers meet homework resistance all the time, so often that the chronic problem and the routine solution have long since fused as the core rationale of schooling, whereby means of enforcement determine the entire assignment package—book reports, exams, and recitation—and what you read at home serves as little more than pretext for disciplinary routines that structure the school day. By-products include mindless obedience, sneakiness, inability to concentrate, and a scorn for books.

With enforcement come grades, report cards, tracking, and various sanctions, guaranteeing that some students will fail. That's what it means to have a ranking system tied to performance: no matter where you stand on the ladder, if you're not at the top, you've lost the game, whether you're second best or last. Pass/fail options are like showdown poker, played by a loser for double-or-nothing stakes.

In their years of schooling, our probationers scored at the bottom so often that most of them stopped trying—thinking of it as their own failure, though of course they hated the regime that put them to the test. The upshot for homework expectations is written on their faces that first night: an assignment of only a few pages of easy reading can stir deep feelings of inadequacy, and reactivate the old choice between obedience and submission. To ask them for homework is like putting them back in Third Grade again, their knees too big for the desks. This is merely to say that the problem is a very thorny one, and deserves lengthy discussion. I will attempt to state here only some of the basic guidelines we've worked out in Dorchester.

First of all, as will become clearer in what follows, our view is that the crucial force for change in our program comes from class discussion, and not the literature that provides its starting point. The reading or writing a student does at home may end up being important, but with us the essential changes grow out of what happens in the classroom, people talking earnestly to one another about their real concerns. We provide a loose framework for these small group conversations in the carefully planned sequence of readings and the questions we pose regarding them, beginning with a focus on childhood, then moving to problems of schooling (including the use of coercion and punishment), considering the plight of the weak or oppressed in today's streets, examining the confusion between manliness and violence, noticing how desperation can lead to despair, and finally questioning the kind of justice dispensed by our society.

Much as we believe that such concerns lie at the heart of our students' predicament, and must be confronted for them to get anything out of their 10 weeks, we are also convinced that the homework assignments raising these issues ought never to be treated as imperatives or guarantees of achievement. Over the years we've made many adjustments in the structure of the course and our own expectations, but we started with one fundamental premise, which we've tried to hold to—that Changing Lives, whether or not it actually changes any lives for the better, should not change them for the worse. It might, for instance, be good for a probationer to learn self-discipline through meeting the requirements of a study program that made reasonable and worthy demands on him, but not at the risk of failing to live up to such demands, and not at the expense of others who might also fail to meet them. We resolved that the course should not be another proof of incompetence or incorrigibility, not even for those who couldn't or wouldn't do the work, good reasons or bad.

The important thing is not to set standards and hold people to them, but to be of genuine use to students at whatever level of achievement they may have reached. The lesson we try to pass on is best described as an attitude toward ideas and experience, rather than any particular block of knowledge or degree of skill. Many of our probationers seem to have missed the key discovery that most children make somewhere between age five and age seven, the discovery of what it means to learn something—to find out what reading is, or how to tell a story, make a map, or act in a play. It's not what you learn, but how it feels to discover something really big, opening new possibilities. Once you learn how history makes the past usable, or how a consensus grows out of earnest debate, or how to see yourself as a potential employer might see you, then you have a new relation to all of life. That's a big order, of course, and to foster the kind of attitude I'm talking about obviously requires taking into account the ideals and aspirations of students, not just their SAT scores and deportment quotients; for it is these ideals that students must discover for themselves, and try to live up to, not the performance goals that teachers or oracular models set for them.

Vital language, trustworthy taste, and practical ethics—the ultimate grounds of all such ideals and aspirations—are not simply inherited from the culture you are raised in, nor can they be constituted by fiat from above. They must be continually created, negotiated, and revised in the public realm, wherever groups of people come together for serious talk. As it happens, for better or worse, the primary forum for such cultural work has become the modern classroom, just as it once was the marketplace or the church, the town meeting or even the theater, in ancient and medieval times when theater was still a civic event.

Whether or not the classroom is better suited than the barber shop for such cultural creation, it is the actual institution that has taken the place of these other formal settings in today's mass society with its suffocating bureaucratic systems organized from on high.

One of our aims, then, is to demystify the whole realm of social control, schooling, and literacy. All their lives our students have been told that they are incompetent readers and writers, and this tends to make them so. But the incompetence is superficial in most cases. Their speech skills are usually more than adequate, and often superb. In fact, their failure in school has protected them from certain kinds of glibness and beating about the bush.

All students, including ours, have the right to success in a truly democratic classroom—not just an opportunity to learn, but active exercise of language, taste, and ethics, in order to explore their own individual powers and ideals in relation to a growing sense of how others speak and judge and evaluate. "Success" means both discovering and making standards, rather than merely living up to them. "Failure" means being left out of the most essential aspects of civic life. Often, the schools fail to do this important work, through a misguided notion of what kind of education is appropriate in an egalitarian society. The men we meet in Changing Lives typically think of themselves as failures. From their earliest experiences in schooling to the regimen of incarceration and probation, they have stubbornly resisted demands and admonishments, have been labeled incorrigible, and have little or no sense of what it might mean to be part of a democratic forum deciding matters of concern for their own lives. We want to establish such a classroom, in which no one will be left out.

Homework, insofar as it fosters this kind of success, is all to the good. But we must not let a coercive or punitive attitude infect our invitation to literary experience. Forced reading is worse than none at all. It kills the spirit of both the reader and the book. Therefore, we have a very permissive attitude toward homework, and usually let delinquents discover for themselves that it's more satisfying to be able to join in the discussion than it is to feel embarrassed and at a loss because you haven't read what the others are talking about. At the same time, we make sure that even those who shirk their homework can contribute something to the conversation. To do this, we spend 10 or 15 minutes at the beginning of every class writing answers to some searching question that grows out of the reading but does not require precise knowledge of a text:

> Please pick one big lesson you learned in your childhood and tell the story of how you learned it and what difference it has made in your life.
> What can people who are "weak" – because of youth, illness, poverty, prejudice, or a history of being in trouble with the law – do to change their lives and make themselves "stronger"?
> How can people survive hitting bottom? Why do some people cling to their anger, pride, or self-pity, while others are able to find something new to believe in?

To meditate and write on such questions briefly before discussing them is something every member of our class can do. In this way, we can function together as a group, regardless of how much or how little individuals have prepared at home. Sometimes the readings figure prominently in discussions, sometimes not at all, but in our small groups no one fails. Some who start out resisting their homework end up discovering they like to read after all; others say something more like this:

> I hate to read, but it was a challenge to myself. I haven't been in school for twenty years! The goal was to eliminate six months from my sentence. The ultimate prize upon completion of the program for me was expressing myself in class, through homework and in groups.

Or this:

> Through the course of this program I've learned how to communicate with people a little better. It seems like before I came to this program I was going numb. I can't remember the last time I picked up a book to read it or even skim through it. I also have a better relationship with my girlfriend. I try to think about other people's feelings now. It isn't just about me any more.

I hope it is obvious that the methods and goals I have been describing here have implications for any classroom, especially in times like our own. I leave it to the reader to weigh the possibilities. Let me move on now to a few final remarks that focus on tone and atmosphere rather than rules, and that may illustrate some of the risks and benefits that come with bringing people back to school long after their original compulsory education.

As I have been arguing, in general it is better to let students find their own way to the give-and-take of the classroom, a setting where few of them have ever been comfortable. Early in every semester, for instance, there are always some in our classes who raise their hands like little children, asking where the water fountain is, or for permission to go to the men's room. It takes two or three times to break them of the habit—Just go! You don't need to ask. But I don't worry about the other habit, also formed long ago, of using a "call of nature" as a brief escape from class. The "numb" student just quoted was invariably the first to finish writing his class exercise, and after a minute or two of staring at the floor, he would get up and amble out. Others did the same thing when they finished, though rarely more than two at any one time. Were they having a cigarette? I never saw anyone in our class smoking, just as I never heard them swearing and cursing, but then I rarely saw them outside the schoolroom or courthouse. My guess is that they often did have to relieve themselves, but that they also felt bored waiting for others to finish writing, and perhaps uneasy about their own lack of more to say. They were uncomfortable just sitting there, quietly thinking, though that was what I hoped people would get used to. Little did they realize that their comings and goings furnished the timetable for our writing stints. I would always wait till everyone was back in the room before calling a halt and assigning people to their small groups for discussion. I wanted everyone present when serious conversation began.

Fewer students left for the toilets once we had broken into small groups, and I remember a comic moment one night that puts all of this in perspective. It was the seventh class, and we were talking about facing crisis, how a man can sometimes come back from hitting bottom a stronger person. One of our most charismatic students was telling his group about living for a few years in an all-White community where his high school classmates shunned him, even in the basketball team locker room. One day he found himself alone in the showers with a white teammate, and opened a conversation. He made a joke and got the fellow to laugh. Soon they were walking home together every day after practice. The suburb was near Chicago, and he offered to take his new friend to visit the black neighborhoods there. Before long, he was guiding tours of his teammates through the South Side.

This student was retelling the story that he had written in his homework that week:

It took a while but the other students started talking to me. It started with the basketball team, because we had more time with each other. I had some of the guys coming to my uncle's house after school, so they could see how I lived. But that wasn't how I really lived, so I got about six guys to come to the city with me. The things they saw were so different – different people, food, houses. One guy told me he saw it on TV before, but they never watched BET (Black Entertainment Television) shows, video, and rappers. They didn't even know what skins (pork rinds) were.

In writing up his story, he compared his high school experience to the way that small group discussions in our class also helped bridge racial boundaries. And, indeed, in his small group that night he was doing the same thing, for he had them all, black and white, on the edges of their chairs. With others picking up the mood, the conversation was very lively. Here, for example, is what another, much older student was saying that night about his experiences across the color line:

> In 1948, I can remember going to town with my mother. We had walked a mile and a half to catch the Greyhound bus. I was tired, and the sun was very hot. When the bus finally came, I was glad to get on and sat in the first empty seat I came to. My mother snatched me by the collar and dragged me to the back. Of course I didn't know why. Later I learned we weren't allowed to sit up front. The back of the bus was full, and black folks were standing up, even with empty seats up front. A white man from up North offered me the seat next to him, and I took it – only to give it up to the next white woman to get on. But I always remember that white man who gave me the seat.

Of course, the white students in the group had their own stories to contribute. (I too had a basketball anecdote I was dying to tell, though I was only an eavesdropper.) One black man summed it up in his homework the following week:

> There's no difference between any man. We are the same, white to black, black to white. We may get raised by intelligent beings or ignorant beings, but we will remain a unified pack of souls, under God's eyes, and whoever preaches differently doesn't know the truth.

In the midst of all this, suddenly the original speaker stood up, and announced that he needed to pee—that he had needed to pee for quite a while, but didn't want to miss anything. They laughed, and as he left, he told them not to talk about anything without him—and in fact he was back in 2 minutes. At the end of the evening, this group didn't want to break up. They kept at it long after all the others had handed in their writing and vanished.

This was our class at its best, the men in the circle establishing their own agenda, mutual trust, and conversational decorum. Much of it in this case was due to the man whose basketball story I've just told. At mid-semester, he wrote the following avowal, not in answer to any assignment, but out of sheer exuberance:

> I really like this class. I think it's the best thing that the court has ever done. I find myself using this class when I'm on the street. Certain things that we read about. I encounter the same things and I think what that person did, and I add that with what I think. And most of the time I come out on top.
>
> I'm also learning about things that black people did that I never knew, thanks to this class. Knowing is half the battle.
>
> Another thing is, I've met white guys that I probably wouldn't have spoke to on the street, but being in this class and breaking off in groups, you get to meet and talk to them one-on-one. By being in small groups, you can get a better understanding of each man's view on life and other situations – black, white, Spanish, or what have you.

Though it means ending on a dissonant note, I must also tell the sequel. This man whose delight in our class was so evident and contagious was the very man mentioned at the beginning of this essay, who had to be informed at the last meeting of the semester that he had collected more than his allowed absences—more than three, in fact—and would not graduate. He had been warned; now it was too late. He argued with the probation officers, was shown the attendance sheet with his five signatures, and stamped angrily out of the room.

I still ask myself: did we serve him well? Was his another failure experience, or not?

Note

1 In 2004, Changing Lives Through Literature received the New England Board of Higher Education's highest award, for "Excellence" in program development. Taylor Stoehr's essay on the Dorchester program, "Is It a Crime to Be Illiterate?" appeared in the March/April 2005 issue of *Change Magazine*. See also Jean Trounstine and Robert P. Waxler, eds, *Finding a Voice: The Practice of Changing Lives Through Literature* (Ann Arbor, MI: University of Michigan Press, 2005).

13

Upward Mobility and Higher Education: Mining the Contradictions in a Worker Education Program

Emily Schnee

Teaching as well as interviewing students in a New York City worker education program taught Emily Schnee a great deal. The conclusions she draws here about the potential contradiction between education for critical consciousness and education for advancement—between, it might seem, the goals of progressive faculty and those of their students—as well as her suggestions for working with this contradiction, have implications for teachers across academia.

For over half a century, a college education has been seen as the conduit to white collar employment in this country. Yet, the expansion of higher education access and degree attainment has created greater expectations for upward mobility than the job market can bear (Anyon 2005; Carnoy and Levin 1985; Lafer 2002; Nasaw 1979). In the last decades, institutions of higher education have consistently produced a greater supply of college graduates than available middle-class jobs. As the number of college graduates has outpaced careers requiring college-level skills, many college graduates end up performing work for which only a high school education is necessary. Not only do increasing numbers of college graduates work beneath their educational qualifications, but also many of those with a bachelor's degree earn close to the minimum wage (Levin-Waldman 1999, cited in Anyon). Hence, the contradiction of unfulfilled expectations is a more widespread phenomenon than is popularly believed (Carnoy and Levin 1985; Clark 1960).

Using the unfulfilled mobility aspirations of adult students in a union-supported college worker education program (WEP) as a lens, this essay aims to explore the tension between education for mobility and education for transformation. While working-class students often come to higher education in pursuit of social and economic mobility, radical educators, including many who teach at WEPs, aspire to teach for critical consciousness and social transformation. The space between these seemingly opposed intentions can be fraught with frustrations on both sides. I argue that honest and explicit consideration of the disparity between students' mobility desires and their realistic prospects for class mobility as a result of their degrees could heighten students' critical consciousness and increase the transformative potential of the worker education program.

Furthermore, I posit that a deeper exploration of students' mobility aspirations reveals that these desires are more complex and nuanced than faculty may assume. Rather than a simplistic vision of higher education as fostering individual economic mobility, the mobility desires of the WEP students I encountered spanned a broad spectrum of ideologies and intentions. Students sought mobility for themselves and their families, for the advancement of their racial and ethnic communities, and for the possibility of pursuing socially transformative work. While the worker education programs' urban and labor studies curricula and progressive pedagogy intersected with students' lived experience to shape their mobility desires in powerful ways, lack of student mobility was ultimately the most potent source of critical consciousness building some students experienced during their tenure in the program. This essay aims to show how a deeper exploration of students' mobility aspirations could provide a basis for critical consciousness building among working-class students and further enhance the radical potential of worker education programs.

Background

The worker education program where I taught for many years and conducted my research is a union-supported college degree program for working adults that is a satellite center of the public university system in New York City. Students at WEP receive a liberal arts education, in either urban or labor studies, that attempts to connect higher education to a vision of social change. WEP describes itself as committed to "opportunity, support, and empowerment" for adult worker education students and for over 20 years has provided union members college access through active recruitment and generous tuition assistance via their labor unions. WEP prides itself on offering adult students a progressive labor and urban studies curriculum, and engaging classes that employ student-centered pedagogies and inspire students to reflect critically on the world. Although vaguely and imperfectly defined, interpreted and enacted differently by all concerned, the program mission assumes that education has transformative potential and attempts to live out its connection to the labor movement by linking higher education not just to individual student mobility, but also to broader struggles for collective social change.

Contrary to the conventional image of a college student, a typical WEP student is a middle-aged black woman with children who works full-time; 87 percent of the undergraduates enrolled in spring 2004 were female and their average age was 45. Although the program does not track the race or ethnicity of students, more than 80 percent of the students who participated in my study identified themselves racially as black; over half are African American, another 24 percent come from the English-speaking Caribbean, and 14 percent are Latino. The vast majority of WEP students are civil servants employed as clerical and secretarial workers by a variety of New York City agencies. Students must be over 25 years of age and members of a labor union to be eligible for admission to the program.

Fourteen students, all of whom had attended WEP a minimum of six semesters, self-selected to participate in this study, which explored the impact of college on adult worker education students enrolled at WEP. Nine students wrote lengthy educational memoirs and participated in semistructured educational life history interviews; another five were only interviewed. Though semistructured interviews were also conducted with 11 faculty and staff, the primary focus of this research was on students' experience of college at WEP.

WEP's structural problems with mobility

The higher education-class mobility nexus so prevalent in our society represents a significant tension for WEP as a union-supported worker education program. WEP both implicitly, and at times explicitly, capitalizes on the assumption that a college degree will lead to career advancement and simultaneously resents the ways in which students' desires for class mobility impinge upon the ideological content and radical potential of the program.

Different versions of WEP's promotional brochures walk the tightrope of enticement and consciousness-raising, alternately promising "growth, opportunity, advancement" to students alongside a mention of developing "a better educated citizenry and union membership to generate new ideas for social change." The director of worker education, like many of the educators employed at WEP, acknowledges this tension, without considering how the program might more fully and coherently respond to this inherent contradiction. He states:

> There is a tension – or disconnect – between student intentions in coming to the program which are often connected to vague ideas of higher education leading to upward mobility and the program intention of preparing better educated union members to participate in their unions and better educated city workers to understand the issues that affect their jobs . . . Our students come to us, in large part, because they want to get a degree . . . they don't come to us because the curriculum says we are going to prepare you to become advocates in your union and your community.

The unions that support WEP further intensify this contradiction, promoting the program as a benefit to their members and readily mentioning career advancement as a possible outcome without having negotiated a promotional ladder that recognizes a college degree as a criterion for advancement. This is compounded by the widespread misunderstanding among WEP students that implicit in the generous tuition assistance the unions have negotiated for them is a commitment to creating avenues for professional advancement for their members. A WEP staff person commented on this contradiction, noting:

> They're [students are] angry at the union, not angry but frustrated, because here you've given me all this, somebody said, the union has given me all this money for my degree, yet they can't negotiate a [promotional] ladder.

This assumed, yet faulty, premise that graduation from WEP will lead to career advancement is exposed in the experiences of the majority of the students who, like my research participants, do not experience significant mobility as a result of their college educations. Of the 14 WEP students who participated in my research, none experienced cross-class mobility as a result of their college education. Seven students gleaned incremental gains from their degrees, moving into higher skilled working-class occupations as a result of their educational attainment, often within their previous workplaces. Seven experienced no career advancement at all.

These students' experiences reveal the contradictions that lie beneath the two opposing conceptions of education—education for upward mobility and education for critical consciousness—at play within the worker education program. They highlight WEP's failure to articulate a coherent vision and practice of education that does not position these conceptions as intractably opposed. While mobility desires are a powerful motivation in most WEP students' return to school, they are rarely openly or explicitly examined in the worker education program. One faculty member reflected on this persistent contradiction in the program:

> One of the problems in WEP is that there's not, there doesn't exist yet, a kind of coherent workable alternative to the dominant ideology among students which is this mobility credential meritocracy. That ideology is extremely potent to people because it is so tenuous. People grab onto it like hell, because it's not sturdy . . . there's a certain desperation in that mobility thing . . . it's possible as a teacher to want to come in and get people off this ideological track which is a real obstacle to people thinking critically and wanting to learn something. And, yet what are you doing? You want to knock somebody off this thing they've worked like hell to get a hold of and what are you offering in return?

The WEP curriculum *implicitly* provides students a vision of education for critical consciousness and social transformation with core courses such as Poverty and Affluence; Community Organizing; and Work, Class, and Culture in which students are engaged in critical analysis of pressing social issues and are asked, through class projects and activities, to connect their learning to their life experiences as city workers and union members. Yet, curricular implementation of this sort is quite uneven at WEP, depending entirely upon the inclinations and ideologies of individual instructors. As a program, WEP does not engage its faculty in sustained or explicit exploration of program mission or the tension between students' desire to use higher education as a tool for mobility and many instructors' aspirations to teach for critical consciousness and social change.

In the absence of a clearly articulated alternate conception of the purpose and value of their degrees, students are left on their own to make sense of the program mission and pedagogy, their own desires for education as a vehicle for mobility, and a civil service promotional structure that does not take their academic credentials into account. While many WEP students have responded thoughtfully and creatively to these tensions (and with a fair share of anger and disappointment as well), I contend that a union-supported worker education program like WEP could do more, both to understand the students' mobility desires in all their complexity and to mine the contradictions between students' aspirations and their realistic prospects for mobility as a potent source of critical consciousness building in radical pedagogy.

The spectrum of students' mobility desires

Compounding the silence surrounding students' mobility desires at WEP is the assumption that students' primary motivation in attending college is their pursuit of individual upward mobility. Yet, unbeknownst to many faculty, and unexplored through formal programmatic structures, WEP students express a complex and varied spectrum of mobility desires. Rather than being a simplistic vision of higher education as fostering individual economic advancement, student ambitions extend from a pursuit of individual mobility, to aspirations for the advancement of their families and racial/ethnic communities, to a desire to pursue employment in socially transformative careers. The WEP students' educational memoirs revealed a startling diversity of aspirations and outcomes that could, if tapped, yield rich material for critical consciousness building within, and beyond, the program curriculum. Of course, many students do enter WEP with typical aspirations for individual mobility. Samuel explained the ideology that impelled him, and perhaps most others at WEP, to get his college degree:

> Well, it [a college education] was and still is, I think, the tool that opens the door for a lot of opportunities in a lot of capacities. I realized at a young age the importance of having a degree. I mean without it your opportunities are limited, so that was definitely a factor. And another factor is economics. You know, it opens the door for you to be able to make more money.

Lisa's initial impetus for enrolling in WEP stemmed directly from her desire for respect and recognition in the workplace. At one point in her career, she left the civil service for a job in which the starting salary offered to her was significantly lower than what was advertised because she did not have a college degree. Indignant that her skills, knowledge, and lengthy work experience were considered insufficient, Lisa left this job almost immediately, returned to her former civil service position, and enrolled in WEP intent on rectifying this perceived injustice. She recalled:

> I took a job as a job developer at a community college and the salary, I'll never forget it because it changed my life forever, the salary they were offering was $40,000 or something like that and I applied. I had all the credentials and the background and the skills, but I didn't have the degree, so they didn't pay me $40,000, they gave me $32,000. And that was such an impact for me. I said to myself, this is the very last time I will *ever* be, or accept a position and not be given the money because I don't have a degree. I'm going to go get my credentials because I don't want that to happen to me again.

Other WEP students sought further education to help them combat ingrained feelings of inadequacy that stopped them from applying for higher skilled jobs, and to make sure that their lack of credentials could not be used as a pretext for retaining them in lower paying, lower skilled jobs. Florence explained:

> There were openings on my job that I thought I wanted to apply for, but somehow or other I always felt inadequate. I wasn't comfortable enough to apply because I thought my writing wasn't good . . . So I figured if I came back [to college] I would be in a better position to apply for the jobs and I wouldn't feel so inadequate.

For other students, their desire for upward mobility was tightly bound to their aspirations for the advancement of their family, community, and ethnic or racial group. Rather than embracing a rugged individualist notion of mobility that severs those who have moved up from their working-class roots, these students conjured up a notion of mobility that sought to bring family and community along on the journey. For mothers, a primary impetus for returning to school was often to be an example for their children and grandchildren. Brenda and her son attended college simultaneously, although at different universities. Their commitment to graduate together kept them straight on the course toward their goal despite obstacles that emerged. In her memoir, Brenda reflected:

> Not only did I continue attending classes, but my son also continued. It was when adversities came in our midst that we promised not to stop halfway through our college education. It was important that we keep our promises, as each other's endurance meant support for each other. He completed his undergraduate degree a year ago and is quite happy he stayed in school.

Florence returned to school only after her daughter had finished college, but they now tag-team child care and other domestic responsibilities as her daughter works to finish a master's degree in early childhood education at the same time that Florence completes her BA

But, upward mobility, for several of the African-American students at WEP, was not simply a struggle to improve the material conditions of their families' lives. It was linked to a larger struggle for freedom from race-based restrictions and limitations (Cole and Omari 2003; Gilkes 1983). As Higginbotham and Weber (1992) note in their study of upward social mobility among white and black women, "many black women expressed a sense that their mobility was connected to an entire racial uplift process, not merely an individual journey" (p. 437). Several WEP students echoed this sentiment.

Deborah's original impetus to return to school came not from work or family, but from her African-American church. From the start, Deborah hoped to use her education to fulfill her "life's objective to serve community and humanity to the best of my ability" in her combined roles as "parent, teacher, counselor, administrator, chaplain, and evangelist." Deborah saw her spiritual and educational achievements as entwined, both strengthening her commitment to lift up those members of her congregation and community who are less fortunate than she is.

The early pages of Florence's memoir detail in depth the hard times her parents experienced as poor African Americans who were denied educational and employment opportunities because of their race and class. Her parents' dream for their children was that they get the education they themselves had been denied. Florence realizes this dream years after both of her parents have died, after decades of start and stop college attendance. She sees her education as a tribute to the legacy her parents left behind: "a legacy of determination" to use education to lift their children—and implicitly the race—out of a life of struggle.

Phyllis's memoir also firmly established her commitment to education as rooted in her experience as a "descendant of slaves." Her pursuit of higher education is a direct challenge to the historical restrictions African Americans faced in both educational and occupational advancement and her desire for upward mobility is a parallel quest for the advancement of her race. In her memoir, this merging of individual and collective desires for uplift is beautifully illustrated through her consistent use of "we" rather than "me." Phyllis sees her own advancement as entwined with that of her people much as the constraints racism places on her are experienced by the collective body of African Americans.

Still other WEP students sought education as a vehicle for mobility to pursue social change work. Rather than seeking earnings or status, these students yearned for employment options and opportunities that would add meaning to their lives and the lives of others. These students found their civil service jobs to be secure, stable, and at the same time stultifying. They desired to use more of their intellects and passions in their work and, in exchange, hoped to do work where they would be respected and acknowledged for what they contribute to others. These students' mobility desires evolved during their tenure at WEP, as they came to new understandings of their lived experiences in the context of the progressive urban and labor studies curriculum to which they were exposed. Sandra is a prime example of this.

A fortuitous intersection of Sandra's work experience, her urban studies major, and the deteriorating conditions in the building where she lives led her head first into the role of community organizer. When canvassers for a housing organization came to her door, Sandra "was gung ho about what I was willing to do . . . as a result I was thrust into the role of tenant leader" in the campaign to improve living conditions in her building (which had been abandoned by a derelict landlord). In this work, she explained:

> I attended meetings with the landlord and represented tenants in meetings with federal, state and city officials. I participated in letter writing campaigns, gathered signatures for petitions, held meetings in my home, delivered public speeches and supported housing legislation.

This parallel work life as an activist brought Sandra the satisfaction and meaning she had sought but had not found through education-related job advancement. Her understanding of the value of a degree changed over time, as she engaged in community organizing and found purpose and meaning there. She wrote in her memoir:

> There are many lessons to be learned from my pursuit of a college degree. I finally realized that I was pursuing status and not an education . . . I started out wanting a degree/status and ended up getting a very special education.

Even Gillian, the only student who had clearly laid plans for upward mobility through law school, rejected the idea of becoming a "career building bureaucrat" and hoped a legal degree would enable her to "be one of the dying few who care about and act on behalf of the well being of the underrepresented and overlooked." She put her own spin on mobility, seeking socially useful work as a public interest attorney. Gillian hoped to become an "advocate within the system" she came to know through her work and grew to understand through her education at WEP.

Lack of mobility and critical consciousness

Though the politically progressive labor and urban studies curricula implemented at WEP clearly influenced some students' aspirations, making them aware of issues and struggles they had previously ignored, it was precisely their failure to attain mobility that became one of the sources of deepest critical consciousness building for several students. It was these students' lived experience—perhaps newly understood in the context of WEP's course curriculum and pedagogy—that unraveled the myth of education as a vehicle for mobility and led several of them to critical consciousness about education, society, and themselves. Phyllis and Sandra best exemplify this transformation.

Phyllis, despite receiving both her bachelor's and master's degrees from WEP, continued to do secretarial work, stymied in her quest for advancement by nepotism, small-minded managers, and racism. Her memoir focused extensively on the evolution of her understanding of the education-mobility nexus and her pain at relinquishing her aspirations for what a degree might mean. She wrote:

> As I embarked upon my last undergraduate semester, there was a profound unhappiness within my soul . . . I began to realize that I was unhappy because I had come to recognize that my degree only meant I had persevered. It was not going to unlock the doors for upward mobility within my career . . . The realization of the aforementioned did bring some solace, as the myth that has been perpetuated by society that education will open the doors to a successful future, one that I sincerely believed in, has now come to fruition . . . education has provided me with the ability to decipher the lies, and I am no longer confused. So yes, the positive end result is that I no longer have to chase after the "American Dream" when the dream was never intended for my people. I can now focus on being happy with what I have obtained as a result of my educational pursuits, because I now also know that money, power, and all the materialistic things will not bring you happiness, but knowing the truth shall set you free from trying to obtain those things.

Yet, Phyllis came to these profound realizations about the limited ability of education to yield class mobility for her as an African-American woman through her own painful personal employment experience, not as part of the curriculum or pedagogy at WEP.

Sandra's memoir also reflected upon a coming-to-consciousness of the limits of education to ensure mobility. As she approached her graduation from WEP, she and Phyllis faced similar barriers to professional advancement. Sandra concluded:

> I used to think that a college degree would open up positions that were otherwise closed. I thought my lack of credentials kept me from advancing. The truth of the matter is that it was not [lack of] credentials that keep me from advancing but supervisors and managers who decided the opportunities I was given or denied.

Sandra's memoir also explored the evolution of her ideas about education. She is aware that her newfound sense of the meaning and purpose of education matches more closely with that articulated in WEP's mission—in great contrast to the expectations she, and her peers, held upon entering the program. In her memoir, she reflected on this transformation:

> [When I started at WEP] Tania [a staff person] kept harping on the community this and the community that. But, we didn't want to hear that

at that time, we didn't want to hear that, we had our own dreams and we knew where we wanted to go and where we wanted to be. We were still in the same mindset that you go to college and you get a degree and you go out and get a job and it was all about self. And you make more money so you can buy more things. And that was basically where we were headed . . . and then I think it began to penetrate, like wait a minute, look at what has been done to us. And then you sort of realize that you are just a product of your experience. And if you don't want to be a participant in your own destruction then you have to change your whole mindset. So, then I stopped thinking in terms of me and started thinking in a bigger and broader sense in terms of us.

Although Sandra was not unique among WEP students in finding her mobility dreams hampered, she was all too rare in embracing this alternate view of education, mobility, and social change. While Sandra credits the WEP curriculum with playing a vital role in her consciousness-raising process, she is quite aware that she is a minority among her peers. Perhaps more students would leave WEP with this deep and critical understanding of the limits of higher education to produce class mobility if the program trusted the complexity and legitimacy of students' mobility desires, and created programmatic space in which they might struggle over and through the meaning of these aspirations and their relationship to WEP's mission as a worker education program.

Conclusion

WEP students' experiences pose important lessons for radical educators interested in weaving working-class students' mobility aspirations into a coherent pedagogical strategy that honors the legitimacy of those desires, educates students about the dilemmas they face in achieving individual mobility, and mines the higher education-upward mobility contradiction as a potent source of critical consciousness building. The WEP students' experiences show us that the seeming contradiction—between students' mobility desires and the goals of radical pedagogy—may, in fact, represent an important, untapped space of educational possibility.

Yet, in a political and economic climate that favors readily measurable outcomes and educational standardization, it is easy to understand why WEP has taught around this tension rather than embraced it. WEP, like many public college programs serving nontraditional students, finds itself vulnerable to downturns in public funding for higher education and under pressure to document quantifiable student outcomes, not leaps in critical consciousness. Its undergraduate student population has experienced a steady decline in recent years[1]—as have many liberal arts programs at universities nationwide—precisely due to market-driven pressures for degrees that, unlike labor or urban studies, promise to yield economic results. WEP has maintained its silence around the tension between student goals and program intentions for more subtle reasons as well: fear of what it means to confront vulnerable students with their dim prospects for attaining mobility through their degrees; concern that open acknowledgment of student aspirations will mean radical educators have to relinquish their goals in favor of the students' goals and worry that students will simply vote with their feet and opt for a degree with ready market potential.

Nevertheless, I argue in favor of open and honest dialogue, in favor of seeing this tension as a space of possibility as well as one of constraint. A series of small but meaningful programmatic changes in WEP could lay the foundation for a proactive and honest dialogue on the connections and contradictions between higher education and upward mobility. Such changes ought to include: the implementation of a core course on social mobility as part of the urban and labor studies curriculum that explicitly explores the relationship between individual mobility and higher education; new recruitment tactics that honestly represent the challenge mobility poses for adult students; frank discussion of program mission, educational philosophy, and student goals starting at orientation and extending throughout students' tenure in the program; and the creation of social change internships and a yearly social change job fair to broaden students' conception of mobility and engage them in assessing their realistic prospects for career change as a result of their degrees. While these suggestions are no panacea for the complex problem of how to align working-class students' mobility aspirations, the goals of radical pedagogy, and the realities of the marketplace, they could be important first steps in beginning to turn this seeming contradiction into a space of radical possibility.

Note

1 According to WEP's internal data, the undergraduate student population decreased from a high of 140 students in 1996 to 62 in 2004 (the last year for which data is available).

References

Anyon, J. (2005). *Radical Possibilities: Public Policy, Urban Education, and a New Social Movement*. New York and London: Routledge.

Carnoy, M. and Levin, H. (1985). *Schooling and Work in the Democratic State*. Stanford, CA: Stanford University Press.

Clark, B. (1960). The Cooling Out Function in Higher Education. *The American Journal of Sociology* 65(6): 569–76.

Cole, E. and Omari, S. (2003). Race, Class and the Dilemmas of Upward Mobility for African Americans. *Journal of Social Issues* 59(4): 785–802.

Gilkes, C. T. (1983). Going Up for the Oppressed: The Career Mobility of Black Women Community Workers. *Journal of Social Issues* 39(3): 115–39.

Higginbotham, E. and Weber, L. (1992). Moving Up With Kin and Community: Upward Social Mobility for Black and White Women. *Gender & Society* 6(3): 416–60.

Lafer, G. (2002). *The Job Training Charade*. Ithaca and London: Cornell University Press.

Nasaw, D. (1979). *Schooled to Order: A Social History of Public Schooling in the United States*. Oxford and New York: Oxford University Press.

PART FIVE

Teaching About Class in the Humanities

14

Working-Class Cultural Studies in the University

Lawrence Hanley

Working-class studies emerged as an academic field only recently in higher education. For Lawrence Hanley, the challenge was to nudge this new field in a direction that avoided what he saw as the co-optation and the de-politicization that had weakened the radical potential of multicultural studies before it. The struggle continues.

Despite their fractious debates, radical critics in the United States have traditionally shared a common understanding of "culture" as "a developed and completely harmonious system of knowledge and of art in all material and spiritual fields of work" (Trotsky 1972: 48). Until the past few decades, radicals essentially agreed with what we now call, by shorthand, an Arnoldian sense of culture as the best that has been thought, spoken, and recorded. Thus, battles within the left, as for instance in the struggles in the 1930s over proletarian literature, often hinged less on redefining culture than on the correlation between "bourgeois" works of art and an emerging "revolutionary" canon of similar artifacts. Culture in its anthropological senses, as in Raymond Williams's fine phrase a "whole way of life," was largely irrelevant to radicals. The absence of this sense of "culture" indicates the extent to which, for generations of American radicals, categories like "proletarian" or "working-class" were political, rather than cultural, identities. Rather than being the grounds of class identity and difference, "culture," like the State, or the means of production, was something to be seized or smashed by the radical social movements.

The invisibility of culture as the everyday medium or "common sense" through which class identities are made and remade also helps to account for the difficulties that radicals often faced when struggling to understand the complexities posed by race and gender. Lacking firm mediations between economy and politics, radicals' approach to race, for instance, veered between an internal colonization paradigm, viewing race as a "special case" of capitalist development (thus producing the famous "Black Belt" or "nation within a nation" thesis), and calls for class unity over race difference, an optimistic but usually ineffective form of voluntarism. Without some analytical framework to understand the imaginary, but real, bases of race and racial difference, radicals often found it difficult to grasp the racialized mediations between class-in-itself and class-for-itself that gummed up both nationalist and "class-based multiracial unity" (Foley 1993: 187) approaches to race and class.

Today, of course, culture is everywhere. Postmodernity, Frederic Jameson notes, is characterized by "a prodigious expansion of culture throughout the social realm, to the point at which everything in our social life can be said to have become 'cultural' in some original and yet untheorized sense" (48). The current moment has largely reversed the oppositions that governed traditional radical thinking on politics and culture: politics itself, in the form of "identity politics" or "new social movements," has been reorganized around issues of culture and cultural identity. Ironically, "cultural studies," for example, which grew out of efforts in Britain to understand and champion a rapidly changing postwar working class, has almost completely abandoned "class" as a central category of interest or analysis. In providing a "Users Guide" to the massive anthology that announced cultural studies' arrival on the American academic scene, the editors of *Cultural Studies* (Grossberg et al. 1992) divide their volume into categories like: the history of cultural studies, gender and sexuality, nationhood and national identity, colonialism and postcolonialism, race and ethnicity, popular culture, identity politics, global culture, etc. In its guide, *Cultural Studies* offers a concise map of the enormous, exciting changes and tensions that are remaking literature, communications, history, art, and other humanities departments across the country.

There is, however, no signpost on this map for class or for the working class. The "Americanization" of cultural studies has been accompanied by gains and losses: just as cultural studies achieved institutional legitimacy, it seemed to refuse the deep, serious engagement with class and the working class that had fueled its original ambitions and excitement (McRobbie 722). On the other hand, class plays the starring role in the new "working-class studies" developed in places like Youngstown State's Center for Working

Class Studies, *Women's Studies Quarterly*, and elsewhere. These efforts grew out of a frustration with contemporary multiculturalism's apparent silence on matters of class. The problem with the arrival of multiculturalism, Tim Libretti notes, is that "the category of class is not overtly articulated in these new literary historical taxonomies" (23). Thus, instead of suppressing class identities, working-class studies proposes to become a site "for analyzing the intersection of class, race, gender, and sexual orientation" (Christopher et al. 1998, "Editorial," 7). To advance into academic legitimacy, working-class critics adopt the conceptual tools left behind by multiculturalism in its struggle to enter the academy. From within the multicultural paradigm, working-class identity is a legacy, an "inheritance," or an "ambiguous gift" (Zandy 1995, "Introduction," 1) that must be recovered. As terms like these indicate, identity is understood less as a social position or process than as a product of shared norms, values, lifestyles, and attitudes; working-class identity reflects identification with a coherent, bounded, integrated, and integrating working-class culture. The chief avenue for recovering and validating working-class identity, as in dominant versions of multiculturalism, lies in exposure to the (anti)canons, (counter)traditions, works, and authors which embody this culture.

How all this works can be glimpsed in an anecdote offered by Constance Coiner. Margaret, a white working-class student in one of Coiner's classes, has consistently expressed resentment toward multiculturalism. After the class reads Denise Giardini's contemporary novel about coal mining and class strife, *Storming Heaven*, Margaret identifies her own family's past with the novel's working-class characters. If this is what multiculturalism is all about, Margaret declares to her teacher, "I'm going to have to reconsider the whole thing" (47). "What is obvious here," Coiner explains, "is that Margaret needs to learn about her heritage as much as Darrell needs to learn about his, as much as Sulan needs to learn about hers [Darrell and Sulan are African American students]. And Margaret needs to find that heritage in literary texts, just as Darrell and Sulan need to find their heritage in literary texts" (47). The effects of such a discovery may be political, though political and social change are not rationales commonly found in the new "working-class studies." If class tends to drop out of cultural studies, working-class studies tends to culturalize class by backgrounding social structures and antagonisms and foregrounding elements of an organic, integrated way of life.

Short of chiding *Cultural Studies* for cutting an important corner from the intersections of race, class, gender, and sexuality, and of scolding "working-class studies" for denying the "last instances" of the social and economic, something that others have already in fact done (Murdock; Clarke), how can we start to resolve this endemic tension between class politics and cultural identity without surrendering real progress accomplished in the "multicultural" moment? One route may be to first consider the current locations of working-class culture and its representations as they are taken up by intellectuals and academics. Until the 1940s and 50s, "literary" authority belonged to critics, anthologists, reviewers, and writers, the "last intellectuals" as Russell Jacoby has called them. Today, "literary" authority belongs more clearly to the university and is most often reckoned in terms of syllabi, curricula, and textbooks. With some exceptions, representations of social difference gain authority as they are institutionalized within the intellectual and pedagogical fields of the university. Recognition of this historical shift and institutional relocation needs to play a larger role in contemporary cultural studies. The ways, for instance, that working-class literature has been transformed, via multiculturalism, into an academic subject points to the need for a closer look at the function of working-class literature within the university.

As John Guillory has argued, multiculturalism's attachment to expressive notions of culture and to a liberal pluralist politics tends to repress an analysis of the distinctions between university and society, or "of what the 'political' means in the context of school as an institution" (9). The institutional function of school, as Pierre Bourdieu and his American followers have argued, hinges on its role in distributing and redistributing cultural capital to sustain social distinction and class hierarchy. In Guillory's analysis, then, the "canon wars" associated with multiculturalism were really being waged not around visions of a more inclusive society or oppression by "dead white males" but around the recomposition of cultural capital for the university's main constituency: the professional managerial class.

Revolutions in syllabi and curricula can come and go, as they have for the past century, so long as the university continues to reproduce class structures and relations by reproducing cultural capital, the cultural taste, languages, and knowledges that serve to distinguish the proper and the "high" from the vulgar and the "low." Pressures from above (an increasing linguistic fragmentation in technical and professional languages) and below (the increasing pervasiveness of mass culture) have, according to Guillory, displaced the "literary syllabus" from its privileged role of reproducing a "vernacular standard" for the professional-managerial class and, hence, have precipitated a "crisis of the humanities." This reconversion of cultural capital thus explains the ironies of multiculturalism's insurgent ambitions: from one perspective, so long as it remains confined within the institutional boundaries of curriculum and syllabus, canon-busting represents a fortification of bourgeois cultural distinction. The ironies of institutionalizing working-class literature in service to the multicultural renovation of the ruling class's cultural capital hardly need to be underscored here. More central to the problems facing working-class studies is the issue of how the multicultural strategy, by focusing its efforts on fuller cultural representation and integration, mystifies the social work of the university. Thus, for instance, the importance in working-class studies of encouraging students to "self-identify" as working class preserves a kind of idealized image of the university, not only as an antagonist to ideologies of "classlessness" that dominate students' extramural lives but also as a sanctioned refuge for ideals of diversity and inclusion. While the difference(s) offered by a multiculturalized university may promote consciousness of injustice, prejudice, or inequity, because these problems are defined largely in cultural, or "representational," terms, they rarely pose obstacles or conflicts to the consolidation of, or ascension into, the professional-managerial class. This discrepancy founds what Guillory calls multiculturalism's "field of 'imaginary' politics" (7), a field defined both by its attention to oppression and resistance and by a repressed consciousness of its own participation in the reproduction of class relations.

In her critique of multiculturalism, Hazel Carby has pointed to this same disjuncture in the institutionalization of writing by black women. Multiculturalism's obsessions with "constructing" identities and with the power of "difference" have largely played themselves out in white, middle-class institutions and classrooms. "Black texts," Carby argues, have thus been employed within the university "to focus on the complexity of response in the (white) reader/student's construction of self in relation to a (black) perceived 'other'; the text has been reduced to a tool to motivate that response" (12). Given the institutional location of multiculturalism's representation of racial difference, Carby writes: "Black cultural texts have become fictional substitutes for the lack of any sustained social or political relationships with black people in a society that retains many of its historical practices of apartheid in housing and schooling" (11–12). There's no reason why working-class literature shouldn't fulfill a similar function of, as Richard Ohmann once phrased it, "sanction[ing] all kinds of nonthreatening nonconformity" (25). Far from being an unfortunate oversight or glitch, the disconnect between Carby s "text" and "society," or the displacements performed by the use of representations, are a specific and necessary effect of the university's social function. In the end, Guillory and Carby are responding to the question of what difference multiculturalism makes where and for whom. What multiculturalism lacks, and what working-class studies needs, is a fuller sense of racial, or class, formation, particularly of the kind that links social structure and textual, or cultural, representation. One final way of understanding multiculturalism's "field of 'imaginary' politics" that has more general implications for working-class studies can be found in Michael Omi and Howard Winant's work on racial formation. There, Omi and Winant posit "racial formation" as a process of linking structure and representation. "Racial projects" are those particular historical efforts to articulate structure and representation into coherent, if provisional, correspondence. Thus, Omi and Winant write:

A racial project is simultaneously an interpretation, representation, or explanation of racial dynamics, and an effort to reorganize and redistribute resources along racial lines. Racial projects connect what race means in a particular discursive practice and the ways in which both social structures and everyday experiences are racially organized, based upon that meaning. (56)

Omi and Winant's notion of racial formation allows us to see, then, that given its academic base, multiculturalism belongs to a professional-managerial class formation; even as it mobilizes largely affirmative images of difference, it articulates these representations to a particular social structure, namely the distribution of cultural capital and social power through the credentializing of the professional-managerial class. More importantly, rather than constituting a break with previous moments of racial representation, a break often figured as a move beyond "stereotypes" or into "self-representation," multiculturalism belongs, despite its affirmative intentions, to a long history of appropriating, managing, and capitalizing difference. Where and for whom images of the working class circulate need then to be both an integral component of working-class studies' self-consciousness and an object of its critical efforts. More and better representations of working-class life won't make a difference if they circulate in the same places with the same effects.

Understanding the value and meaning of something like "working-class literature" needs to involve, for instance, a series of difficult questions about the realities of its circulation: when working-class writing becomes "literature," how does it reward writers with connections to new audiences and alienation from other readers and readings? Writing "literature" implies what kinds of readers doing what kinds of things to a writer's narratives? In short, what social relations are altered by the circuits of cultural capital when (working-class) writing becomes (bourgeois) "literature"? Working-class writing, whether written by, for, or about the working class, is almost always writing driven to distraction by these anxieties about its own legitimacy and value. Following Guillory and Carby, proponents of a multiculturalized working-class literature must think their project through two necessarily linked questions: (minority) representation for whom? greater access to what (curriculum)? In other words, how do minority representations ultimately function within the university? And, how does more "diverse" literary representation correspond to, or not correspond to, minority access to the university? Seeking answers to these questions might encourage us to see that the university itself needs to become a site of political struggle, not just over representations, but also over ways of making and certifying knowledge and pedagogies, and over the means of access for working-class students. Working-class students enter the university, when they do, as already cultured and classed beings, as "people with experiences, with backgrounds, with linguistic resources" (Fox 1990, *Social Uses,* 20). Working-class identity, conceived as ongoing process, rather than recoverable product, might serve both as a source of knowledge and as a way to interrupt the traditional social relations of education and pedagogy. Acknowledging the creativity and expertise of working-class people, curricula, and syllabi might become occasions for collaboration, and the university might eschew its traditional work of sorting, standardizing, and conforming in favor of producing new, critical knowledges and subjects.

Three-quarters of the students at the college where I teach are either immigrants or the children of immigrants. By any definition, they are overwhelmingly working class. This experience, however, rarely condenses into a discrete, recoverable "heritage." Eduardo, a student in one of my American Studies courses, for instance, is a punk rocker who works in a hotel kitchen. His father is Ecuadorian; his mother is Dominican. Eduardo tells me that he's happy to have escaped Camden, New Jersey, where he spent most of his high school years, for the relative peace and quiet of Bathgate Avenue in the Bronx. While he's a devoted fan of Rancid and the Dropkick Murphys (a hardcore, militant working-class punk band from South Boston), Eduardo and I sometimes trade compact discs of the latest *son* music from Cuba. Eduardo tells me he can relate to and enjoy the Latino literature course he's taking this semester, but he's also eager to tell me about the classes he's taking this semester on film noir and liberation theology. (Both his parents are evangelical Christians. This significant alienation from their native cultures and traditions supplies an important subtext for their emigration to El Norte.) Clearly, Eduardo's porous, syncretic, and dynamic cultural and social experience would only confound the multicultural paradigm, with its need for coherent, bounded cultures and "heritages." Eduardo is also upwardly mobile. His matriculation at City College is a conscious, if hard-fought, stepping away from his working-class home, neighborhood, and experience. College for him is an initiation into an alien world; this is a perception he shares with most of his professors. Confronted by working-class students like Eduardo, radical teachers might typically ask: what cultural identity can be preserved or salvaged against the backdrop of the university's relentless work of reproducing bourgeois status and social hierarchy? This question, however, not only implies a simplification of Eduardo's experience, but also misses an important opportunity to challenge the ideologies and epistemologies that underwrite the university's work of reproducing class difference. Instead of viewing ourselves as merely supplying textual opportunities for working-class students to re-appreciate their experience or thinking about successful learning as the proper reception of syllabus-sanctioned texts, what if we viewed working-class students as the producers of new knowledges? Our work, in this view, would be closer to developing what Antonio Gramsci called "organic intellectuals," intellectuals who transform their subordinate experience into insurgent knowledge.

My American Studies class includes a unit on genre and on the power of cultural genres to shape both our perceptions of the social world and our self-perceptions. The particular genre we analyze is the "immigrant narrative" or American *bildung*. The first task is to figure out how this genre works its way into and through a variety of disparate texts. We read fiction and poetry by writers like Anzia Yezierska, Sandra Cisneros, Edwidge Danticat, Junot Diaz, Gary Soto, and Garren Hongo. We analyze films like *Crossover Dreams* (1985), *Avalon* (1990), and *Neuba Yol* (1996). And we end this part of the unit by reading Richard Rodriguez's meta memoir, *Speak Memory: The Education of Richard Rodriguez* (1983). The questions that drive our reading of these texts are analytical: what narrative patterns constitute the core plot of the American *bildung*? What is the character system that generates the genre's protagonist(s) and antagonist(s)? What are the motifs that often signal membership in the genre? What are the variations on the grammar of the *bildung*'s generic plot? The overarching question here is: how does the American *bildung* offer a convenient, functional, and useful set of resources for transforming social and historical experience into cultural recognition? This leads of course into questions of how this narrative transformation also encodes particular ideological values and pleasures.

The second part of our work on immigrant narratives, however, asks students to collect stories from their neighborhoods and families. Armed with tape recorders, my students seek out relatives and peers, asking them to describe how they made the passage from place to place and how they experience the displacements involved in migration. The students transcribe these stories and then compare them to the generic narrative that we've pieced together from literary and filmic representations. Thus, a new set of questions becomes relevant: to what extent are these vernacular narratives shaped by more powerful generic narratives? How do these narratives expose silences and omissions in the dominant, generic narrative? How consonant are the ideological values and pleasures between the two kinds of narrative? What function does vernacular narrative seem to fulfill for its tellers? After an initial surprise at the strong points of identity between generic and vernacular stories, students are quick to notice how the stories they've collected often exceed the American *bildung* and, so, question its power to capture and signify the social experience of migration.

In this unit, students are learning about one of the most cherished of literary institutions—genre. Yet studying the generic inflections of stories from local neighborhoods, families, and friends also helps to demonstrate that there is no "experience" there to be recovered in some pure, original form; experience is always already shaped by narrative forms and by the ideologies more or less encoded within these forms. But there's something more at stake in this project. Working within vernacular narratives means bringing this new, cultural material into the academy and taking these representations seriously as sources of new knowledge, knowledge that often complicates and relativizes academic knowledge. As the organic intellectuals in control of making this knowledge, students who normally experience their liminal status—one foot planted in the university and one foot planted in their neighborhoods and communities—as a liability are able to convert this liminality into an asset. This process opens up the possibility for new subjectivities, but it also redraws the classroom as a site for the emergence of new forms of cultural capital, forms which are not exclusively grounded in the authority of academic knowledge or of subaltern experience. Of course, one classroom can't overturn the ideological apparatus of higher education. (And we need, as radical teachers, to start thinking beyond the classroom, the course, and the syllabus to understand our work in terms of broader institutional structures and arrangements.) However, seeing students as organic intellectuals who can produce new knowledges helps to interrupt the logic of upward mobility and social reproduction by undermining the dichotomy of school and "street" that this logic depends on.

Finally, to return to the programmatic issue of "working-class cultural studies," my argument implies that we need to worry less about putting "class," in some textual incarnation, back into the "Users Guide" of cultural studies and more about the relations between the ways and places that cultural studies has been institutionalized. In a late essay, written in response to the emergence of "cultural studies" as an academic field, Raymond Williams described how, "in the very effort to define a clearer subject, to establish a discipline, to bring order into the work—all of which are laudable ambitions—the real problem of the project [of cultural studies] as a whole, which is that people's questions are not answered by the existing distribution of the educational curriculum, can be forgotten" (169). The "Americanization" of cultural studies has largely been the story of its growth in certain, select institutions; the questions that have driven its growth in the United States have belonged to the particularly classed location of these institutions.

As Williams points out at the beginning of his essay, innovations like cultural studies, or for a preceding generation, literary studies itself, "occurred outside the formal educational institutions," in adult education or among educationally disenfranchised women (169). The way to put "class" back into cultural studies is to pay more attention to those places where educational institutions impinge on working-class experience, often producing the kinds of contradictions, frustrations, resentments, and withdrawals chronicled by writers from Thomas Hardy to Jack Conroy to Ernesto Quinones, each of whom has contributed to a staple genre of working-class literature—the narrative of failed cultural ambition. In other words, working-class cultural studies needs to begin with working-class people's demands on institutions, curricula, syllabi, and pedagogy. In previous decades, these demands were likely to be explicit and unavoidable—student takeovers, protests, and manifestos. Today, they are more likely to be expressed through acts and arts of omission: silence, withdrawal, and boredom. This resistance is everywhere in the American higher educational system, but like working-class students, it's concentrated in places far removed from top tier public and private universities and colleges. These are places, incidentally, where proletarian student bodies are most likely to be taught by proletarianized, part-time, contingent faculty. It's here that the contradictions of class and culture find their fullest, most immediate expression. And, it's here that working-class cultural studies needs to find its enabling problems, its urgency, and its politics.

References

Carby, Hazel. (Fall 1992). "The Multicultural Wars." *Radical History* 54: 7–20.
Christopher, Renny, Lisa Orr, and Linda Strom. (1998). "Editorial." *Women's Studies Quarterly* 26.1 and 2: 4–12.
Clarke, John. (1991). *New Times and Old Enemies: Essays on Cultural Studies and America*. New York: HarperCollins.
Coiner, Constance. (1995). "Class in the Classroom: Transcription of an American Studies Association Workshop." *Radical Teacher* 46: 46–8.
Foley, Barbara. (1993). *Radical Representations: Politics and Form in U.S. Proletarian Fiction, 1929–1941*. Durham, NC: Duke University Press.
Fox, Thomas. (1990). *The Social Uses of Writing: Politics and Pedagogy*. Norwood, NJ: Ablex.
Grossberg, Lawrence, Cary Nelson, and Paula Treichler, eds, (1992). *Cultural Studies*. NY: Routledge.
Guillory, John. (1993). *Cultural Capital: The Problem of Literary Canon Formation*. Chicago, IL: University of Chicago Press.
Jacoby, Russell. (1987). *The Last Intellectual: American Culture in the Age of Academe*. New York: Basic Books.
Jameson, Frederic.(1992). *Postmodernism, or, The Cultural Logic of Late Capitalism*. Durham: Duke University Press.
Libretti, Tim. (1995). "Is There a Working Class in U.S. Literature? Race, Ethnicity, and the Proletarian Literary Tradition." *Radical Teacher* 46: 22–6.
McRobbie, Angela. (1992). "Post-Marxism and Cultural Studies: A Post-script." In Grossberg, Lawrence, Cary Nelson, and Paula Treichler, eds, *Cultural Studies*. NY: Routledge, 719–29.
Murdock, Graham. (1989). "Cultural Studies: Missing Links." *Critical Studies in Mass Communication* 6: 436–40.
Ohmann, Richard. (1996). *English in America: A Radical View of the Profession*. Hanover: Wesleyan University Press.
Omi, Michael and Howard Winant. (1994). *Racial Formation in the United States*. 2nd ed. New York: Routledge.
Trotsky, Leon. (1972). *Leon Trotsky on Literature and Art*. Ed. Paul Siegel. New York: Pathfinder Press.
Williams, Raymond. (1996). "The Future of Cultural Studies." In *What Is Cultural Studies? A Reader*. Ed. John Story. New York: Arnold.
Zandy, Janet. (1995). "Introduction." *Liberating Memory: Our Work and Our Working-Class Consciousness*. New Brunswick, NJ: Rutgers University Press.

15

All That Hollywood Allows: Film and the Working Class

Linda Dittmar

Writing at a time when virtually no attention was being paid to issues of class in cinema studies, when postcultural criticism was hogging the camera and class analysis played at best a bit part, Linda Dittmar describes a number of teaching approaches that might give class the attention it deserves. Her analyses of classic postwar films such as On the Waterfront *and of more recent films, like* Blue Collar, *are models of forceful yet nuanced interpretation, the kind of work that should be and has been continued.*

To design a college-level film course that focuses centrally on class is to break new ground. A two-volume collection of more than 70 current film course outlines and reading lists does not list even one such course, and there is almost nothing in print in this field that has the word "class" in its title, let alone mention of the working class.[1] This does not mean that no one is teaching film from this perspective, but it does mean that class gets subsumed under other considerations and so pushed away from the public arena.

Determined to prevent these issues from dropping out of sight altogether, two members of the Society for Cinema Studies organized panels on working-class representation for two consecutive annual meetings of this academic organization, and they have edited a book on this topic.[2] Still, what struck me on both occasions was the edgy, even peevish tone of their invitation.

Unfortunately, their impatience was not misplaced, for amidst euphoria over virtuoso breakthroughs in poststructuralist film theory on the one hand and over the opening up of film studies to feminism, multiculturalism, and more recently Queer revisions on the other, attention to working-class issues has not yet found its rightful place.

Resistance in film studies

Of course, the avoidance of a class perspective has been endemic in the United States, where individualism and capitalism have long provided the cornerstone for political practice and ideology. It is easier for us to talk about "poverty" than about exploited classes, about "termination" and "downsizing" than about firings, about "the economy" but not about class conflict. Even with the end of the Cold War, class awareness continues to be shunned as a potential conduit for communism. When the Society for Cinema Studies established a special Task Force on Race and Class, thereby registering that racism and economic disenfranchisement are partners in oppressing people of color, those present at the Task Force's founding meeting voted to drop "class" from its title. Though the vote passed by a very narrow margin, the message was clear: we will support the progressive agendas of identity politics (i.e. concerning ethnicities, genders, sexualities, etc.), but we hesitate to do so in relation to the systemic effects of capitalism.

For me, mulling over these anecdotes, the initial question was whether film studies as a discipline resists class analysis in ways that do not apply to feminist and other anticolonizing scholarship. Put differently, I wondered whether the immensely productive influence of poststructuralist theory on film studies, including its melding of attention to apparatus, form, and social use, might not conflict with a materialist and activist class perspective. Knocking about here may be an unvoiced recoil from Marxist criticism, as if it is necessarily mired in an outmoded predilection for thematic readings and at odds with the cutting-edge discourses of ideology and refracted meanings elaborated by Althusser, Foucault, Machery, Jameson, Bakhtin, and others. Mas'ud Zavarzadeh makes this point forcefully in *Seeing Films Politically*, where he argues that the self-absorbed pleasures of contemporary theory affected a shift in the meaning of "ideology," "power," and "hegemony" which turned them into abstractions detached from a materialist analysis of social class.[3]

I dwell on this problem at the start of this essay because what happens in the classroom is informed by broader inquiries circulating in the academic world. In this respect, Zavarzadeh's argument is not as rarefied as it might seem, for it concerns choices, not inevitabilities. His focus is on individuals' choice to immerse their work in self-referential theories (derived from semiotics, psychoanalysis, deconstruction, etc.) at a cost to politics. To this

I add the choice to foreground decolonizing perspectives in ways that end up driving a wedge between considerations of class and identity politics. Yet none of these divisions is necessary. If anything, in each case inclusion of class analysis is compatible with the very practice that at present excludes it. That this divisiveness affects the teaching of a popular medium friendly to progressive analysis is particularly ironic. Thus, while feminist film courses are increasingly in evidence, and while the teaching of other aspects of diversity is clearly on the rise, within this general embracing of egalitarian agendas the issue of class remains marginalized, as though there might be competition between class and other group positionalities.

Film theory and identity politics are not inherently resistant to class analysis, but they have tended to function this way, even if inadvertently. They have helped us be critical consumers who understand the politics of representation—notably the representation of disenfranchised groups such as women, African Americans, Latinos and Latinas, Asians, Native Americans, lesbians and gays, and myriad others. But they also let film studies remain relatively unreflective about the role of class in scenarios of disenfranchisement and about the possibility of materially based conflicts and alliances across such groups and within them. That is, despite their emphasis on liberatory discourses as key to social change, both poststructuralist theory and identity politics ended up participating in the broader silencing of class-focused discourse in the United States.

Though I review these pitfalls to suggest that we must look to ourselves as partly complicit in the erasure of class, it is worth remembering that Hollywood and its satellites, including films made for television, further muddy the waters. It is not that films fail to depict characters from all walks of life, but that they discourage awareness of the fact that "walks" translate into classes, and that classes are defined by incompatible interests responding to gross inequalities and injustices. In this respect, film studies, so steeped in Hollywood's glamour industry, is particularly susceptible to the seduction of artifacts constructed to deflect viewers from class awareness. This construction occurs at all levels of narration. Most obviously, it is evident in films' thematic preference for middle- and upper-class protagonists and perspectives. More subtly, it is also evident in ways in which films diminish working-class characters and disregard the conditions affecting their lives. But permeating each narrative are also commentaries inscribed by each film's audio and visual "languages"—by the costumes, sets, lighting, film stock, color filters, editing, music, camera positions, selective amplifications, and much more—which often tilt films toward a seemingly depoliticized reception that favors identification with ruling-class interests.

In this sense, then, any and all films are available for class analysis, from *Schindler's List* (1993) to *Tongues Untied* (1989), and from *The Age of Innocence* (1993) to *The Joy Luck Club* (1993). The very effacing of class relations proves instructive, once students learn to see how our films mystify the positionality of their characters within class. Working-class people in particular, students can discover, are often made the butt of jokes, a cause for distaste, or objects for admiration, but rarely initiators of in-depth debate concerning social justice or the possibility of social change. Considered in aggregate, our films glorify wealth, dismiss or primitivize the working class, criminalize the poor, and pass off the heterosexual and patriarchal white middle class as a norm barely distinguishable from the upper classes. To help students become aware of this prevailing practice is to help them see how the film industry produces false consciousness—how it buries the vernacular of ordinary lives in myths of a universal human condition that supposedly transcends class considerations.

The politics of cinematography

While the above argues that any film or film course can be taught from a class perspective, this essay concerns feature-length fiction films made in the United States that focus on working-class issues centrally. (Films made in Europe and elsewhere bring up related but also different issues this essay cannot address.) Almost invariably, close analysis shows, our films work to normalize existing class relations in order to contain our understanding of workers' agency. Consider, for example, what Hollywood does with one of its all-time screen idols, Marlon Brando, in his McCarthy-era working-class roles, notably in *A Streetcar Named Desire* (1951), *Viva Zapata* (1952), *On the Waterfront* (1954), and *The Wild One* (1954). With his flesh pressing against denim, leather, checkered flannel, or the frayed gossamer of a cotton T-shirt, as the case might be, and with the camera closing in on his sensuous face as it gropes for comprehension, this degraded Prometheus mingles the pessimism of the postwar era with Cold War capitalist agendas. In the case of *On the Waterfront*, the Brando character ends up as a Christ-like savior who must stumble to a working man's Calvary before he delivers the cowering longshoremen from their corrupt union and back to the paternalistic safekeeping of the state, church, and family. Seen against the historic background of the McCarthy hearings, contemporary unrest at the waterfront, and the gearing up by the United States for its newly staked out position as a world power, this was meant to be a happy ending.

Viva Zapata was also scripted to reassure its predominantly North American and western-identified audience. Concluding on a note of sadness for this folk hero's betrayal and fall, the film nonetheless writes off the Zapatista uprising as uncivilized and corrupt, and it further comforts viewers with the apotheosis of Zapata's white horse as the reincarnation of the man's spirit. Seen against the history of the relations of the United States with Mexico from the Mexican Revolution to the 1990s' Zapatista insurrection in Chiapas, the film posits the necessity of a North-American intervention and hegemony south of the border. The Mexicans, it suggests, are not ready for self-government, and their grassroots organizing for land reform are bound to founder on greed and treachery. Focusing on the individual leader rather than on the peasants he represents, the film uses Brando's gift for slackening his facial muscles and slurring his speech to discredit him. Posing him as an icon of things Mexican, it has him project a magnificent primitivism lit up with flashes of intuition and it stresses his landed gentry origins. Nowhere do we find the articulate intelligence or informed communal solidarity which defined the historic Zapatistas' struggles.

While each of these films has a particular political agenda, their shared practice of suppressing class consciousness, disempowering workers, discrediting collective bargaining, and invoking religion as a stand-in for social change is standard practice in Hollywood films. *The Deer Hunter* (1978) is just a more recent example. Produced shortly after the Vietnam War and focusing on a group of working-class friends impaired by horrifying ordeals suffered in Vietnam, this film uses the spectacle of exotic warfare and nostalgia for a supposedly Edenic prewar past to obscure the plot's immediate context, namely the collapse of Pennsylvania's steel industry and the unemployment crisis increasingly affecting workers nationally. The film has war, but the class position of this war's victims on either side does not lay exclusive claim to our emotions. The returning veterans' relation to their country, community, and jobs is shaped by physical and psychological wounds acquired overseas, not by their place in an economic system that left miles of rusting steel mills along Pennsylvania's waterways. In this connection, the plot's initial celebration of a homogeneous ethnic community (Slavic) combines with the deer hunt and the closing sequence's singing of "God Bless America" to put forth an essentialist view of this country as vulnerable only to the brutality of others. Invoking the rites of marriage in the industrial landscape, male bonding in the wilderness, and the salve of patriotism when all else fails, the film provides an ersatz healing that offers audiences no lasting comfort.

Bringing class analysis to bear on these films allows students to see how each of them pursues an agenda relevant to its historic moment. *On the Waterfront* promotes the subordination of labor to government regulation and capitalist interests; *Viva Zapata* taps anti-Communist anxieties and a racist view of the nonwestern Other to justify US intervention in Central America; and *The Deer Hunter* invokes family, nature, and flag in its response to a controversial war and as a coverup for a faltering economy. Such readings, focusing mainly on the use of the working class to serve particular national agendas, can only benefit from a further broadening of the inquiry to include attention to gender, ethnicity, and related categories of inequality and exploitation as implicated in the construction of class relations. Note, for example, these films' ambivalent representation of male workers' physical power, where admiration and even covert desire mingle with the need to debase and contain workers' intelligence, articulation, and therefore agency. Consider, too, the symbolic function of women in these films as conservators of hearth and home, and the ways in which this role advances the cause of law and order within narratives geared to affirming the political status quo. Or consider how the foregrounding of ethnicities (Irish, Mexican, and Slavic in these instances) lets cultural and religious identity—at once sentimental and racist—displace class consciousness.

Once we normalize attention to such issues, the possibility of teaching film from a working-class perspective materializes at every turn. Key here is not simply what one might select for teaching, but the questions brought to bear on this selection. Assembling a filmography is just a first step, then. The more difficult task is to teach students (and ourselves, especially if not trained in film analysis) to appreciate the extent to which the very process of representation constructs meanings. That is, everything the apparatus can do and all that we prepare for it is active in the construction of meanings which interlace with a film's thematic concerns, supplementing, modifying, and sometimes contradicting the position apparently taken by its plot. Whether we use an occasional film to illustrate some aspect of a broader inquiry or teach an entire course on working-class issues, we need to understand the medium's resourcefulness in using cinematography to inscribe ideology and politics.

The function of religion in *On the Waterfront* and *The Deer Hunter* can serve as just one example of this activity. Though both films use religion to define the working class by race and ethnicity, they do so to different ends. In *On the Waterfront*, religion is at once a galvanizing force (mediated through Father Barry's and Edie's characters and speech) and a metaphoric reminder of redemptive agony (conveyed through images ranging from the bleak rooftop crucifix-shaped antennas to Terry Molloy's final "passion" as he stumbles up the gangplank that is the waterfront's Via Dolorosa). In *The Deer Hunter*, religion is opaque, impenetrable. Its contents withheld, its ritual beautifully filmed but disrupted with choppy editing—here cinematography stresses the exotic otherness of the working class and its worship, using the very process of representation to distance the viewer from comprehension. Though of course much more distinguishes these cinematographic treatments (e.g. the difference between the lush expressionism of black and white film and golden wash over soft color, or differences in sound track and verbal content), even this truncated analysis suggests that each film uses religion to define working-class prospects differently. *On the Waterfront* argues for a docile workforce, anchoring this agenda in a spiritual commitment to the existing order as a matter of divine rightness; *The Deer Hunter* holds on to ritual without comprehension, yearning nostalgically for the reassurance of a church and hearth which by the film's end have lost their power to heal or inspire.

Designing a unit on working-class representations

So far, my own college-level teaching has not included a course devoted solely to working-class representations. I teach diverse commuting students at an urban university come on hard times, and my courses are inclusive, focusing on social class as interwoven with gender, ethnicity, region, sexual orientation, occupation, and the like. While this arrangement normalizes attention to class as routinely applicable to all films, a systematic focus on working-class issues pulls this group out of the periphery and into the center of our work. One way of doing so is to create a unit that studies working-class representations centrally for part of a given course. This was my solution in two courses, "America on Film" and "The Politics of Film." But there is enough material for a whole course on this subject, let alone similar units which can be designed for a variety of courses in and out of film studies. The rest of this discussion will concern, first, the potentials of the unit I developed and, second, the possibility of reworking this configuration to different ends.

It was my choice to focus my working-class unit on organized labor and the politics of employment. The films I selected—*The Grapes of Wrath* (1940), *On the Waterfront*, *Salt of the Earth* (1953), and *Matewan* (1987)—concerned traditional labor issues as we know them in the public sphere: salaries, safety, job security, class consciousness, solidarity, and collective bargaining. This is not the only direction to go. One can teach about filmic representations of the working class in the domestic sphere, about work in situations that traditionally precluded collective bargaining, or about the poor as an underclass, for example. One can teach about the working class through the lens of gender or analyze it with an eye to racism. While the films listed here allow for all of this, I selected them partly because of ways they fit into the needs of each course as a whole and partly because they foreground class consciousness and solidarity. This investment in activism proved helpful in these particular courses. It countered representations of injustice and conflict with ideals of social amelioration, and it encouraged us to probe each film's ideological position in relation to such prospects.

Because *Salt of the Earth* and *On the Waterfront* were made within a year of one another and yet assume diametrically opposite positions on the question of class struggle, their pairing is central to this unit. Produced at the height of HUAC's investigation of Hollywood, and by a director implicated as a friendly government witness (Elia Kazan), *On the Waterfront* embraces a straight capitalist and McCarthyist agenda. Bestializing its workers, it insists on a compliant workforce, it affirms the rightness of being a "stool pigeon" for a government shown to collaborate with private capital, and it offers a familial/religious model of redemption as its comfort to the masses.

Salt of the Earth, in contrast, was made by Hollywood renegades (Michael Wilson, Herbert Bieberman, and others), several of whose careers were shattered because of their socialism and because they refused to cooperate with HUAC. This film stresses workers' need to resist containment by joint capitalist and government interests, it shows how the seemingly private functions of sexism and racism play into this containment, and it argues for grassroots organizing and solidarity across gender and ethnicity as a way to win workers material gains. There is nothing in *On the Waterfront* to suggest that workers are capable of acting on their own behalf, that unions serve workers, that solidarity is a useful tool, or that collective bargaining can win better income and working conditions. Everything in *Salt of the Earth* suggests as much. Paternalism, brawn, and individual martyrdom hold no charm here; practical needs, dialogue, collective wisdom, and mutual respect do.

It is not an accident that these two films differ stylistically as well as politically. *On the Waterfront* is a dazzling film, resonant in its symbolic use of the cinematic apparatus on top of Marlon Brando's star status. Its predominantly nocturnal settings bathe the gladiatorial struggles it depicts in metaphysical implications, while its claustrophobic enclosures—tenements, alleyways, a barren playground, or a cavernous ship's hold—turn the waterfront into a latter-day hell. Even the soundtrack seems to enact a primal battle between good and evil, where the shriek of a foghorn, the heartbeat throb of percussion, and an Irish jig's invocation of a preindustrial (and in this film's context, prelapsarian) past mingle with jazz to encode the outlaw seductions of urban life. *Salt of the Earth*, in contrast, enjoys the unexpected benefits of a low-budget production. Denied the comforts of sophisticated technology, a large professional crew, or wasteful footage ratios, its use of barren New Mexico hills and miners' housing as its set, and of miners to enact aspects of their own lives, is compelling. The very simplicity of the soundtrack here contrasts with *On the Waterfront*'s density. Most important to this largely Mexican-American union struggle is the use of intertwined musical strains derived from the Mexican Revolution and folk traditions, and from Anglo union songs and popular culture. In short, what *Salt of the Earth*'s semidocumentary procedures lose by way of gloss they more than regain by way of clarity and honesty. Form, in either case, functions as a metaphor for the human situation at hand and as a conduit for reception. In *Salt of the Earth*, the recourse to cinematographic authenticity ends up supporting the workers' struggles; in *On the Waterfront*, the very exuberance of its formal operations creates a conceptual overload appropriate to its murky politics.

Produced at the height of the Great Depression, *The Grapes of Wrath* makes for a useful introduction to this pair because its tangled political contradictions anticipate the definitive parting of ways we see in *On the Waterfront* and *Salt of the Earth* some 14 years later. It shares *Salt of the*

Earth's affection for the dispossessed but not its faith in militancy. Rejecting what intimations of collective action Steinbeck did include in the original novel, it nods toward New Deal politics and embraces a fast disappearing notion of the "family" and an ill-defined idea of "the people" as its redemptive hope. Moreover, while its representation of migrant workers aspires to the truth-claims of documentary, the effect is rather contrived both because the film is nonetheless obtrusively crafted and because it quotes too directly the studied and aestheticized images Dorothea Lange, Walker Evans, and others bequeathed us as the iconic distillations of the working class. Even the leitmotif of "Red River Valley" rings false here. A cliché "western" motif, this "red maiden's" love song to a feckless cowboy has no substantive relation to anything in the film beyond folksy pretense. Not incidentally, this film, like *On the Waterfront*, rejects collective proletarian action and embeds political discourse in nocturnal scenes, high contrast lighting, and claustrophobic sets that signal moral and political confusion. Indeed, its most artfully crafted footage is assigned to Muley's incoherent explanation of how the banks repossessed the land. Composed in bold diagonals and unfolding through dramatic superimpositions, fades, and rhythmic editing, this elaborate sequence awes one with its epistemological instabilities. Not as paranoid or disdainful of workers as *On the Waterfront*, *The Grapes of Wrath* nonetheless evinces no confidence in them. In keeping with Depression-era liberal humanism, not socialism, it mourns human suffering without acknowledging the collusion of government and private enterprise in producing that suffering in the first place.

Whether it is taught alone or as part of a cluster of films concerning labor struggles and the dispossession of working-class people, it is especially useful to probe ways *The Grapes of Wrath* refuses to acknowledge that workers can make gains through militant solidarity. Whatever few nods the original novel makes in that direction, the film resolutely sidesteps. *Matewan*, in contrast, is an out-and out prounion film, a warm paean to what has come down in American mythology as the purest and best of our leftist traditions. A prolabor film concerning a historic strike in West Virginia of the 1920s, it complements both *Salt of the Earth* and Barbara Kopple's milestone documentary *Harlan County, USA* (1976) in its unqualified support for organized labor and in its appeal to its audiences' reason as well as empathies. A gently loving film, beautifully awash in the greens of fresh vegetation and the soft discolorations of faded 1920s clothing, it uses unknown actors of striking physiognomy and a soundtrack replete with melodious ethnically coded folk music to draw us to the miners' side. Among these symbolically laden tropes, the soundtrack is particularly eloquent. As with *The Deer Hunter*'s Russian music, *On the Waterfront*'s Irish jig, *The Grapes of Wrath*'s "Red River Valley," and *Salt of the Earth*'s militant union chants and Mexican songs, *Matewan*'s Appalachian, Italian, and African-American tunes encode a diverse ethnic heritage, affirm the "folks'" right to well-being, and in one memorable episode weave the miners' different musical "languages" into a beautifully harmonizing trope of "unity" and "solidarity."

Yet for all its inspired socialism, *Matewan*'s appeal is also its downfall. This may be hard to see, given its evident affection for working people and its unswerving political dedication to their struggle. This may be harder yet to see given this film's thoughtful treatment of racism and ethnicity. Indeed, it is the first film since Salt *of the Earth* to address this divisive issue and argue for workers' ability to build solidarity across ethnic differences. At the same time, *Matewan*'s imputing an essential goodness to folk tradition inscribes nostalgia for a Wobbly past that late capitalism is rapidly rendering useless. Such faith in traditional unionism is heartening but insufficient. It harkens back to a prelapsarian leftist Eden—not the Eden of *On the Waterfront* or *The Deer Hunter*, but the heyday of labor militancy as it existed before multinationals, before the flight of industry to the Third World, before NAFTA. It speaks to the left's dreams at a time when the conditions of working-class life raise different questions and require different answers.

Moving beyond units

Students at a school like the University of Massachusetts Boston are not conservative. They approach films about labor struggle without the indifference or even hostility that might emerge in other settings. For me, teaching the film clusters I review above (only the first three films in "America on Film," all four in "The Politics of Film"), the hardest task is not winning them over to a sympathetic viewing, but to the challenge of critical readings. However briefly, the discussion above foregrounds instances of cinematographic manipulation to illuminate the importance of this perspective to decoding each film's stance toward its subject matter. At issue here is a methodology, a way of reading film "language" as a repository of politics and ideology. Applicable to both mainstream and independent oppositional films, it is our sole defense against manipulation. For students, to master these processes and become able to separate the melded layers of each film's discursive practices is to become selective consumers of filmic representations.

For viewers untrained in film analysis, this approach does not come easily. Unlike literature, which our schools treat as a crafted art form in need of expert analysis, films are assumed to be naturally decipherable. As "mere" popular entertainment—slap-dash concoctions of opportunistic panderings to lax minds and depleted imaginations, as cultural conservatives would have it—films don't have the aura of "texts" in need of close readings. It is hard to counter this attitude without a critical mass of evidence. Though one can make a case for close reading by teaching a single film (for instance, *The Grapes of Wrath* in a history course about the Great Depression), students benefit from the opportunity to cross-reference several films. The above model centers on the paring of *On the Waterfront* and *Salt of the Earth*, and it is further enriched by the addition of *The Grapes of Wrath* and *Matewan*. This is just one option, open to countless variations and alternatives.

What follows is a brief survey of some of these options. It is necessarily a sketchy and incomplete survey, leaving out various films for lack of space (notably the marvelous yet barely known film, *Northern Lights* (1979), concerning farmers organizing in North Dakota at the turn of the century, and the poorly made *Hoffa* (1992), which disappoints at every turn). Documentaries, so important in working-class representations, are also left out. They require a detailed discussion as a separate genre because their cinematography rests on different codes concerning "truth" and ideology. Nonetheless, this overview suggests myriad possibilities for clusters which can fit the needs of particular courses and for entire film courses focused on working-class issues. The preceding discussion privileges organized labor, but other configurations can privilege questions of gender, ethnicity, family, migration, militarism, sports, and myriad other topics that galvanize working-class identities and experiences.

Blue Collar (1978) would make for a particularly apt addition to the cluster above. Focusing on rank and file paralysis, petty ambitions, and small-time corruption, this film's cynical recoil from labor militancy is diametrically opposed to *Matewan*'s romance. *Blue Collar* denudes unions of their viability as a political tool and a model of intelligent self-government. Teaching it side by side with *Matewan*, one can analyze two very different ideological responses to a period of profound economic dislocation and increasing working-class despair. Here, the narrative concerns the failed attempt of three friends to take over their Local's leadership and it does so against the background of shallow demands, incompetence, stupidity, and corruption. The greedy bunglers are just too dumb to function in a political arena that has no interest in workers' welfare. Both their personal friendship and their union "brotherhood" disintegrate quickly in the face of individual ambition and external pressures. That this threesome happens to be interracial further stresses the fragility of cross-race alliances and the unshakability of racism. When the going gets rough, the men turn on each other with a hate that confirms the film's suggestion that unions have outlived their usefulness.

While *Matewan*'s cinematography responds to the postindustrial crisis of the labor movement by keeping alive the romance of militancy as it existed in a remote past, *Blue Collar* uses its cinematography to depoliticize the contemporary work place (a Checker cab factory). The decline of labor is axiomatic here, and with it the death of liberal humanism. Instead, it is the process of production itself that holds fascination for us, alongside the workers' doomed struggle to better their lives. As occurs in *On the Waterfront* too, *Blue Collar* constructs for its audiences a superior voyeuristic viewing position that relishes the protagonists' gladiatorial struggles within claustrophobic sets that spell disaster. The opening sequence establishes this viewing position by reducing the factory floor to a beautifully composed formalist arrangement of primary colors and neutrals, and by accompanying its prowling camera and rhythmically edited shots with the driving pulse of the blues. At more or less regular intervals, this momentum gets blocked, trapped in aestheticized freeze-frames of machine parts abstracted from their use and of black workers coded erotically (a muscular torso in a tight yellow tank top) or associated with drugs (a hazy shot of a man inhaling from a rubber hose). No whites get singled out for this treatment, though whites are evident on the floor. Reminiscent of the machine aesthetics of modernist and futurist renditions of the industrial landscape, *Blue Collar* promotes visual pleasures to which the broader political and economic consequences of its narrative are irrelevant. Condensed in the sensory caress of its rhetoric are its central propositions: the elemental power of machines, the labyrinthine workplace, the fetishized and homoeroticized laboring body, and the severing of work from its product.

Interestingly, the difference between *Matewan* and *Blue Collar* concerning the prospects of unionism extends to their treatments of racism. *Matewan*'s humanist socialism has faith in unions' ability to eradicate racism, while *Blue Collar* is utterly sardonic in this regard. But the juxtaposition is also useful as a potential seed of yet another cluster of films—ones dealing centrally with ethnicity and racism as a working-class issue. In this regard, it is worth noting that traditional representations of organized labor in the United States presuppose a white nation and a white workforce. Whiteness, it would seem, is our human norm. *The Grapes of Wrath* concerns white Oakies; *On the Waterfront* has only one black character, an unspeaking "extra"; and Depression-era films like *Our Daily Bread* (1934), *The Crowd* (1928), or *Suliivan's Travels* (1944) similarly normalize whiteness as a defining quality of this nation. Stereotyping and essentializing people of color in terms of racist presuppositions, their place within the economic relations of production—that is, their class—becomes an invisible consideration. Even *An Imitation of Life* buries the questions of class it so obviously raises in the pathos of maternal melodrama (in its 1934 version) and in anxieties over female empowerment (in its 1959 version). Overall, race and ethnicity function quite distinctly on the silver screen, with "ethnicity" generally referring to European origins and "race" referring to African, Asian/Pacific, and Native American origins. "Ethnicity," in the United States, invokes sagas of immigration that allow for upward mobility and class consciousness, while "race" invokes a stringent genetic heritage that locks people into a perpetual underclass. Our films include characters of color who remind us that employment is race bound, but they rarely address the relation between race and class centrally.

The Killing Floor (1984), an American Playhouse TV Production concerning labor organizing and racism in the Chicago stockyards early in this century, is a noteworthy exception. A wistful, loving narrative focusing on the politicization of an African-American protagonist, this film explores in-depth race relations within unions and the ways in which capitalism divides ethnicities and fans racism to disempower all workers. But this film has been a sleeper, as have several others that combine considerations of race and class centrally: *Nothing But a Man* (1964), *Bush Mama* (1976), *The Killer of Sheep* (1977), and *Bless Their Little Hearts* (1984), for example. That "race" in these instances concerns African-American descent is no accident. Until recent demographic and political shifts in the nature of racist ideology and antiracist activism, the cultural consensus tended to equate "race" with African-American identity in ways that filmmakers are finally beginning to question. *Stand and Deliver* (1988) and *Mi Vida Loca* (1993) are two striking examples of films focusing on Los Angeles's Latin communities from a working-class and underclass perspective, but at present, the number of African-American films centrally implicated in working-class issues clearly outstrips them.[4]

The function of gender within class is easier to identify, considering that all people are gendered. That the films discussed above tend to focus on male protagonists and put forth a masculinist perspective on work and social class is in keeping with the general culture of the labor movement. *Salt of the Earth*—an exemplary feminist film in this respect—is clearly atypical. With the exceptions of *Norma Rae* (1979) and *Silkwood* (1983), films which focus on the workplace tend to privilege masculine agendas. This in itself does not preclude feminist perspectives in labor films, but a women-focused study of the working class tends to invite a shift in emphasis from the public arena to more circumscribed spheres, as evident in domestic melodramas like *Stella Dallas* (1937) or *An Imitation of Life*, dramas like *The Marrying Kind* (1952) or *A Catered Affair* (1956), and the seemingly more public but in fact still largely personal contours of such films as *Heart Like a Wheel* (1983), *The Accused* (1988), *Thelma and Louise* (1991), *Rambling Rose* (1991), *Gas, Food, Lodging* (1992), or *Ruby in Paradise* (1993). As even this very incomplete list suggests, fiction films rarely focus on female protagonists' relation to work, let alone to organized labor. Encoding them mainly as people whose identity derives from personal relations, these treatments essentialize gender as defining identity and subordinate class as a secondary or even invisible consideration.

Though this essay cannot extend the discussion of gender and class, or race and class, the above begins to sketch out the kind of questions one might raise in this regard. As we already saw in the commodification of primitivized male bodies in *On the Waterfront* and *Blue Collar*, "gender" includes more than a simple "male" and "female" distinction. The social construction of the working class, we saw, gets further inflected through outlaw sexual fantasies and illicit desires that often remain unnamed. Race, we must remember, is similarly constructed through myriad definitions of masculinity, femininity, and anything between and outside such categories, all of which get commodified in our society in relation to class. In short, interrelations of race, class, and gender turn out to be much more complex than the mantra-like recitation of these three words might suggest. Indeed, it is the very complexity of their interrelations, together with the misguided impression that surely one of these categories must be the key to identity, that plays into the effacement of class in a culture where class consciousness is gutted to begin with.

But in addition to myths of physical destiny and legacies of allied hates that construct working-class representations—and thus realities!—are also the particulars of history. As the preceding discussion suggests, filmic representations of working-class people are embedded in history and can be studied in relation to national or group agendas at given points in time. The combat film genre, for instance, is predicated on class divisions that it must reconcile or cover up in the interest of national security; and Depression-era films include coping mechanisms that range from reformist humanism to countless comedies, dramas, melodramas, and entertainment extravaganzas invested in total denial. Each version of *An Imitation of Life*, for instance, is replete with opportunities to study the interrelations of gender, race, and class, but each is also a case study in evasion. Indeed, once one starts looking, there is no shortage of what to teach concerning working-class representations and there certainly is no need to be hampered by the kind of resistance I discuss at the start of this essay. For me at least, what emerges most clearly from this overview is an awareness of how a critical reading of filmic representations enables us to reconceptualize working-class identities and politics.

Notes

1   Erik S. Lunde and Douglass A. Noverr, eds, *Film Studies and Film History: Selected Course Outlines and Reading Lists from American Colleges and Universities*, two vols. (New York: Marcus Wiener, 1989).

2   Rick Berg and David James, eds, *The Hidden Foundation: Cinema and the Question of Class* (Minneapolis: University of Minnesota Press, 1996). See also Hill, John, *Sex, Class, and Realism: British Cinema 1956–1963* (London: British Film Institute, 1980); and Stead, Peter, *Film and the Working Class: The Feature Film in British and American Society* (New York: Routledge, 1991). Since this essay was originally published, other valuable books have some out, including Tom Zaniello, *Working Stiffs, Union Maids, Reds, and Riffraff; An Expanded Guide to Films about Labor* (Ithaca, NY: Cornell University Press, 2003); and Tom Zaniello, *The Cinema of Globalization; A Guide to Films About the New Economic Order* (Ithaca, NY: Cornell University Press, 2007).

3 Mas'ud Zavarzadeh, *Seeing Films Politically* (Albany, NY: State University of New York Press, 1991).
4 With the exception of *Nothing But a Man*, these are formally experimental and polemical films which make no concessions to the prevailing taste for clear narration, visual pleasure, and conformist politics. In this respect, they have more in common with the feminist avant-garde or Cuban cinema of the 1970s, for example, than with the African-American films screened theatrically.

Films cited

The Accused. Jonathan Kaplan. 110 min. (color), 1988.
The Age of Innocence. Martin Scorcese. 138 min. (color), 1993.
Bless Their Little Hearts. Billie Woodbury. 90 min. (b/w), 1984.
Blue Collar. Paul Schrader. 114 min. (color), 1978.
Bush Mama. Haile Gerima. 97 min. (b/w), 1976.
A Catered Affair. Richard Brooks. 92 min. (b/w), 1956.
The Crowd. King Vidor. 93 min. (b/w), 1928.
The Deer Hunter. Michael Cimino. 183 min. (color), 1978.
Gas, Food, Lodging. Alison Andrews. 101 min. (color), 1992.
The Grapes of Wrath. John Ford. 129 min. (b/w), 1940.
Harlan County, U.S.A. Barbara Kopple. 103 min. (color), 1976.
Heart Like a Wheel. Jonathan Kaplan. 110 min. (color), 1983.
Hoffa. Danny DeVito. 138 min. (color), 1992.
An Imitation of Life. John Stahl. 106 min. (b/w), 1934.
An Imitation of Life. Douglas Sirk. 124 min. (color), 1959.
The Joy Luck Club. Wayne Wang. 138 min. (color), 1993.
The Killer of Sheep. Charles Burnett. 87 min. (b/w), 1977.
The Killing Floor. Roland Joffe. 142 min. (color), 1984.
The Marrying Kind. George Cukor. 96 min. (b/w), 1952.
Matewan. John Sayles. 130 min. (color), 1987.
Mi Vida Loca. Alison Andrews, 92 min. (color), 1993.
Norma Rae. Martin Ritt. 115 min. (color), 1979.
Northern Lights. John Hanson/Rob Nilsson. 95 min. (b/w), 1979.
Nothing But a Man. Michael Roemer. 92 min. (b/w), 1964.
On the Waterfront. Elia Kazan. 108 min. (b/w), 1954.
Our Daily Bread. King Vidor. 80 min. (b/w), 1934.
Rambling Rose. Martha Coolidge. 112 min. (color), 1991.
Ruby in Paradise. Victor Nunez. 115 min. (color), 1993.
Salt of the Earth. Herbert J. Biberman. 94 min. (b/w), 1953.
Schindler's List. Steven Spielberg. 185 min. (b/w and color), 1993.
Silkwood. Mike Nichols. 131 min. (color), 1983.
Stella Dallas. King Vidor. 106 min. (b/w), 1937.
Stand and Deliver. Ramon Menedez. 102 min. (color), 1988.
A Streetcar Named Desire. Elia Kazan. 122 min. (b/w), 1951.
Sullivan's Travels. Preston Sturges. 90 min. (b/w), 1944.

Thelma and Louise. Ridley Scott. 129 min. (color), 1991.
Tongues Untied. Marlon Riggs. 55 min. (b/w), 1989.
Viva Zapata. Elia Kazan. 113 min. (b/w), 1952.
The Wild One. Laslo Benedek. 79 min. (b/w), 1954.

(Special thanks to Karen McGovern, of the Media Center at the University of Massachusetts Boston, for her invaluable help in compiling this filmography.)

16

Canon Issues and Class Contexts: Teaching American Literature from a Market Perspective

Janet Galligani Casey

Janet Galligani Casey describes a recent effort to encourage her students at Skidmore College, despite their own mostly privileged and largely taken for granted class positions, to understand the class nature of literary production and reputation. A creative and unusual project she assigned enabled them to break loose from the view, absorbed through years of schooling as well as from the culture at large, that literary value transcends issues of class.

How do we make class issues relevant for literature students in a way that is not just about what is inside a text, and thus conveniently distanced from their own lives and influences and choices? This question has long troubled me, especially since I teach at a selective liberal arts college, Skidmore, where the majority of students—the children of educated parents from relatively affluent communities, with an established interest in the arts—would be considered privileged. While these students are eager to study literature and earnest in their desire to consider texts that focus on socioeconomic conditions different from their own, they too often seem safely removed from any of the class tensions represented. How might I engage their class positions more fully within the parameters of a literary studies course?

As one response to this problem, I have developed an advanced course, titled "Literature, Class, and Culture," which not only showcases class-oriented texts but also pays particular attention to class-inflected aspects of literary history, especially the politics of production and dissemination. Guiding questions in the course description indicate that the term "class" will have multiple valences:

> To what extent do class dynamics shape not only individual literary works, but also the ways in which those works are received and promoted? How did the novel come to be associated with the middle class, and how has it been seen by some as advancing bourgeois interests? What practical and theoretical problems arise in the creation of a working-class literature? How has the notion of canonicity hinged on implicit and explicit attitudes toward class?

Especially provocative to students, however, is the course emphasis on how texts are situated within the bookselling and critical establishments, wherein writers, publishers, critics, advertising executives, and academics participate in a complex negotiation of literary stratification that often emerges from or resonates with class attitudes and aspirations. This frame of reference broadens students' perceptions of how class as a sociocultural phenomenon manifests itself in the literary arena. It also surprises and challenges them in its departure from the typical undergraduate English course, which privileges the internal dynamics of texts. One student wrote in an end-of-semester reflection, "I never would have thought to look at literature from this [outside] direction." Others suggested that the course not only made them "see class issues everywhere," but also redefined their notions of what literary studies itself might mean.

The course focuses particularly on the early twentieth century, when emerging readerships (notably the expansion of middle-class literacy) altered the status of books in the cultural mindset, provoked new interest in class themes as a topic for literature, and lent fresh energy and urgency to the bookselling industry. Through analyzing the critical and promotional environments within which texts were framed, the course helps students see the literary field as fluid rather than fixed, shaped in part by socioeconomic forces that may have little to do with literariness. And these issues have relevance for their own learning: on the very first day I point out that the course's title is borrowed from the American literature anthology of the same name edited by Paul Lauter and Ann Fitzgerald.[1] That an anthology might be organized around issues of class, and that such an anthology has been far less frequently adopted in college courses than more generalized anthologies of American literature, introduces key questions about how the academic establishment itself generates and sustains interest in texts. It also links two separate avenues of investigation that are central to the course: how does the concept of class assert itself as a theme in literature, and how is it that literary texts—even those ostensibly about class—often evade examination as artifacts embedded in a class culture?

One of my first hurdles is to broaden students' understanding of the complexities of class structures and the varied ways that they operate within culture. Typically, my students have not interrogated their own class positioning especially deeply; the idea that their behaviors, preferences, and even their decision to study literature might be related in part to class formations is often new to them, and they find it both intriguing and unsettling. Moreover, they have had little exposure to a market-based understanding of literary history. On the contrary, everything in their academic experience works against such an understanding, and serves to mystify literature not as a potential or partial product of economic forces, but as an inspired creation that somehow "naturally" evidences its cultural value. To be sure, my students are generally aware that certain social prejudices—based on race, gender, region, etc.—have affected the status of literary works, and they perceive the "canon wars" (a term with which they are familiar) as a corrective to such prejudices. Yet an understanding of books as commodities either eludes them entirely or is deemed offensive. In short, they are more likely, and more eager, to see literature as critiquing capitalist culture than as influenced by it.

My purpose is to help them see books not only as vessels of ideas, but as material artifacts in a competitive commercial arena. This requires a close examination of market factors: the dynamics of buying and selling, of creating and then nurturing specific audiences, of slickly packaging some books and even sabotaging others, all to gain a foothold among consumers. Clearly, even the "high" critical establishment participates in these processes (who would argue that book jacket blurbs don't matter, or that a well-placed review doesn't affect sales?), although we might like to pretend that art somehow operates beyond the reach of market forces. And, indeed, this tendency to separate the literary from the commercial is one of our earliest course topics. We examine how and why, at a certain point in literary history, successful sales came to be devalued as a sign of corrupt aesthetic standards—an attitude that framed genuine literature as external to the marketplace. (One highbrow critic of the early twentieth century, quoted in the *Atlantic Monthly*, suggested that a book selling a hundred thousand copies signaled "disgrace" for the author.)[2] To trace this development, we look carefully at early twentieth-century book reviews, which could be surprisingly direct in their class commentary and their concern with reading as status. We also consider the nascent economy of bestseller lists and literary prizes, which proved powerful for marketing purposes but which, some argued, contributed to an erosion of "literary value."

A key point is that class is often linked to taste. One way I demonstrate this is by focusing on the creation in 1926 of the Book-of-the-Month Club, an organization that my students are aware of but that they are reluctant to connect to their study of serious literature. (Many assume, mistakenly, that the Club peddles "light weight" or even "trashy" works, which feeds nicely into the discussions about taste and class that will follow.) We study the origins of the Club as a business enterprise, the creation of the infamous "jury" charged with making monthly reading recommendations to the Club's clientele, and, most compelling of all, the hostilities that the Club generated within the critical establishment. On one hand, some commentators felt that the Club vulgarized the literary enterprise by nurturing a purely consumerist attitude toward books (and not very good books at that), and by encouraging middle-class readers to rely on a panel of experts rather than on their own considered judgments about literary value. On the other hand, the Club was hailed as a boon to the average literate citizen, who, it was claimed, lacked the time, energy, and/or expertise necessary to wade through the rising sea of published books, and who was less interested in avant-garde themes or techniques than in a good story.[3]

My students, initially inclined to see the Club as irrelevant to their studies, find its history nonetheless engrossing. They quickly perceive that opposition to the Club often translated to resentment of its commercial power and, by extension, the purchasing power wielded by middlebrow book-buyers. Hence, they are alerted to the fierce competition for readers and dollars that took place within the literary arena of the early twentieth century, as well as to the ways that competing audiences were imagined in class terms. As with Oprah's Book Club today, the early years of the Book-of-the-Month Club provoked uneasy commentary about the perceived need to separate "serious" literature from the supposedly second-rate books consumed by an indiscriminate public. Yet students also see that they themselves are implicated in this ongoing battle between a "high" and a "middle" book culture, and they come to understand that their vague perceptions of the Book-of-the-Month Club as an inferior cultural institution have been shaped in part by its absence from academic consideration, and are furthered through class-inflected details such as the venues in which the Club is typically advertised today. Not coincidentally, they discover that advertising is an especially rich site for exploring how book-loving audiences have been and continue to be fractured in class terms. As a particularly blatant example of a book promotion that hinged on class anxieties or aspirations, I share with them some of the advertisements for Edna Ferber's 1924 blockbuster, *So Big*, which played pointedly not on readers' aesthetic sensibilities, but on their social apprehensions: for example, "How big are you? . . . Measure yourself against Edna Ferber's mighty novel"; or "Look over your neighbor's shoulder – he's probably reading it."[4]

Of course, none of this is to argue that market forces are entirely responsible for shaping definitions of the literary (the case of Emily Dickinson being but one example to the contrary). Yet it exposes students to a particular context for literature that is usually obscure to them, and that, when revealed, compromises their tendency to see the canon as ineluctable, or as based wholly on literary standards. It also urges them to consider the various ways that literary "success" has been defined, and how those definitions might have been informed by assumptions about social hierarchies. We analyze carefully, for instance, the pejorative use in period reviews of terms such as "middlebrow" or "sentimentalism" or "propaganda," all of which signaled, in different ways and at various moments, a substandard literature. As our investigations reveal, it was not merely minority writers who were excluded from the realm of high art, but also white mainstream and popular writers whose works may have been intended for an average readership rather than an elite one, and whose financial success was often in inverse relation to long-range critical success within the academy.

In my experience, students become especially engaged—though also somewhat defensive—when they realize that they have internalized academic attitudes about such texts. Some of the most successful classroom moments emerge when I teach a noncanonical, middlebrow novel, such as *So Big* (which, by the way, is about generational class dynamics) and allow students to air their initial frustrations with its "easiness." My advanced English majors often find this novel deceptively flat compared to works by, say, Eliot or Faulkner; one student even protested emphatically, "I didn't come to college to read stuff like this." Fuller contextualization, however, can lead them to see that there is no absolute measure of literary value, and that their attitudes and academic training inevitably manifest a class positioning. (Ferber's text is particularly germane, since she satirizes the 1920s' era university as a site of unimaginative standardization.) In a related exercise, for instance, I ask students to read a classic literary text studied in the college curriculum—perhaps a short poem by Wallace Stevens or Emily Dickinson—and work in groups to generate a list of the types of readers who are unlikely to appreciate it. Their responses—for example, "the uneducated," "those who want to get a clear message," "those who dislike complex symbolism"—lead us to consider how a text is pitched to an implied readership, and how it works to fulfill the expectations and ideals of that readership. From there, it is only a short step to the point where they can imagine alternative canons and alternative types of literature as having legitimate and even sophisticated claims on a different kind of reading public.[5]

These and other concerns converge in the course's final project, in which I ask students to design a class-oriented American literature anthology. With the notable exception of Lauter and Fitzgerald's text, the market boasts almost no examples of such a book, a situation that immediately raises intriguing questions. Why has this particular organization of literary material—as opposed, say, to anthologies oriented around gender or race—been less than compelling in the academic market place? The general submersion of class issues in American life and the mythology of America as a "classless" society are surely relevant here. Yet ultimately I want students to grasp the extent to which consumer choice drives the bookselling market, even in academic contexts: that is, individual professors decide what they think will be interesting and worthwhile for their students to read. Thus, faculty members, in concert with publishers, both determine and delimit the range of study materials available. This brings to the foreground what many students have never thought about, namely the existence of an academic book market that is governed by its own power relations as well as by economic realities similar to those of the broader book market, even as it remains more attuned to values of literariness.

Some may object that asking students to design and "sell" an anthology requires them to inhabit a capitalist role, compromising the intellectual analysis of marketplace dynamics that has been central to the course. But this project proves useful for two reasons. First, grappling with the complications of creating such a volume gives students an inside perspective on the varied considerations, literary and nonliterary, that structure their own learning as English majors, calling into question the naturalized authority of texts and canons and providing a better understanding of the intricate interactions between the marketplace and issues of culture and aesthetics. Second, the project demonstrates that, in the academic market, selling a book is considerably more complicated than appealing to trends. Not the least of the students' challenges is to decide what it means to conceptualize and "teach" class concepts through literary materials.

Thus, the project asks them to contend simultaneously with literature, culture, and pedagogy, as well as with market economics. It requires them to think carefully and deeply about the nature of class (what exactly is it, and how might it be represented and taught?), the marketing of textbooks (what makes them attractive to professors?), and the relationships between the two. A detailed assignment sheet suggests only some of the interlocking questions that must be explored, gesturing toward the enormous difficulties involved in the real-world creation of such a book:

> What sorts of texts will you include? Long or short? By authors from different classes, or primarily from one (e.g., middlebrow)? From a limited time period, or from a broad historical span? Written texts only, or images too? Fiction? Nonfiction? Poetry? Drama? Journalism? Other kinds of texts? Critical analyses? On a basic level, are you aiming for *variety*, or *similarity*?
>
> How exactly will class be made a focus? Through primary selections that obviously foreground issues of class? Through critical commentary

that uncovers the class dimensions of apparently "neutral" texts? In other ways?

Will your proposal depend on experts to compile your anthology (as is common), or will you compile it yourself? Why? What types of expertise do you think are important for this type of volume? What sorts of experts would you seek?

To whom will this book be marketed? College students in liberal arts colleges like ours? High schools and community colleges? Large research-oriented universities? How might a particular target audience shape your inclusions and exclusions?

How will you convince professors to order your text for their courses? How will you distinguish your text from others on the market? How will you make your anthology affordable?

What kinds of "extras" will you include that will help students contextualize the primary selections? For example, will you make space for author biographies? If so, why, and what will they include? Some anthologies have historical time lines; if you choose such a route, will your timeline(s) note literary events, events in labor history or class consciousness, or both?

Above all, remember that your anthology will need to be portable. If your proposal seems likely to result in an enormous and therefore unwieldy text, it will not seem attractive to your potential publisher (i.e., me).

This last point—that an anthology must be portable in order to sell—is often an enormous eye-opener for students, since its very obviousness usually eludes interrogation. Yet its impact on literary studies is unmistakable: the anthology form necessarily privileges shorter texts, potentially distorting the literary-historical record.[6] In case students have missed the idea that market issues may indeed play a part in shaping the discipline of literary studies, the anthology project brings that point home in a very tangible way.

Students in my course have approached this project with excitement (because it departs so thoroughly from the standard end-of-semester literary paper) and misgivings (because it forces them to confront issues for which they generally feel ill-equipped, even after a semester of conversations about the relations among class, culture, and commerce). Yet many manage the assignment with insight and creativity. They spend a great deal of time on their projects, producing portfolios that include not only the required pieces (an 8–10 page proposal justifying the volume's title, general arrangement, and basic editorial choices; a statement on marketability and marketing strategies; and a 5-page Introduction to the anthology itself) but also such elements as cover art, sample entries, detailed timelines, annotated tables of contents, and even accompanying compact disks with music, video, and/ or images. And the range of organizing principles can be vast: some of the more imaginative projects have included an anthology focused on food and cooking as a way to investigate the power of class (with recipes matched to literary texts), and an anthology on contemporary working-class literature that also draws on film and rap music.

What I did not anticipate, however, is the way that this assignment gives students room to unpack their own relations to class issues and/or literary study. For example, one memorable anthology project, created by a student who had emigrated from China, proposed to explore the relation between class positioning and immigrant assimilation. While the project's execution was less than stellar (largely due to the student's relatively limited knowledge of American literature and his still-developing English writing skills), the theoretical questions raised in his Introduction were quite creditable. First, he asked, what difference is there between assimilating into the working class of a given culture and assimilating into the higher classes? Second, what tensions are created when one's class status in one's native community differs from one's class status in the aspirant community? These questions prompted a lively discussion among his American-born classmates, who had assumed that "American" literary materials would be by and about "native" people. Hence, the project raised a fundamental question that is often unexamined in literature classes: namely, what exactly is meant by American literature?

As this example suggests, the real value of the project becomes clear when the students present their proposals to the class as a whole. The larger group is a kind of editorial collective, challenging the creator of each anthology to defend his/her vision and using specific details of the individual project to raise further questions about the conceptualization, teaching, and marketing of class themes. The resulting discussions are highly instructive and sometimes highly charged. Students become surprisingly forthright in their assessments, making comments such as "It's a great idea from a student perspective, but would large numbers of professors actually buy it?" or "It may be marketable, but that doesn't mean it's a good book for college literature students." Foremost among their concerns is the way class becomes explicitly and implicitly defined within a given proposal, and their rigorous debates make it clear, once again, just how volatile that topic is. One student objected, for example, to the general avoidance of an upper-class perspective in virtually all of the proposals under review, arguing that class identity issues had become unfairly reduced to working- and middle-class concerns and representations. Others wondered aloud about what they saw as the diminished role of traditional literary assessment (i.e. "quality"), questioning the ways that purely thematic concerns might pressure the literary selections. ("Is it really more useful to read recent stories on the working class than to read Dreiser?" asked one.) Hence, students' investment in the course and its ideas is indexed through the probing and often defensive nature of their discussions, which force them to formulate their own viewpoints about issues that have undergirded their literary educations but on which they have rarely been asked to comment. Among the broad implicit questions that structure these debates, and ultimately the course as a whole, are these: What exactly should the study of (American) literature entail? How do we define the literary as against the cultural? Do texts have cultural value that is nonliterary? Do they have meaning and status apart from that which the market imposes upon them?

Of course, the anthology project is not without its challenges. In particular, I have been somewhat chagrined to note the ease with which my students take on the role of salespeople, as demonstrated by the care lavished on their proposals; I worry that the critical stances I have so carefully nurtured throughout the semester will be blunted by the pleasures of what one referred to as "the selling game." In my next iteration of the course, I plan to devote more time (perhaps even requiring a written response) to the postpresentation discussions, thereby throwing the weight of the exercise onto the critique sessions. (The trick, I believe, is to channel appropriately their enthusiasm for thinking about business and marketing into a project that enhances, rather than undermines or neutralizes, their discerning stance toward the interactions of literature, class, and consumerism.) Admittedly, too, the course as a whole may suffer a bit from the necessarily disparate applications of the idea of class. But if a single course cannot hope to consider fully all of the possible applications of this term within a literary studies context (is class primarily related to modes of production? readerships? reception? thematics?), neither can it restrict itself productively to a single, refined usage, given the subtle and complicated ways that socioeconomic phenomena inform the discipline—and indeed, just about everything else.

Perhaps the most unexpected outcome of this course for me as a teacher, however, is that it has caused me to reflect on the relationship between what I teach and the developmental stage of my students. While I am eager to demonstrate that the literary as a category is larger and more elastic than they may have thought—a notion that I find exciting—I am forced to recognize that their inevitable resistances to this idea may have less to do with their privileged class positions than with their status as undergraduates. A more capacious definition of the literary—one that includes middlebrow works, for instance, rather than just "high" canonical texts, and one that acknowledges the influence of such nonliterary forces as the consumer marketplace—necessarily calls into question the stature and judgment of an informed intellectual elite; yet, isn't the implied end-point of higher education admittance into that very group? For my students, then, who are still striving to earn what we might think of as intellectual and cultural legitimacy, the challenge to a "pure" or "absolute" aesthetic standard threatens not merely their definition of literature, but their entire enterprise as students. Perhaps it is only those of us who have earned our intellectual stripes, so to speak, who can plunge exuberantly into an interrogation of the ways and means by which literary-cultural status is perpetuated.

But while these reflections have made me aware of the need for sensitivity in teaching from this perspective, they have not undermined my hope that a course such as Literature, Class, and Culture can deepen students' understanding of how class issues inform both their studies and their lives. On one level, the course and its final project seek merely to stimulate students' awareness that socioeconomic conditions, in addition to being treated thematically within texts, also help to situate those texts within a literary-cultural field. But, in the best cases, our discussions also prompt students to consider more carefully the various ways that the authority of a literary canon may be built, sustained, and deconstructed, and to think more deeply about their own class positioning and its relation to what they read—a process that has applications beyond the narrow confines of literary studies. The point, of course, is that neither texts nor their audiences can escape wholly the structuring dimensions of class perspectives.

Notes

1   Paul Lauter and Ann Fitzgerald, *Literature, Class, and Culture: An Anthology* (New York: Longman, 2000).
2   Quoted in Frank Luther Mott, *Golden Multitudes: The Story of Best Sellers in the United States* (New York: Macmillan, 1947), 3.
3   On the Book-of-the-Month-Club, see Janice Radway, *A Feeling for Books: The Book-of-the-Month Club, Literary Taste, and Middle-Class Desire* (Chapel Hill: University of North Carolina Press, 1997).
4   Ferber's novel was the #1 bestseller of 1924, received the Pulitzer Prize for Fiction, and was made into three films (1925, 1932, 1953). For these advertising examples, see the *New York Times* 12 October 1924 and 25 January 1925. For more on Ferber's novel and on the economy of literary best sellers generally, see Janet Galligani Casey, *A New Heartland: Women, Modernity, and the Agrarian Ideal in America* (Oxford University Press, 2009).
5   Literary success, then, has something to do with how well a particular work yields to the typical reading practices of its implied audience. Thus in other sessions we specifically address the politics of "close reading"—the primary interpretive mode of literary studies classes—as necessarily privileging a certain approach and thus a certain type of reader.
6   Students in this course are familiar with the work of John Dos Passos, an excellent case in point. Dos Passos's best-known novels—especially the weighty *USA* trilogy—are typically represented in anthologies by very brief segments that, as my students can easily discern, fail to provide a full sense of his narrative experimentation.

17

Teaching *Howards End* to the Basts: Class Markers in the Classroom, and in the Bourgeois Novel[1]

Ed Wiltse

Even a literary work that clearly and explicitly explores class difference can present interpretive challenges to students whose own (not fully acknowledged) class positions often make understanding harder than it ought to be. Ed Wiltse's approach to overcoming the obstacles he encountered—getting to class by way of gender—has applications far beyond the literature classroom.

[I]ndependent thoughts are in nine cases out of ten the result of independent means.

– Margaret Schlegel, *Howards End*

Radical academics frequently observe that class is harder to talk about in the classroom than other axes of oppression, and although I'm wary of the tendency of such truisms to play into what Henry Giroux dubbed a cynical "pedagogy of the depressed," I've experienced this too.[2] While my students leave Freshman Orientation—which I've come to think of as a kind of "diversity boot camp," with squads of new recruits in new haircuts marching about the campus for drills in respect and open-mindedness—fully prepared, even expecting to talk about issues of race, gender, and sexuality, they are much less forthcoming or articulate when it comes to questions of class, in literature and culture, and in their own lives. This is somewhat ironic, since in my estimation Nazareth College, where I teach, is a good deal more "diverse" in terms of class backgrounds than in terms of race. But of course "my estimation" is part of the problem, since the college publishes statistics on racial diversity ("7.6% minority enrollment"), but not on class.

Nazareth is a small, private liberal arts college rapidly adding the preprofessional undergraduate and graduate programs that pay the bills these days; we're formerly Catholic and all women, now independent and coed, though still about two-thirds women among the undergraduates. We draw the bulk of our first-year students from the Thruway cities and surrounding towns of upstate New York; a substantial number of transfer students come from the local area via 2 + 2 programs with community colleges, which streamline the process of admission and transfer credit upon completion of an Associate's Degree. The Admissions Office tells me that about one third of our first-years are the first generation in their family to attend college (that number seems significantly higher among transfer students), and that over half of incoming students are eligible for New York State's Tuition Assistance Plan. And, in my highly unscientific sample, their family narratives, as told to me in class or personally, or as written about in journals and first-year composition essays, most often suggest backgrounds we'd likely think of as ranging from working to middle class. Those who market the college make much of its "affordability"—in addition to the usual, annual noise about our overall *U S News and World Report* ranking, we sometimes hear about our placement on their list of "Great Schools at Great Prices."[3]

I include all this about my institution and its students by way of preamble, or perhaps backstory, to a narrative about teaching E. M. Forster's 1910 novel *Howards End* to 16 upper-level English majors in a class on Twentieth-Century British literature, and the questions about class in the classroom, and in the bourgeois novel, that emerged in the process. *Howards End* is well known for its indictment of the philistinism of the new mercantile elite, at a moment of tumultuous social and economic change. The novel's two central families are laid out in Manichean terms that only an undergraduate compare-and-contrast essay could love: the Wilcoxes represent materialism, commercialism, industry, empire, and "the great outer life of telegrams and anger," whereas the Schlegels embody idealism, high culture, spirituality, and "personal relations" (23). In clearly preferring the social and cultural sophistication of the Schlegel sisters to the commercial and material impulses of the Wilcox family, Forster positions himself in the then raging "Condition of England" debate, grudgingly acknowledging the necessity of the Wilcoxes' prosaic industriousness to keep the society's wheels turning, but insisting that the Schlegels must be the true inheritors of England and Englishness. Showing students these oppositions is as simple as a chart on the blackboard—so perhaps it's not only undergrad essays that appreciate Forster's schematic design.

However, there's another combatant in this "culture war," complicating its simple binaries—poor Leonard Bast, a clerk living "at the extreme verge of gentility" (38), but with a hunger for the easy cultural capital that the Schlegel sisters possess as a birthright. Despite some moments of withering condescension, on the whole, Forster clearly wants to be sympathetic to this character, whose "mind and . . . body had been alike underfed" (39), and to record the difficulties of those whose dream it is "to acquire culture! . . . to pronounce foreign names correctly!" (34) Moreover, it is Bast who pushes Margaret Schlegel to realize, as she tells her sister Helen, that "You and I and the Wilcoxes stand upon money as upon islands. It is so firm beneath our feet that we forget its very existence . . . I stand each year upon six hundred pounds, and Helen upon the same . . . and all our thoughts are the thoughts of six-hundred-pounders" (51–2). However, neither Margaret nor Forster is able to do much with this surprisingly astute insight into the self-erasing ideological work of capital, and Forster soon belittles Margaret's notions of political economy in a scathing and rather sexist representation of a ladies' discussion club meeting in which the Schlegels and their friends consider how they might help Bast, had they a million pounds to give away. Ultimately, the novel insists, Bast's attempts to master elite culture are doomed, and such Modern cultural climbers, and those who would assist them, are as prone to cause disaster as the social climbers of a thousand Victorian novels before them. Bast dies, appropriately enough, under a landslide of books in the parlor of Howards End, the house that epitomizes an England where people knew their places in the social order.

Critics have long noted a kind of bad faith in Forster's critique of the shallow mercantilism of the Wilcoxes, since Forster's readers were certain to be more like the Schlegels and less like the Wilcoxes. But what about a group of readers far more likely to sympathize with Bast than either of the two wealthy families at the novel's center? Most of my students, after all, also can't pronounce foreign names, don't know how to act at the symphony, and find themselves distracted from the joys of clever conversation by material realities a good deal more pressing than Bast's lost umbrella. And to my horror, our class discussions (and discussions of class) quickly made it apparent that understanding the ironic distance at which Forster holds the character of Bast, and the failures and blindnesses of a bourgeois critique of bourgeois materialism, required exactly the cultural capital that the Basts in my classroom didn't have. It became steadily more evident to me that the wealthier students, who weren't spending the bulk of their time in the low-wage jobs that enabled many in our classroom to be there at all, were at something of an advantage, both in terms of their background in reading multilayered ironic prose and in terms of the time they could dedicate to decoding Forster's winding sentences and free, indirect style.

From what I could discern, recognizing that these are dangerous generalizations that may say as much about my own class biases as about my students' actual understanding, the closer my students were to Bast in class background, the more likely they were to struggle to see the ideological contradictions in his story. For such students, Bast's tribulations—his struggle to parse a sentence of Ruskin and then his ludicrous meditations on how to use its structure in a letter to his brother—were simply accurate reflections of their own encounters with high culture, not least with *Howards End* itself. Of course, this presented an irony of its own, as it seemed to reinforce Forster's point about the Basts of this world, forever locked out from the parlors and drawing rooms of elite culture.

Of course, my story of teaching *Howards End* to the Basts, unlike Forster's story of Bast himself, has a happy ending, or I probably wouldn't be writing about it. Ultimately, the key to unlocking those drawing rooms, and revealing the sham logic and shoddy construction behind them, proved to be finding a back door. My students and I were able to get at the novel's contradictory class politics by looking first at its gender politics. The detour through gender to get to class may seem a bit of a cop-out, but I like to think of it as strategic, at this reactionary moment in American political life, in my institution, where our history as a women's college and current gender imbalance makes feminism a natural entrée to political consciousness (though, even here, students struggle with the "f" word).

During our first class on *Howards End*, when I discovered that some students were struggling to understand the role of social class in the novel, I launched into my standard, quick overview of the three classes as they consolidated in the early nineteenth century in terms of their relationship to the means of production, and then offered some suggestions about how globalization, flexible accumulation, and the rise of the service economy have complicated the traditional model today. At our next meeting, I circulated a brief handout that simply describes demographic and lifestyle characteristics (parents' educational levels and careers, housing location and type, and a few details to suggest degree of economic security) for "five Nazareth College students I've known," carefully selected and presented to suggest typical class fractions and backgrounds, so my students were likely to recognize versions of themselves and their friends somewhere on the list. After asking students to read through the list and identify (silently) the person whose background most resembles their own background, we discussed how each of the five could be described in terms of class, and what that might have to do with each one's experience of college—and this is where my trouble started.

While, as noted above, students were willing, even eager, to see connections between Bast's struggles with elite culture and their own ("yeah, we had to read Ruskin in Survey—totally hard"), they were much less willing to see connections between Bast's economic struggles and their own, especially in terms of class mobility and their postcollege lives. Even for those students willing to admit (to themselves or to the class) that their backgrounds were working class, I found that they, like most Americans today, saw themselves, today and into the future, as solidly middle class, entirely irrespective of their actual living conditions. All of the standard American mythology about mobility and a classless society stood in the way of our discussion of class's structuring role in the lives of Forster's characters, and in our own, making it hard to even approach the questions I had begun with, about the ideological underpinnings of Forster's characterization.

But of course my students all "have" gender, in a way that they do not see that they "have" class, and I have found that my students are generally much more willing to acknowledge gender's role in everything from life choices and opportunities to reading preferences and strategies, making gender an easier place to begin ideologically situating *Howards End*. And on its surface, the novel has much to offer the feminist reader: a female protagonist who is at once intellectual and likable (a rare combination, even in 1910), an open critique of society's double standard with respect to male versus female sexual behavior, an embedded critique of conventions of wooing and marriage, and even some vague suffragist leanings. And in the end, Margaret has her "triumph. She, who had never expected to conquer any one, had charged straight through these Wilcoxes and broken up their lives" (291). She is to inherit the house that she was destined to have all along, and her discovery of that destiny's arrival prompts a new mystical awareness: "Something shook her life in its inmost recesses" (293). She declares her plan to leave the house to the child of Helen and Bast's illicit encounter, and the novel's famous final words belong to Helen, asserting a jubilant fertility in this bizarre household, populated by the Schlegel sisters, a broken Henry Wilcox, and Bast's bastard: "'The field's cut,' Helen cried excitedly – 'the big meadow. We've seen to the very end, and it'll be such a crop of hay as never!'" (293)

My students found this ending a bit hokey, and I found that a good place to begin decoding it ideologically, to unpack the leaps and lapses by which Forster produces it. Most obviously, for all Forster's critique of the conventions of marriage, the novel's resolution depends on a marriage plot worthy of Trollope. The students were quick to see that Margaret's "destiny" at Howards End is accomplished not by the fulfillment of Ruth Howard Wilcox's final wish, nor by Margaret's own endeavors, but by marrying a powerful man and then being lucky enough to see him decimated by his son's bad judgment and bad luck. They were then led to ask whether a man like Wilcox would really remain under his wife's control, or whether her aesthetic and ethical superiority, familiar enough to them from other Angels in other Houses, would inevitably take a back seat to his pragmatism and economic power. More broadly, Margaret's decision to engage with the world by means of her influence over her husband, first through love and finally through force of will, seemed to my students to negate much of the feminist energy of her earlier characterization. Of course, Forster beats us to this punch, as he so often does, having Margaret recognize and regret her newfound affinity with "Mrs. Plynlimmon [who], when condemning suffragettes, had said: 'The woman who can't influence her husband to vote the way she wants ought to be ashamed of herself'" (196). But, my students were quick to point out, just because Margaret recognizes her compromises with patriarchy doesn't make her any less of a sell-out, especially since the novel was written at a moment when actual "suffragettes" were hunger-striking and being force-fed in British prisons.

In their thin veneer of feminist sensibility overlying myriad contradictions, the gender issues in the novel provided a kind of blueprint for the same contradictory pattern of bourgeois liberalism evident in the novel's class politics. My students, who were used to thinking about gender issues in terms of the work of ideology, felt renewed confidence in their decoding skills, despite the twists and turns of Forster's ironic sensibility, when we talked about gender roles in the novel in terms of individual passages or the broader plot. I then worked to convince them that those same decoding skills would work for class issues, by focusing on the character in whom the two patterns intersect most tellingly, Jacky Bast, Leonard's wife. By a coincidence that might have made Dickens blush, Leonard, whom the Schlegel sisters meet at the symphony, turns out to be married to the woman with whom Henry Wilcox had an affair some years before in Cyprus, and Henry's later condemnation of Helen's out-of-wedlock pregnancy gives rise to Margaret's famous feminist critique of the sexual double standard. But the representation of Jacky herself is unlikely to win the hearts of feminists, beginning with her introduction, which I'll quote in all its glorious length, as she returns home and interrupts Leonard's well-meaning but doomed effort to imitate Ruskin's prose style:

A woman entered of whom it was simplest to say that she was not respectable. Her appearance was awesome. She seemed all strings and bell-pulls – ribbons, chains, bead necklaces that clinked and caught – and a boa of azure feathers hung round her neck with the ends uneven. Her throat was bare, wound with a double row of pearls, her arms were bare to the elbows, and might again be detected at the shoulder, through cheap lace. Her hat, which was flowery, resembled those punnets, covered with flannel, which we sowed with mustard and cress in our childhood, and which germinated here yes, and there no. She wore it on the back of her head. As for her hair, or rather hairs, they are too complicated to describe, but one system went down her back, lying in a thick pad there, while another, created for a lighter destiny, rippled around her forehead.

The face – the face does not signify. It was the face of the photograph, but older, and the teeth were not so numerous as the photographer had suggested, and certainly not so white. Yes, Jacky was past her prime, whatever that prime may have been.(43)

The contrast between the colorless Leonard and the Technicolor Jacky couldn't be greater, and the narrator's horror at her gauche accoutrements couldn't be more pronounced. Students were quick to see the sexism in the different images of this couple—Leonard's Ruskin versus Jacky's azure boa, Leonard's desperate fumbling for culture and philosophy versus Jacky's complete absence of an inner life: "the face does not signify." And then it's a fairly simple step to see the interplay between sexism and class elitism at work here—what the students called Jacky's "cheap tackiness" is the more horrific for its being feminized, even as her attempts at feminine seductiveness are the more repellent for their being tacky and cheap. Students were quick to see how in this passage Forster recruits the reader into a bourgeois subject position in order to look down on Jacky: "we" in this passage are the people who "sowed mustard and cress in our childhood," presumably not for food but as some kind of science project; "we" are quite clearly not the people whose hats resemble the ill-fated results of such projects.

Once my students began the process of denaturalizing the novel's representation of the Basts, they found evidence of its class contradictions at every turn. In particular, they were able to see how in the abstract we find some incisive critiques of the precarious position of people whom today we would call the working poor, and how easily chance could topple them into the "abyss" of poverty and despair, and to find connections to their own lives in our "rust belt" region where layoffs and plant closings abound. But, in *Howards End*, when such despair comes closer, what Margaret tellingly describes as "the odours from the abyss" become a bit much, and the novel turns away (197). Leonard, who is earlier characterized as "grandson to the shepherd or plough boy whom civilization had sucked into town; as one of the thousands who have lost the life of the body and failed to reach the life of the spirit" (98), is replaced in the novel's conclusion by a dreamy-eyed rendering of the plough boys who stayed behind. Forster's closing celebration of the land and its people relies on a vague idealization of yeoman virtues embedded in a mythic past: "Here men had been up since dawn. Their hours were ruled, not by a London office, but by the movements of the crops and the sun. That they were men of the finest type only the sentimentalist can declare. But they kept to the life of the daylight. They are England's hope" (276). Ultimately, I believe, it was the students from outside the inherited world of economic and cultural capital—students who have experienced not just "the odours from the abyss" but have felt its pull on their own lives—who were more likely to resist the seductions of this nostalgic, aestheticized version of the English countryside and its inhabitants, in order to see the novel's conclusion most clearly. It was those students who were most inclined to ask, in response to Helen's jubilant closing pronouncement that "it will be such a crop of hay as never," "who cut and baled that hay?"

Such questions redounded not only through our discussion of *Howards End* but also throughout the semester. Students' enthusiasm for the more explicit and energizing feminism of Virginia Woolf's *A Room of One's Own* was tempered as they found echoes of Margaret's ideas on "independent thoughts" deriving from "independent means" (109) in Woolf's pronouncement that "[o]ne cannot think well, love well, sleep well, if one has not dined well."[4] Once again, students realized that their own dinners were more likely to be current equivalents of the women's college's beef and prunes so disparaged by Woolf ("ramen noodles and day-old bagels," suggested one student) than the Oxbridgean sole and partridges that she finds necessary to light "the lamp in the spine" (18), and so, with some prompting, they began to consider the questions of class at stake in the esthetic judgments by which Woolf evaluates women's literary history, and, more broadly, in the process of canonization itself. Woolf, after all, was neither the first nor the last critic to define an esthetic purity she memorably calls "incandescence" in terms of writing that is "without hate, without bitterness, without fear, without protest, without preaching" (71), and to go on to lament the rarity of that quality in the writing of women or the working class—of course, later, non-White authors would be perceived to have these same "impediments." And as we marched through a century of British literature and culture, my students continued to wonder about the questions of class at stake in the different academic and marketplace status of the novels of Kingsley Amis and Alan Sillitoe, or Salman Rushdie and Beryl Gilroy, or the films of James Ivory and Ken Loach. Of course, they needed continual reminders that what we were likely to encounter as questions of esthetics, or audience, or educational level (of characters, and cultural producers and consumers) were ultimately questions of class. And for some students, this interrogation of the ongoing, pervasive role of class politics in culture and society ran so directly counter to all they'd been taught about this "land of opportunity," and to their own upward mobility quests within it, that class remained for them an English problem, if indeed it was a problem at all. But for at least a few of the Basts in my class, such questioning gave them heart both to resist the economic determinism of Bast's futile encounter with Ruskin and Woolf's beef and prunes dinner as they tackled the opacities of *The Waste Land* and to think for themselves about what's worth reading, and why.

* * *

It would be nice to end on that note of slightly muted triumphalism (indeed, an earlier version of this essay did end there), but of course the gap between what we think happens in our classrooms and what students think is often vast. In responding to that earlier version of this essay, the board member readers for *Radical Teacher* rightly suggested that an essay like this one would benefit from more direct quotation of student voices, a suggestion I've mostly been unable to address, because the idea of writing about this particular teaching experience only came to me some months after completing the semester. But the suggestion sent me back to the students' semester-ending course evaluations as a possible source of insight. After finding to my usual dismay that most students ignored the narrative portion of the evaluation and stuck to the "bubble sheet," I did glean a few useful responses. Among the half-dozen, mostly positive notes, three students responded to the course's emphasis on class issues in particular. One simply indicated that it was "a nice change from always talking about race and gender," which, alas, sounds a bit like switching from barbecue to honey-mustard sauce for his or her literature McNuggets. Another student liked the "connections between our lives and the books and movies," noting that "those construction workers [presumably in Ken Loach's film *Riff Raff*] could be my cousins." She or he went on to ask, "since they're elitist and 'problematic' (your favorite word), how come we spent so much time on stuff like *Howard's [sic] End* and *The Waste Land* (yuck)?"—and in posing that question, suggested an inkling of the sort of class consciousness that I am seeking to nurture. The third student who responded explicitly to the course's focus on class suggested that I "stop talking about class and money all the time. It gets old, and I don't really think it affects us that much."

But for all the (necessary) deflation of one's dreams of radical and radicalizing pedagogy that such comments inevitably provoke, for me the larger feeling evoked by the experience of teaching *Howards End* to the Basts is hopeful. Since that somewhat fumbling effort to help students understand ideologies of class using the example of ideologies of gender, I've become a bit more conscious and controlled in my efforts to work through, or around, student resistance to thinking about class, in literature and our lives. I imagine that for other teachers, successful strategies will depend on their personas and the composition of their classrooms—much as we adapt our strategies for analysis of race and gender depending on who we are and who's in the room. But of course class is far more than an "identity category," through which our students may have experienced solidarity, or exploitation, or both. As the proverbial water through which we fish swim, all the more invisible for its omnipresence, the precondition of our existence and primary determinant of its character, class is far harder for our students to see, and for us to see in our students. And for students like mine, for most of whom upward mobility through higher education is an article of faith, as well as an increasingly risky bet, making visible the ideologies and determinations of class is all the more difficult—and all the more crucial. My students know too well that the "conditions are not of their own making"; I hope and believe that by putting class at the center of my pedagogy, I can help them begin to find better ways to "make their own history."

Notes

1   This essay began as a presentation at the Modern Language Association's 2001 Radical Caucus panel on teaching the bourgeois novel; I'm grateful to the organizers of that panel, the other panelists, and the audience, as well as to *Radical Teacher*'s board member readers, for suggestions about the paper. References in text to E. M. Forster's *Howards End* refer to the Penguin Twentieth-Century Classics edition (New York: Penguin, 2000).

2   Henry A. Giroux, "Pedagogy of the Depressed: Beyond the New Politics of Cynicism." *College Literature* 28(2001): 1–32.

3   If my response to our marketing sounds a bit snide, that's no doubt due to the usual academic discomfort with the commercial side of our enterprise, which is itself symptomatic of some of the broader questions about class and education that this essay will touch on. But for the record (and for my upcoming tenure review), I should say that I'm really quite grateful to be teaching at a "great school at a great price," not least for the opportunity to teach students who can't afford great schools at less-great prices. In particular, I'm grateful to teach in an English department where some two thirds of our majors pursue certification to teach in the public schools, offering at least the hope that whatever radicalizing force arises from those students' experiences here will be passed on to future students in other settings.

4   Virginia Woolf, *A Room of One's Own* (New York: Harcourt, 1957), 18. Further references in text.

PART SIX

Teaching About Class Across the Campus

18

Empathy Education: Teaching About Women and Poverty in the Introductory Women's Studies Classroom

Jennifer Scanlon

Faculty often try to persuade their students of the importance of class by displaying statistics, many of which provide a stunning picture of inequality. But for most students, numbers have little emotional impact, in fact, little impact at all. Jennifer Scanlon tried another way; and, though the numbers in her essay come from the Clinton years, her creative approach to teaching "empathy rather than numbers" is no less useful today.

Many traditional-aged college students solidly identify with an individualist ethos, a renewed creed of the American Dream. Often accustomed to and sometimes eager for discussions of gender and race, they become uncomfortable when class issues are raised. Whether middle or working class, they are reluctant to acknowledge the demographic, political, or economic factors in the United States that may make their future work lives unstable financially. Working-class students usually are certain that they will achieve a class status higher than their parents; middle-class students seem equally certain of attaining at least the same status as their parents. And a college degree, they believe, will largely eradicate any sexism or racism in employment opportunity, wages, or advancement.

Women's Studies faculty attempting to teach about the realities of women and poverty in the United States try to challenge these myths, as well as the notion that the poor suffer from a lack of character rather than a lack of money. After several unsuccessful attempts at breaking through the stereotypes and having students recognize the realities of poor women's lives, I designed a group workshop for the classroom. This essay outlines what I hoped to teach about class in an introductory-level Women's Studies course, presents the workshop, and discusses some of the results. I have found that the workshop succeeds in providing what might be called "empathy education" and could be used by other Women's Studies faculty.

The setting for this workshop is a 4-year public college, part of the state university system of New York. Many of the students are first-generation college students. A large percentage rely heavily on state-supported education, not being able to afford the expense of a private college. In a course like "Introduction to Women's Studies," many of the students are in their first year, but there often is a balance between them and more advanced students. With the great demand for Women's Studies classes, some students must wait several semesters before gaining admission to the introductory course. As our program has gained a reputation for excellence in teaching across the campus, we have also gained greater diversity in student enrollment. As a result, the student composition of the classes in many ways mirrors the composition of the student body as a whole. Most of the students are white and many are members of sororities or fraternities. The one way our students do not mirror the general student population is in terms of gender: about one quarter of the students in our introductory courses, on the whole, are male.

Through this introductory course, the Women's Studies Program reaches approximately 200 students each year. Our goals for the course include encouraging an understanding of issues relating to race, class, and sexuality in addition to gender. In keeping with the goals of our General Education program and the goals of feminist pedagogy generally, the course contains many opportunities for active learning: group activities, the use of music and films, group presentations, and a great deal of in-class discussion. This exercise is one of many that engage the students in finding answers to, or at least further questions about, social issues.

In the postelection environment of 1995, with the State University of New York (SUNY) under assault, it is in some ways strange that students should fail to respond to issues of class identity and class struggle. Busloads of our students descended on Albany to speak their minds about budget cuts. Many others participated in teach-ins and college-wide discussions of the potential impact of our new governor's proposed cuts for SUNY. At the same time, though, students remain uneasy about considering the long-term consequences of political decisions based on class. It might appear bewildering to many faculty members that events directly affecting students should prove to be impediments to, rather than opportunities for, questioning and learning.

In defense of the students, steeped as they are in contemporary media and political rhetoric about the poor, they have good reasons for keeping to their misconceptions about social class. In the 12-year assault of the Reagan-Bush years and, unfortunately, in the rhetoric of the Clinton administration thus far, poor people are blamed for their problems. The current mood in the United States, with an emphasis on "welfare reform" but little discussion of needy people, encourages students to believe that poor people lack not money but morality, not jobs but souls.[1] Although the students are often blind to the supports they receive as participants in a heavily subsidized state-supported higher education system, they are acutely aware of the ways in which the poor secure taxpayer supported services.

After discovering repeatedly that students responded to my discussions of class issues and of poverty by introducing racist and sexist examples of welfare mothers and Cadillacs, someone they know who cheats the system in order to have a television set and a VCR, or poverty as a "lifestyle," I realized I needed an approach that would get beyond the stereotypes and at the personal side of poverty. I had to do two things: first, as Ardeth Deay and Judith Stitzel argue, I had to get beyond my own feelings of frustration with the conservative environment and my students' conservative attitudes (Deay and Stitzel 1991: 29); next, I had to change my approach: if what I was doing in the classroom was not working, I had to try something else.

Feminist pedagogy, fortunately, provided me with several strategies. I am not an expert on the statistics about women and poverty. Since, in any case, statistics just seem to elicit from students examples of apparently well-off poor people, I looked for an approach that would actually teach empathy rather than numbers, understanding rather than abstraction. I searched for a way to provide "connected learning" (Hayes 1989: 57) by forgetting about my own lack of expertise in social stratification or economic theory and concentrating instead on my ability to engage students in a process that provides the tools for critical reflection (Hayes 1989: 55). From my experience, in-class workshops, where students work in groups and then present their findings, promote that kind of engagement. I decided to approach the problem using what Weiler calls the three major themes of feminist pedagogy: to make no claims of objectivity, but instead place women firmly at the center of analysis; to emphasize the lived experience of women; and to have as a goal social change (Weiler 1998: 58–9).

The format I now use in teaching about women and poverty evolved both from my reading on feminist pedagogy and from my classroom experience. First, I introduce students to key concepts, arguing that the concepts are not objective, probably differing significantly from what the students have heard in or out of the classroom about poverty in the United States. I then introduce them to the workshop, hopefully forcing the students to get outside themselves for a bit and enter the lives of others in order to feel their struggles. We end the class by making a collective attempt to identify new social policies that could meet the needs of poor women and facilitate positive social change.

Introduction to women's lives in poverty: Just the facts

To provide a bit of context for the group activity, I provide some statistics, as well as my argument, about women and poverty in the United States. I ask whether or not poverty has a gender, a race, an age. I provide a few statistics to help complicate the students' analysis. A single parent of two children who works for the minimum wage earns $2300 a year below the federal poverty line. There are 13 million people on AFDC, but only four million are adults, and 90 percent of those are women. The average salary needed to keep a family of four out of poverty is $7.00 an hour. Nearly one of two Black children lives below the poverty line (Astor 1993: 5). I try then to get them to talk about some of the reasons why people of color and white women and children are overrepresented in the statistics. Together, we identify some of the issues, including child care, part-time work, and low wages. Inevitably, though, some of the stereotypes arise, so I provide only a few statistics and then divide them into groups, giving each member of the class a copy of the following worksheet:

The group activity worksheet

Your group will discuss the life of one of these women and/or children. Give your characters names and other identifying characteristics (age, ethnicity, race, sexual orientation, etc.). Make them as real in your minds as you can. Then take out a calculator and construct a monthly budget for the family. Include all possible expenses, making a separate list for expenses the family has but cannot meet. Talk about how the economic situation affects each individual involved. Prepare to introduce your woman and/or children to the class; when you do, make any relevant connections between your characters' situation and the issues we discussed at the beginning of class.

1. Single parent with two children

This woman has a high school education and is employed as a receptionist at a local want ad newspaper. She earns $6.00 an hour but receives no medical or dental benefits. Her ex-husband is supposed to pay child support but has moved out of state and pays her one or two times a year, if that. Develop a budget for her and her children. Describe a typical day for this mother. What does she do if one of her children is ill? What does she do during school vacations?

2. Single mother receiving AFDC and food stamps

This single mother has two children under six. She did not complete high school. Like many other women, she left her partner because he was violent. Her AFDC allotment is $334 a month with $182 a month in food stamps. Where will she live? How is she perceived by the society around her? Describe a typical day in this woman's life, and discuss how and when she might move toward self-sufficiency. Identify social supports that could help her in such a transition.

3. Child of single parent

This junior high school child lives with her/his mother and younger sister. The mother earns minimum wage at a manufacturing job, a job which provides no health or dental insurance. The child is not old enough to work but lacks many of the extras other kids have in school. Create a monthly budget for the family, including rent, food, utilities, etc.; then figure out what money is left over for the child. Consider things like school trips, video games, haircuts, movies, sports activities, etc.

4. Married couple with two children

This couple has been married for 6 years, living month to month primarily but saving about $3000 along the way. The man lost his job 9 months ago and has been unable to find another. His unemployment benefits are about to run out. The woman works part-time at a department store, but she receives no benefits. Right now, with the wife working, they are not entitled to receive any social service support. In addition, the automobile they have paid off is worth $5500, and in order to receive benefits your car must be worth less than $4800. If they spend all their money and go on welfare, they will receive $516 a month for a two-bedroom apartment, including all utilities. What steps should they take?[2]

My role in the group activity

I move around the room, talking briefly with each group as the students work. My objective during this time period is to put hitches in their solutions. For example, if they decide one of the children is a baby, thinking they will cut food costs, I bring up the issue of diapers, pediatrician visits, and clothes that fit for short periods of time. If they talk about women doubling up or moving in with family members to save money, I let them know that the woman will most likely lose her benefits as a result, since the income of all people living together will be counted for food stamps, even if they do not share food (Clarke 1994: 44). If they argue that the woman receiving AFDC can get a part-time job, I let them know that in order to keep any benefits she must, in 29 states, earn less than 60 percent of the federal poverty level (Amott 1993: 123). If they argue that a single parent can sue her ex-husband for regular child support, I ask them if she is entitled to take time off from work, if there is room in her budget for court fees, if she has money for child care so she can go to court. I purposefully look for what they leave out and I disturb their accounting as I walk around the room. This frustrates them in what I consider positive ways: they see that as tightly as they may construct their budgets, things come up that they had not considered.

Group introductions of characters, situations, and budgets

When the groups report back, some are smug about their ability to have their characters live within their means. Most, however, are quick to point out just how difficult the women's and children's lives must be. When two separate groups have the same characters, they advice each other about how they calculated expenses or complain about how they could not handle the child care, transportation, and medical care. They introduce strategies the poor women might use, and as a group we discuss the good and bad points of those strategies. The discussion is light years away from the blaming-the-victim approach they took at first. Most of the students now identify with their characters; they want them to make it. Suddenly, social service supports are necessary and humane, rather than supplementary and debilitating. Not all the students take this exercise seriously; some defensively find no connections between themselves and these imaginary characters, but most take up the challenge and make the connections. "She can't even go to the movies," one student woefully remarked, while another pointed out that a receptionist has to look nice but earns too little money to buy the clothing and cosmetics necessary to pull it off.

The public policy agenda

The last part of the workshop, after the characters have been introduced and discussed, is to make a list, collectively, of what kinds of public policy and social change would help these women and children. Now on-site day care, a higher minimum wage, health insurance, affordable and accessible public transportation, job sharing, job training, and other issues make some sense—and come from the students, not just the professor. We talk about the ways in which middle-class women are encouraged to stay at home and take care of their children, but poor women are not. We talk about the work and value of mothering, in contrast to the social validation of work that pays, no matter how inconsequential or even detrimental it is for the society. I introduce a quote by Pat Gowens, founder of the Welfare Warriors, who argues, "There is no recognition of mothering as work. Raising children is invisible in this society" (Astor1993: 4). We discuss, perhaps briefly, sex segregation in employment and the need for pay equity programs; sexual harassment on the job; and proposals for securing child support through the Internal Revenue Service or other agencies. What might otherwise be an almost meaningless list on the board has now become a list of solutions for the people these students have in their heads. The problems as well as the solutions become both meaningful and urgent.

Evaluation

Although I consider the exercise effective, I see several weaknesses. These students have been trained to see poverty as something that affects people outside the American Dream. They see themselves as people living inside the American Dream. One day's exercise cannot overturn years of conditioning. Also, traditional-aged students, partly because of their youth, are unlikely to feel vulnerability—or at least admit vulnerability. This exercise, like many I use, benefits from the participation of nontraditional students, who often can attest to the accuracy of some of the life stories we discuss.

I have learned, in doing this exercise with students and in discussing issues of social class, that I have to tread carefully over the issue of their futures. Although I wish for them a more comprehensive understanding of poverty, I do not wish to discourage them from pursuing their studies or fighting to improve their lives. I recognize the need for anger and the power of anger for propelling social change; I also recognize the debilitating effect of resignation and depression. My long-term goal is to get students to engage with issues of class for a sustained period of time without fostering in them a listless and apathetic approach to great social problems.

Another difficulty arises when the students' racism emerges. Sometimes students remark that these women do represent the "deserving poor," but they know that many others abuse the system. They bring up women living like "queens," a common reference to African-American women on welfare. The real women they have discussed get lost behind the more familiar stereotypes. I address this by asking them about the ways in which race might influence a woman's visit to a social service agency or to a job interview. Poor

African-American women, of course, do not have the luxury of choosing to deal with one identity at a time; they are poor, African American, and female simultaneously. I ask students to think about why it is that they have a race-based image in their minds when they think of welfare, when in fact the majority of welfare recipients in the United States are white. I ask them about the high percentage of welfare recipients in our area, almost all of whom are white. I have found that the best approach to the stereotypes is to get them out in the open and then examine them. Students seem better equipped to do this after conducting this in-class exercise than before it.

Conclusion

The characters and situations for this worksheet could be as varied as the faculty who invent them or the students whose individual life experiences they might or might not reflect. I offer these only as a starting point and a pedagogical approach for others. This exercise provides students with an opportunity to actively think about the contradictions between the messages they receive in the media and the messages they hear in a Women's Studies classroom. It provides one more piece of evidence encouraging students to see that multiple readings of societal issues are possible. My greatest fear is not that these particular examples are not the best; my greatest fear is that faculty, because of student apathy or even hostility, will shy away in their classrooms from addressing the same class issues that the feminist movement has yet to address adequately outside the classroom. Diana Pearce writes that our task is "not about finding out how poor women are different or how they need to be changed, but to recognize the universal and embedded nature of women's poverty in the gender, racial, and class inequalities that characterize American society today" (Pearce 1993: 94). Feminist faculty can accomplish this by educating for empathy as well as for knowledge. This workshop is one way to approach that task with respect both for the students, through engaging feminist pedagogy, and for the subjects, poor women and children, who must form more than simply a footnote in the work that goes on in the Women's Studies classroom.

Notes

1   The literature on welfare mothers, orphanages, and the poor who cheat the system proliferates. For background reading to help provide reality checks for students completing this exercise, see Wahneema Lubiano, "Black Ladies, Welfare Queens, and State Minstrels: Ideological Warfare By Narrative Means." In *Race-Ing Justice, En-Gendering Power*, Ed. Toni Morrison (New York: Penguin, 1992), 323–63; Renu Nahata, "Persistent Welfare Stereotypes."

In *Issues in Feminism*, ed. Sheila Ruth (Mountain View, CA: Mayfield Publishing Company, 1995), 347–349; and Gina Tessier, "Whose Welfare?" *Ms* 4(2) (September/October 1994): 90–2.

2   The automobile figure of $4800 has not been adjusted since the 1970s. That and other current figures are supplied by Clarke 1994: 43.

References

Amott, Teresa. (1993). *Caught in the Crisis: Women and the American Economy Today*. New York: Monthly Review Press.

Astor, Kathy K. (January-February 1993). "Punishing Women Who Break the Rules of Patriarchy." *New Directions for Women* 22(1): 3–5.

Clarke, Kevin. (1994). "Hunger in America is Increasing." In *Poverty: Opposing Viewpoints*. Ed. Katie de Koster. San Diego, CA: Greenhaven Press, 37–45.

Deay, Ardeth and Judith Stitzel. (Spring 1991). "Reshaping the Introductory Women's Studies Course: Dealing Upfront with Anger, Resistance, and Reality." *Feminist Teacher* 6(1): 29–33.

Hayes, Elisabeth, (ed.) (1989). *Effective Teaching Styles*. San Francisco, CA: Jossey-Bass.

Pearce, Diana M. (1993). "Something Old, Something New: Women's Poverty in the 1990s." In *American Women in the Nineties: Today's Critical Issues*. Ed. Sherri Matteo. Boston, MA: Northeastern University Press, 79–97.

Weiler, Kathleen. (1998). *Women Teaching for Change: Gender, Class and Power*. South Hadley, MA: Bergin & Garvey.

19

Teaching an Interdisciplinary Course on the American Upper Class

Richie Zweigenhaft

For over three decades, Richie Zweigenhaft has been teaching (and revising) a course focused on a widely hated, endlessly envied, often caricatured, but rarely analyzed class, one that wields immense but not always visible power in shaping American society. His students come to understand their own class position better by studying a class that they're highly unlikely to join.

I teach a course titled The American Upper Class. I first taught the course in the early 1980s after having spent the previous few years writing about the extent to which Jews were and were not allowed into the Protestant Establishment. Drawing especially on the work of E. Digby Baltzell, an upper-class sociologist from the Main Line of Philadelphia, and the work of C. Wright Mills, a radical sociologist from Texas, whose father sold insurance, I had written a series of articles, and also coauthored a book titled *Jews in the Protestant Establishment*.[1] In the process of studying upper-class Protestants, and the ways they had and had not allowed Jews into their midst, I began to focus more on the relationships between the

American upper class (including elite boarding schools, exclusive city and country clubs, and debutante balls) and the American power structure.

Most colleges have sociology courses on "Stratification" that seek to teach students that there is a class structure in the United States (a big surprise to some students). By the 1980s, most colleges had courses titled Race, Class, and Gender (I have taught that one, too, though I title my course Class, Race, and Gender). So, too, do most colleges include courses that focus on poverty in the United States. Not many have courses on the American upper class.

In this course, I have sought to address some basic issues. First, though most students, like so many Americans, deny its existence, I try to help students understand that there is a class system in this country and that it has for the most part worked in rather predictable ways throughout the last 110 years. Second, I hope to show students that those in the upper class not only have a lifestyle that is much admired and much emulated, but also that they are clearly connected to, but not the same as, those who run the institutions of power in the United States. Third, I hope that students will come to realize that those who are not in the upper class, and especially those who are at the bottom of the class structure, are very much affected by the advantages that those in the upper class have and work to maintain. Fourth, although the course differs substantially from the one I teach called Class, Race, and Gender, I try to help my students understand that one cannot really understand class without also considering race and gender—the three (and other forms of oppression or discrimination) interact in complex ways. Fifth, I encourage students to think about how the American upper class is now part of an international upper class, and the ways by which those atop the class hierarchy in this country connect with those in the upper classes around the world. (Hint #1: there are now far more international students at the most elite boarding schools in the United States than there used to be. Hint #2: there are now a number of foreign-born CEOs of Fortune-level corporations, men from upper-class backgrounds in their home countries).

I teach at Guilford College, a Quaker liberal arts school in Greensboro, North Carolina. Guilford is somewhat selective, but not nearly as selective as many New England colleges. The students are geographically diverse (mostly from up and down the east coast, but some from the west, and some international students), and there is considerable diversity in terms of their class backgrounds. These days the tuition, room, and board runs about $33,000, though most students do not pay the full rate, and some are here mostly or fully on scholarships. Some students are from very wealthy families, many are from the upper middle class, and many are from middle- and working-class families. Many students are from rural North Carolina, or from small southern towns, and they see Greensboro as the big city. Therefore, when I teach this class, I do not assume that my students are from economically privileged backgrounds, or that they have ever heard of schools like Choate, Andover, or Exeter, though some have (and one or two may have attended those schools).

I use a chronological approach in this course, not only because it makes intuitive sense, but also because I have become more and more aware of how limited my students' knowledge of American history is.[2] Although I have varied the reading in different iterations of the course, I have tended to use four books that I consider classics, published in 1899, 1924, 1956, and 1984. This allows us to consider what was going on in the country at those times, to examine the ways in which the upper class was portrayed in these works, and to explore the extent to which things seem to have changed (or not) since then.

I lead off with Thorstein Veblen's *Theory of the Leisure Class*.[3] Veblen's book provides historical perspective, not only because he wrote it in the late nineteenth century, but also because he begins with an anthropological look backward to earlier civilizations and a (very) hypothetical treatment of the evolution of systems of stratification. His erudite and flowery (but also humorous) language is very much of a bygone era, but, surprisingly, most students like his book and appreciate his sense of humor. Many of the concepts that Veblen introduced, most especially "pecuniary emulation," "conspicuous leisure," and "conspicuous consumption," are quite useful as we move to the other books and move forward chronologically to the present.

When we finish reading Veblen, I ask the students to take a driving tour of Greensboro and to use Veblen's ideas to write a paper about what they have seen ("Thorstein Veblen Comes Back From the Dead and Takes a Driving Tour of Greensboro, NC"). Like every American city of about 240,000 people, Greensboro has opulent houses (mansions really) and it has crowded projects. I detail a route for them which takes about an hour to drive. It sends them through the downtown, right past the Woolworth's where in 1960 four students from nearby North Carolina A&T University sat in at a segregated lunch counter in a protest that is generally considered to have sparked the sit-ins and economic boycotts that were central to the Civil Rights movement. The route also includes the projects where, in 1979 at a "Death to the Klan" rally sponsored by the Communist Workers Party, five people were killed, and several others were injured, by members of the Ku Klux Klan and American Nazi Party (six Klansmen and Nazis were later acquitted in a state trial). The route also includes working-class neighborhoods, middle-class neighborhoods, and the neighborhood that surrounds "the" country club (this neighborhood, with the unlikely name of Irving Park—which always reminds me of one of my Jewish relatives in Brooklyn—provides ample opportunity to write about conspicuous consumption).

We then read Fitzgerald's *The Great Gatsby*, published in 1925 and set in New York during the years following World War I. Many students previously have read this book—it is a favorite in high schools[4]—but they have not focused on the text as a source for a class analysis. They know Daisy and Tom Buchanan are rich, and that Nick is not so rich, and that Tom's mistress, Myrtle Wilson, is from the working class, but they have not really thought much about Nick's family background and why it is important to understanding what Fitzgerald is saying about the Buchanans, about Gatsby, and about the Wilsons. They know that Gatsby is rich, and that he grew up poor and that the source of his wealth is shady. This book provides a nice opportunity to look at the relationship between class and wealth, the distinction between new money and old money, the difference between celebrity and power, and the way that the relationship between wealth and class can change over two or three generations. (I ask my students if Bruce Springsteen is part of the upper class. What about LeBron James? What about Ice Cube? How might the children of these wealthy athletes and entertainers become part of the upper class? Would sending them to Lawrenceville, or Andover, help? Why?)

Bringing us into the 1950s is C. Wright Mills's *The Power Elite*, a book that resonates now, over 50 years after it was written, more than one might think. Mills addresses directly some of the questions raised by *Gatsby*. He presents a readable, though extensively documented, argument that by the 1950s, power in America no longer resided in wealthy families but was in the hands of the white Anglo-Saxon Protestant men who held the highest positions in three institutions—more specifically, those who were in the corporate elite, the political elite, and the military elite. Mills showed empirically that those in the upper class were very much overrepresented in these powerful positions, but he also showed that they were not one and the same (there were some Horatio Alger stories, but not as many as the publicists claimed). Still, he argued, the system functioned to perpetuate the wealth of those who had it, and those in the power elite who were not from the upper class were typically, though not always, doing the bidding of those in the upper class. Mills admired Veblen (he called him "the best critic of America that America has produced") but he also provided an important critique of Veblen's limited portrayal of the upper class (and indirectly of Fitzgerald's as well).

The fourth book that I assign, published in 1984, is Susan Ostrander's *Women of the Upper Class*. Through interviews with 36 upper-class women in a Midwest city, Ostrander looked at how these women fit into their families and into the local upper class. The book includes poignant descriptions of their work with the Junior League and other volunteer organizations, their relationships with their husbands and children, and their attitudes about the cultural changes taking place around them. They were clearly privileged economically, but many were also quite subservient to their husbands, and Ostrander's portrayal is rich with nuance. Here, especially, given the considerable changes in women's worlds that have taken place in the decades since the book was written, my students have a great deal to say about the changes they think have occurred, and we often spend time designing the follow-up study on this topic that I would love to see someone do.

I have taught this course three times since 1999, and in those classes the last book I've assigned has been either the first edition or the second edition of a book that I coauthored; the first (published in 1998) was titled *Diversity in the Power Elite: Have Women and Minorities Reached the Top?* And the second (published in 2006) was titled *Diversity in the Power Elite: How it Happened, Why it Matters.*[5]

This book updates C. Wright Mills's *The Power Elite* by examining the extent to which Jews, women, African Americans, Latinos, Asian Americans, and gay men and lesbians have become a part of the corporate, political, and military elites. When Mills wrote his book, all three institutions were run by white Anglo Saxon Protestant men, but, as was quite obvious in the spring of 2008, as Senators Barack Obama and Hillary Clinton vied for the Democratic nomination, there are now some African Americans and some women in positions of power. In the book, we detail just how many people from these various groups have made it to the top of these three institutions of power, and we look at the class backgrounds of those who have made it. It may not be a surprise to faculty that each of the Republican and Democratic Presidential nominees in the twenty-first century attended an elite boarding school (Bush: Andover; Gore: St Albans; Kerry: St Paul's; Obama: Punahou; McCain: Episcopal; Romney: Cranbrook), but it is news to some of my students, and as we read and talk about this book, we put the role of elite boarding schools into the larger context of understanding the upper class and the power elite.

The end-of-semester evaluations indicate that the students very much like the class, and think that they have learned a lot. Guilford uses a standardized form with both quantitative measures (24 questions, answered on a one–six scale) and open-ended questions asking for narrative comments. The numerical ratings have been consistently high, with scores higher than the averages for the college and the social science division and, in fact, higher than the evaluations I receive in many of the other classes I teach.

The narrative responses to the open-ended questions indicate that, for many students, the class is an eye-opener. As one student put it, the course "completely changed my perceptions of the class structure." In response to a question which asked what aspects of the course contributed the most to their learning, many students wrote about the short response papers that they were required to write and hand in at the beginning of each class. These short papers were designed to increase the likelihood of students actually reading the assigned material before they came to class, and to enhance the quality of the discussions. It seems to have worked. As one student wrote, "We had assignments due every class which forced us to do the reading and generated GREAT class discussion."

Many students mentioned the class discussions, at times focusing on the way they were structured ("The class discussions were set up to encourage us to interact with one another") and at times emphasizing the diverse makeup of the students in the class ("The varied back grounds and perceptions of classmates reflected great diversity, and therefore provided an opportunity to learn").

Only one student raised a concern about bias, and this concern seemed to apply to the comments of students instead of (or perhaps in addition to) the choice of the readings or the views I expressed. In response to a question about how the course could be improved in the future, this student wrote that I should "encourage the class to be open-minded about the upper class."

I, of course, do not tell them what to do with what they have learned, but I do encourage them to think about the choices they make. For those few very wealthy students, I'm always sure to mention *Robin Hood Was Right: A Guide to Giving Your Money for Social Change*, a book published in 2000 that encouraged extremely wealthy progressives to give their money away in ways that promote social justice rather than spending their lives trying to accumulate more.[6]

I also try to get them to think about the symbiotic relationship between social protests (e.g. sit-ins during the Civil Rights movement) and legislative changes (e.g. the Voting Rights Act of 1965). The next time I teach the course I plan to tell them about Adam Hochschild's 2005 book about the end of the slave trade in England, *Bury the Chains: Prophets and Rebels in the Fight to Free an Empire's Slaves*. Although his book is not about the American upper class, it does show just how important it is to have both disruptive protest from the outside and people of commitment on the inside to bring about meaningful change.[7] Whether my students disrupt from the outside, or try to work from the inside, is, of course, up to them, but I do hope that they will do what they can to bring about much-needed change in the way the class system is stacked in favor of those born into the upper class in America.[8]

Notes

1   Richard L. Zweigenhaft and G. William Domhoff, *Jews in the Protestant Establishment* (New York: Praeger, 1982).
2   One of my students wrote recently in a paper, "As was the case during Benjamin Franklin's presidency. . ." Another student, in a response to Frederick Douglass's slave narrative, wrote the following: "The amount of beatings,

and the severity of the beatings for simply walking by a mistress watching television, or whatever, is still hard for me to comprehend."

3   One of my friends, an economist, tells me that in his graduate program this book was generally referred to as "The Leisure of the Theory Class."

4   *The Great Gatsby* is especially popular these days with high school students from immigrant families. Apparently, they see it more as an inspirational tale than as a cautionary tale. See Sara Rimer, "Gatsby's Green Light Beckons a New Set of Strivers," *New York Times*, 17 February 2008.

5   Richard L. Zweigenhaft and G. William Domhoff, *Diversity in the Power Elite: Have Women and Minorities Reached the Top?* (New Haven: Yale University Press, 1998); *Diversity in the Power Elite: How it Happened, Why it Matters* (Lanham, MD: Rowman & Littlefield, 2006).

6   Chuck Collins, Pam Rogers, and Joan P. Gordon, *Robin Hood Was Right: A Guide to Giving Your Money for Social Change* (New York: W. W. Norton, 2000).

7   Adam Hochschild, *Bury the Chains: Prophets and Rebels in the Fight to Free an Empire's Slaves* (Boston, MA: Houghton Mifflin, 2005). Hochschild was raised in a very wealthy family (as a boy he was driven to the Princeton Country Day School in the chauffeured family limousine), but, after attending Harvard in the 1960s, went on to help found the left magazines *Ramparts* and *Mother Jones*. He has written about this in a memoir, *Half the Way Home: A Memoir of Father and Son* (New York: Viking, 1986).

8   A few years ago, I was asked to give a talk at Middlesex, an elite boarding school in Massachusetts. This was a very different audience than the students I typically have in my classes at Guilford in that many of them, probably most of them, were from the wealthiest and most socially exclusive families in America. For that talk ("Social Class and Social Justice: Changes From Within and Pressures From the Outside"), I focused primarily on the creation of the *A Better Chance* (ABC) program and on Hochschild's *Bury the Chains: Prophets and Rebels in the Fight to Free an Empire's Slaves*. If you'd like a copy of that talk, send me an email at rzweigen@guilford.edu.

20

Teaching About Class in the Library

Emily Drabinski

*Class can make itself felt in ways only the most devoted
are likely to notice, even in the way the library is organized.
Emily Drabinski describes teaching at Sarah Lawrence College
and at Long Island University, two institutions at very different
places on the class hierarchy, about the hidden class ideology of
the seemingly neutral Library of Congress classification system.*

Structures of social and economic class are notoriously difficult for students
to see, laboring as they do under the powerful myth that America is a
country of endless opportunity, where anyone can triumph over obstacles to
be anything they want to be. This is the rhetoric emanating everywhere from
American Idol to the presidency of the United States, and it is a powerful
story. Library classification schemes can be a useful classroom text in this
regard. Brief examination reveals them to be nearly invisible structures that
determine what it is possible to know in the library. Librarian-instructors
can scale this idea to help students understand that other structures are
at work in our social, economic, and political lives too, even if we cannot
always see them.

Library materials are arranged according to classification structures that
determine where individual titles are placed on library shelves as well as their
relation to other materials. Generally, public and elementary and secondary

school library materials are classified according to the Dewey Decimal system, while college and university libraries are arranged according to the Library of Congress (LC) system. The classification scheme functions as a kind of scaffolding, an abstract map that generates the physical layout of the library. In the case of the LC system, books about social and economic class are located in class H, the category for Social Sciences. This broad class is divided into 16 narrower classes, called subclasses. Subclass HB contains books related to Economic Theory and Demography, subclass HC contains Economic history and conditions, and so on. Books about class delineations are housed in subclass HT, Communities, Classes, and Races.

Initially, these divisions appear quite objective. Books about class can certainly be subsumed under the broader category of the social sciences, and pairing class and race in the same subclass makes some sense. Still, a closer analysis reveals some problems with this arrangement, problems that are reflected in the lived reality of class as well. For example, LC places books about class in HT. The subclasses on either side of this are HS (Societies: secret, benevolent, etc.) and HV (Social pathology. Social and public welfare. Criminology). Books about class, then, are most prominently related to social pathology and secret societies rather than economic theory (HB), commerce (HF), or public finance (HJ). Used as a teaching text, LC can helpfully demonstrate the way class in the United States is often thought of as something malleably related to the individual rather than causally related to economic theory or public financing, not to mention the even further obscured relationship between class and politics (class J) and the law (class K).

Perhaps as telling as where class shows up in LC is where it does not. Its invisibility in other parts of the classification scheme parallels its invisibility in the social world, and an articulation of these silences can help students understand class as something operating even if we do not see it. Subclass HT contains books that are explicitly about class. For example, Larry Bartels's recent *Unequal Democracy* is in HT because it explicitly addresses the question of class in America. A book like *The Bell Curve*, however, is classed many shelves, even floors, away in BF, where it is shelved along with other books that address the topic of "the intellect." Jonathan Kozol's *Savage Inequalities* is shelved in LC, alongside books about urban education but far from works of class analysis that would contextualize his work. And literature, long the place where stories of American exceptionalism take the clearest shape, is shelved in PS, in another (library) world altogether.

In my experience, teaching library skills in a variety of classes at Sarah Lawrence College and at Long Island University's Brooklyn campus, treating the LC structure as a text to be critically engaged rather than simply accepted and regurgitated, is compelling to students. They can see quite clearly that structures they did not know existed have a lot of influence on what they can discover in the library. The implications are vast—these structures not only govern the library, but what and how we know, and in turn, what we can be.

POSTSCRIPT

In the fall of 2011, the Occupy Wall Street movement exploded into the news. Media coverage, whether friendly or hostile, was extensive, and the expression "we are the 99%" soon became as familiar as "Got Milk?" It seemed for a while that the discourse would be changed forever, that Occupy's critique of the class structure might become a permanent feature of American political debate.

The economic crisis that fueled the Occupy movement was severe. In 2011, official US unemployment stood at 8.9 percent, home foreclosures numbered nearly four million, and student-loan debt passed the one-trillion-dollar mark. But people were talking, and acting. Words like "bankster" were making a comeback, and protest was spreading.

Coming as it did close on the heels of the Arab Spring and of protests across Europe challenging newly intensified austerity measures, the rapidly spreading Occupy movement brought hope of deep political change. Occupy groups sprang up in hundreds of cities in the United States and around the world, often building alliances with labor unions. In Wisconsin, a bill to deny collective bargaining rights to teachers and other public sector workers had led tens of thousands of protesters to occupy the State Capitol Building. Campuses across the United States flowered with demonstrations and occupations; University of California students, to take but one example, had gone on strike across the state to protest tuition increases. Occupy Our Homes actions were halting many foreclosures and evictions.

But at this writing (September 2012), it's hard to look to the future with the optimism of a year ago. Though decentralized Occupy work continues, police repression, as well as cold weather and the simple toll of time, just about ended last winter's occupations of public spaces; a hopeful resurgence of occupying in the spring of 2012 didn't last. Public debate, especially in the campaign for the Presidency, is muddling and distorting class issues beyond recognition. Talk has shifted from reducing inequality back to balancing the budget; a distressing number of talking heads in the corporate media are taking Tea Party ideology seriously; Ayn Rand's books are selling wildly. The call for justice for "the 99 percent" is losing ground to fear-mongering about the deficit, empty promises of "job creation," and paeans to the wonders of small business. Recent activism has clearly changed some people forever, but the sense of historical possibility many felt a year ago is fading.

And, of course, the destructive operations of class continue. In higher education—to return to the particular focus of this volume—profoundly unequal access for students and deteriorating employment conditions for many faculty are likely, in the near future at least, to continue. As for what goes on in the classroom—it remains to be seen how deeply and lastingly recent events will have influenced the content and methods of higher education. Many essays in *Class and the College Classroom* address resistance to the acknowledgment of issues of class, and though recent events have pushed them into the spotlight, those of us who consider these issues essential need to continue our efforts to spread and deepen understanding of what class means and to work for change.

CONTRIBUTORS

Vivyan Adair, the Elizabeth J. McCormack Associate Professor of Women's Studies at Hamilton College, is coauthor of *Reclaiming Class: Women, Poverty, and The Promise of Higher Education in America*, and the author of *From Good Ma to Welfare Queen, A Genealogy of the Poor Woman in American Literature, Photography and Culture.*

Carolina Bank Muñoz is an Associate Professor at Brooklyn College and The Graduate Center of the City University of New York. Prior to coming to New York, she was a Project Director at the UCLA Labor Center. Her work focuses on immigration, globalization, labor and work, and race, class, and gender. Her book, *Transnational Tortillas: Race, Gender and Shop Floor Politics in Mexico and the United States*, is the winner of the Terry Book Award. She is currently working on a book project about Walmart in Chile.

Janet Galligani Casey is Professor of English and Director of the First Year Experience at Skidmore College, where she also oversees a faculty development initiative on civic engagement funded by the Arthur Vining Davis Foundations. She is the author of *Dos Passos and the Ideology of the Feminine* (1998) and *A New Heartland: Women, Modernity, and the Agrarian Ideal in America* (2009), and has edited *The Novel and the American Left: Critical Essays on Depression-Era Fiction* (2004). She is a founding member of the Middlebrow Research Network, and served as the first senior cochair of the Modern Language Association's Committee on Contingent Labor in the Profession.

Born in Nacogdoches, Texas, **Carlos Dews** received his BA in Humanities from the University of Texas at Austin and an MA and PhD in American Literature from the University of Minnesota. He taught American literature and creative writing at the University of West Florida from 1994 to 2003 and served as the Chair of the Department of English and Foreign Languages there from 2000 to 2002. Tenured and promoted to Associate Professor at the University of West Florida in 1999, he served as the Founding Director of the Carson McCullers Center for Writers and Musicians at Columbus State University in McCullers's hometown of Columbus, Georgia, from

2001 to 2003. After completing an MFA in Fiction Writing at the New School University in New York in 2008, he relocated to Rome, Italy, where he is now an Associate Professor and Chair of the Department of English Language and Literature at John Cabot University.

Linda Dittmar is a long-standing member of *Radical Teacher*'s editorial group and Professor Emerita at the University of Massachusetts Boston, where she taught literature and film studies for 40 years. Her writing includes the books *From Hanoi To Hollywood: The Vietnam War In American Film* and *Multiple Voices in Feminist Film Criticism* as well as many book chapters and articles. Her current research and teaching concern literary and film representations of the Israeli-Palestinian conflict and a memoir in progress.

Emily Drabinski is the Coordinator of Library Instruction at Long Island University, Brooklyn, and coeditor of *Critical Library Instruction: Theories and Methods*.

Joseph Entin teaches English and American Studies at Brooklyn College, City University of New York. He is the author of *Sensational Modernism: Experimental Fiction and Photography in Thirties America* (2007) and coeditor of *Controversies in the Classroom: A Radical Teacher Reader* (2008). He is working on a new book about representations of low-wage workers in contemporary US fiction, photography, and film.

Kristen Gallagher is a writer, editor, and educator. Recent essays have appeared in *Criticism: A Quarterly for Literature and the Arts*, *Jacket2*, *Radical Teacher*, *The Paulo Freire Journal*, *The Salt Companion to Charles Bernstein*, and *Reading the Difficulties*. She has published two books of poetry, *We Are Here* (Truck 2011) and *Grand Central* (forthcoming). Recent creative work has appeared in *Dear Navigator*, *West Wind Review*, *The Brooklyn Rail*, *Matrix*, *Joyland Poetry*, *P-Queue*, and *Poetic Labor Project*. She received a PhD in Poetics from SUNY Buffalo in 2005 and is now Associate Professor of English at City University of New York-LaGuardia Community College, where she teaches Composition and Creative Writing. She is also the Director of LaGuardia's Writing Center.

Larry Hanley teaches in the English department at San Francisco State University, and has served as editor of *Academe*, the magazine of the American Association of University Professors.

Susan Jhirad is a retired Professor of English from North Shore Community College in Lynn and Danvers, Massachusetts, where she taught for 30 years. She received her PhD in Romance Languages and Literature from Harvard.

She is a long-time political activist from the Civil Rights, antiwar, Women's Liberation, and Welfare Rights Movements. She helped form Welfare Education Training Access Coalition (WETAC) with Erika Kates, PhD, which advocated for the rights of welfare recipients to count education and training as "work." Currently, she is completing a book, *Dickens's Inferno: the Moral Universe of Charles Dickens*. It connects Dickens's moral-religious concerns with Dante's, as well as with social issues of today.

Michelle LaPlace taught history at the College of San Mateo and served on the Executive Committee of the American Federation of Teachers, Local 1493. She wrote for *Processed World* under the name Sofia Furia.

Carolyn Leste Law is Dissertation Advisor at Northern Illinois University. She is coeditor (with Carlos Dews) of *This Fine Place So Far From Home: Voices of Academics from the Working Class* and of *Out In The South,* both published by Temple University Press.

Kat Meads is the author of *For You, Madam Lenin* and other books of prose and poetry, including *The Invented Life of Kitty Duncan, Born Southern and Restless,* and *Little Pockets of Alarm.* Her short fiction and essays have appeared in *Drunken Boat, Southern Exposure, American Letters & Commentary, Gargoyle,* and *Chicago Quarterly Review.* She has received an NEA award, writing residencies at the Fine Arts Work Center in Provincetown and Yaddo, *Chelsea* magazine's fiction prize, and the Dorothy Churchill Cappon Essay Award from *New Letters.* She currently teaches in Oklahoma City University's low-residency Red Earth MFA program. See www.katmeads.com.

Laurie Nisonoff is Professor of Economics at Hampshire College, and coeditor of *The Women, Gender and Development Reader.*

Richard Ohmann helped found *Radical Teacher,* in 1975, and remains on the board. He taught English and American Studies at Wesleyan University, and is the author of *Politics of Letters* and of *Politics of Knowledge: The Commercialization of the University, the Professions, and Print Culture,* among other books.

Robert C. Rosen teaches English at William Paterson University in New Jersey and is coeditor of *Literature and Society: An Introduction to Fiction, Poetry, Drama, Nonfiction* and of *Against the Current: Readings for Writers,* and author of *John Dos Passos: Politics and the Writer.* He is a member of the *Radical Teacher* editorial board and coeditor of *Politics of Education: Essays from Radical Teacher* and of *Controversies in the Classroom: A Radical Teacher Reader.*

Jennifer Scanlon is the William R. Kenan, Jr. Professor of the Humanities in Gender and Women's Studies at Bowdoin College. She has published widely on aspects of women's and girls' cultural and consumer practices, including beauty parlors, chick lit, board games, and online book reviews. Her most recent book, *Bad Girls Go Everywhere: The Life of Helen Gurley Brown* (Penguin), explores the working-class roots of Brown's controversial form of feminism. The book was named a "Book of the Times" by the *New York Times*, and a business book of the year by American Public Media's Marketplace, and it was reviewed widely and to significant acclaim nationally and internationally.

Emily Schnee is Assistant Professor of English at Kingsborough Community College of the City University of New York, where she teaches composition and developmental English. For many years, she taught writing to adults in union-supported worker education programs in New York City. Her research focuses on questions of educational equity and social justice.

Erin A. Smith is Associate Professor of American Studies and literature at the University of Texas at Dallas. She teaches courses in nineteenth-and twentieth-century American literatures and cultures and in gender studies. She is the author of *Hard-Boiled: Working-Class Readers and Pulp Magazines* (Temple University Press, 2000). Her current book project, *What Would Jesus Read?: Scenes of Religious Reading and Writing in Twentieth-Century America*, is under contract with University of North Carolina Press.

Taylor Stoehr's most recent books include *The Paul Goodman Reader* (edited for PM Press), *I Hear My Gate Slam* (translations from Classical Chinese poems, published by Pressed Wafer), and *Changing Lives: Working with Literature in an Alternative Sentencing Program* (Paradigm Publishers). The latter is a full-length account of the experimental program for probationers which the essay reprinted here discusses. Stoehr is Emeritus Professor of English at the University of Massachusetts Boston.

Susan J. Tracy is Professor of History and American Studies at Hampshire College and the author of *In the Master's Eye: Representations of Women, Blacks, and Poor Whites in Ante-Bellum Southern Literature*.

Stanley Warner is Professor Emeritus of Economics at Hampshire College. He has also taught at the University of California at Santa Cruz and at Bucknell University, and has done research on the environmental and social impacts of hydroelectric development in Quebec.

Ed Wiltse is Professor of English at Nazareth College, where he teaches Crime and Detective Fiction, and twentieth-century British and Irish

Literature. He has published essays about jail prisoners' reading strategies, Thackeray's *Vanity Fair*, and the Sherlock Holmes stories. He recently coedited the volume of essays, *Hope Against Hope: Philosophies, Cultures and Politics of Possibility and Doubt* (Rodopi 2010), which contains an essay about the work he does with Nazareth students and prisoners at Monroe Correctional Facility.

Richie Zweigenhaft is the Charles A. Dana Professor of Psychology at Guilford College in Greensboro, North Carolina. He received his BA at Wesleyan University, his MA at Columbia University, and his PhD at the University of California, Santa Cruz. He is the coauthor, with G. William Domhoff, of *Jews in the Protestant Establishment* (1982), *Blacks in the White Establishment?: A Study of Race and Class in America* (1991), *Diversity in the Power Elite: Have Women and Minorities Reached the Top?* (1998), *Blacks in the White Elite: Will the Progress Continue?* (2003), *Diversity in the Power Elite: How it Happened, Why it Matters* (2006), and *The New CEOs: Women, African American, Latino, Asian American Leaders of Fortune 500 Companies* (2011).

INDEX